Northumberland County, Virginia

Order Book Abstracts

1683–1686

Ruth and Sam Sparacio

HERITAGE BOOKS
2019

HERITAGE BOOKS
AN IMPRINT OF HERITAGE BOOKS, INC.

Books, CDs, and more—Worldwide

For our listing of thousands of titles see our website
at
www.HeritageBooks.com

Published 2019 by
HERITAGE BOOKS, INC.
Publishing Division
5810 Ruatan Street
Berwyn Heights, Md. 20740

All rights reserved. No part of this book may be reproduced or transmitted in any form or by any means, electronic or mechanical, including photocopying, recording or by any information storage and retrieval system without written permission from the author, except for the inclusion of brief quotations in a review.

International Standard Book Number
Paperbound: 978-0-7884-5887-3

NORTHUMBERLAND COUNTY, VIRGINIA
ORDERS
1678-1698

p. 183 - At a Court held for Northumberland County the 20th of June 1683 Annoque Regni Regis Caroli secundi 2d, 35th &c.

Present

Lt. Coll. SAMUELL SMYTH   Capt. THOMAS MATHEW
Capt PETER KNIGHT   Mr. PHILIP SHAPLEIGH
Mr. PETER PRESLEY   Capt. JOHN HAYNIE   Justices
Major JOHN MOTTROM   Mr. CHRISTOPHER NEALE
Capt. LEONARD HOWSON   Mr. RICHARD KENNER
Mr. NICHOLAS OWEN

- CHURCHILL agt FLYNT Whereas it appeares to this Court that PETER FLYNT, Administrator of JOHN KNOTT, deceased, standeth indebted unto SAMUELL CHURCHILL two hundred pounds of tobacco and cask for making a Coffin for the said KNOTT, Judgment is granted SAMUELL CHURCHILL against the Estate of JOHN KNOTT for the said sume with costs als Execution

- Constable appoynted Ordered that HENRY BOGGAS be Constable for CHERRY POINTE,
CLOUD TULLOS for CHICACONE,
RICHARD BRADLEY for MATTAPONY,
ZACHARIAH THOMAS for NEWMAN's NECK;
THOMAS ROUT for the Upper Precincts of Fayrfeild Parish; and
JOHN COLES for the Lower Precincts thereof;
CHRISTOPHER BAYLES for the South side of GREAT WICOCOMICO and
Mr. JOHN EUSTACE for the lowest Precincts of this County

- JOHN PASKALL's Will proved On the Petition of HANNAH, the Executrix of JOHN PASKALL, deceased, a Probate is granted her of the Last Will and Testament of the said JOHN the Will being proved by the Oath of Mr. THOMAS [? GASKOYNE] Executor of and witnesse to the said Will

- Negroes's age adjudged Jenny, a Negro of Mr. PETER PRESLEY, JUNR. is adjudged to be six yeares of age; Jack a Negro of Mr. RICHARD KENNER to be seaven yeares of age; JOHN WALTERS's Servant to be twelve yeares of age

- Mr. CAMMELL's Certificate Certificate is granted WILLIAM CAMMELL to the Assembly for twenty ells of Linnin Cloath he haveing made Oath according to Act that it was of his owne manufacture

- MRS. JANE WILDEY's Certificate Certificate is granted MRS. JANE WILDEY to the Assembly for for fourteen yards and an half of woolin cloath she haveing made Oath according to Act that it was of her owne manufacture

- WILL: DOWNING's Will proved On the Petition of MARY, Executrix of WILLIAM DOWNING, deceased, a Probate is granted her of the Last Will and Testament of WILLIAM DOWNING theWill being proved by the Oathes of WILLIAM SOUTHING and JOHN ATKINS, witnesses to the said Will

- RICH: BURGESS freed from Levy Ordered that RICHARD BURGESS, a poor and impotent person be freed from the Levy

p. 184 Northumberland County Court 20th of June 1683

- THO: JONES agt Mr. GEO: KNIGHT Whereas on an Order dated the 22d of March last Mr. THOMAS JONES had an Execution against the Estate of Mr. GEORGE KNIGHT for fifteen pounds sterling with costs which Execution was filed on two Servants to which Mr. PETER KNIGHT layeth claime and did prefer a Petition into this Court wherein he comlayned that Collo. THOMAS BRERETON bad by the Execution seized on ye said Servants which he did averr was his owne proper Estate and soe to make it out did produce assignments of the Servants from the said Mr. GEORGE KNIGHT to him to which the said THOMAS JONES did plead that that conveyance or assignment was clandestinely and fraudulently done to deny him of his right, the Court cannot find the fraud as alledged and therefore doe order that Collo. THOMAS BRERETON, Sheriffe as aforesaid deliver the Servants to Mr. PETER KNIGHT and pay him five hundred pounds of tobacco and cask for the damages with costs als Execution [Mr. PETER PRESLEY disents from this Order]

- Appeale Collo. THOMAS BRERETON and Mr. PHILIP SHAPLEIGH oblige themselves in the penall sume of ten thousand pounds of tobacco and cask that the said BRERETON shall prosecute his said appeale

Capt. JOHN HAYNIE is bound with the Appealer in the same sume that he shall appeare to answer the said appeale

- Capt. KNIGHT's Bond to Collo. BRERETON Capt. PETER KNIGHT, Capt. LEONARD HOWSON and Capt. THOMAS MATHEW doe oblige themselves joyntly and severally in the penall sume of ten thousand pounds of tobacco and cask unto Collo. THOMAS BRERETON to save him harmeless from any damages that he shall susteyn by delivering the Servants in dispute to the said KNIGHT

- Capt. HOWSON and Capt. MATHEW agt Capt. KNIGHT Capt. PETER KNIGHT confesseth Judgment for the present payment of twenty thousand pounds of tobacco and cask unto Capt. LEONARD HOWSON and Capt. THOMAS MATHEW in case he defend them not from any damages they may susteyn by their assumpsit as abovesaid

- THO: WAUGHOP agt THO: BEECH An Attachment is awarded Mr. THOMAS WAUGHOP for two hundred pounds of tobacco and cask returnable to the next Court

p. 185 Northumberland County Court 20th of June 1683

- THO: BOWYER Servt to JNO: NICHOLS THOMAS BOWYER doth in Court bind himself to serve JOHN NICHOLS or his assignes seaven yeares JOHN NICHOLS to provide for him cloathing lodging and dyett during the tearme fitting for an Apprentice and forthwith to deliver to him a Heyfer which during the said tearme JOHN NICHOLS is to marke the like eare of her increase so he doth of his owne cattle and at the expiration of the said tearme to deliver her and her in-creas unto THOMAS BOWYER in consideration for his service as aforesaid

- MRS. WILDEY agt NICH: SEABORNE MRS. JANE WILDEY being arrested to this Court at the suit of Collo. THOMAS BRERETON, the Attorney of NICHOLAS SEABORNE, for fower hundred seaventy pounds of tobacco and cask and made Oath that she was indebted to NICHOLAS SEABORNE for nothing but

NORTHUMBERLAND COUNTY ORDER BOOK, 1678-1698   -3-

one pound of candlewick; a non suit is granted MRS. JANE WILDEY against Collo. THOMAS BRERETON, Attorney as aforesaid, with costs and damages according to Act

- TIPTON agt WILDEY Whereas it appeares to this Court by a Bill under the hand and seal e of WILLIAM WILDEY dated the 12th of June 1680 that WILLIAM WILDEY stood indebted unto Mr. SAMUELL TIPTON the sume of three hundred fifty pounds of tobacco and cask; Judgment is granted to Collo. THOMAS BRERETON, the Assignee of SAMUEL TIPTON against JANE WILDEY, the Executrix of WILLIAM WILDEY, for the said sume als Execution

- MEDCALF to have her Child Whereas SARAH MEDCALF had a bastard Child after her terme of service was expired but became bound to serve some yeares for a cure on her which she haveing served, it is ordered that she be free and that she have her Child with her, Mr. JAMES CLAUGHTON engaging to save the Parish harmeless from the said Child

- REBECCA, Servt. to MRS. JANE WILDEY freed from the Levy Ordered that REBECCA THOMAS, Servant to MRS. JANE WILDEY, being a runaway Servant and noe way beneficial tov her be freed from the Levy

- The Court adjourneth till the 3d Wednesday in the next month

- Widdow WALTERS freed from the Levy ELINOR WALTERS being a very aged woman industriously endeavouring to [   ] charging the Parish, it is ordered that she shall have one person whome she shall buy to work for her freed from the Levy

p. 186 - At a Court held for Northumberland County the 18th July 1683 Annoque Regni Regis Caroli secundi 2d, 35th &c.

                    Present
Capt. PETER KNIGHT   Capt. THOMAS MATHEW
Mr. PETER PRESLEY   Capt. JOHN HAYNIE
Major JOHN MOTTROM   Mr. CHRISTOPHER NEALE   Justices
Mr. NICHOLAS OWEN   Mr. WILLIAM ROGERS

- Jack, an Indian slave of JOHN COCKERELL, is adjudged to be seaven yeares of age

- CH: FALLONS agt Mr. GEO: KNIGHT Whereas it appeares to this Court by a Bill under the hand of Mr. GEORGE KNIGHT dated the 30th of March 1682 that Mr. GEORGE KNIGHT standeth indebted unto CHARLES FALLONS by assignment of THOMAS BURBURY the sume of twelve hundred pounds of tobacco and cask; Judgment is granted CHARLES FALLON against GEORGE KNIGHT for the present payment of the said sume with costs ald Execution unlesse GEORGE KNIGHT gives CHARLES FALLONS good security for the payment thereof the 10th of 8br next according to Act

- WADE agt KNIGHT Whreas on a Judgment obteyned against Mr. GEORGE KNIGHT by JOHN WADE for fower thousand pounds of tobacco and cask an Injunction was granted GEORGE KNIGHT to stop further proceedings at the Common Law untill he had a hearing in Chancery and GEORGE KNIGHT haveing this Court put in his Bill and the Defendant his Answer to which the Plaintiffe prays time untill the next Court to reply to it, which is granted the Plaintiffe then fitting all things that may any way clear ye business that a finall determination may be had of that difference

- HARCUM agt HARTLAND Whereas Mr. WILLIAM HARCUM obteyned Judgment against WILLIAM HARTLAND for sixteen hundred twenty pounds of tobacco and cask for makeing a cure on one ABRAHAM NORRIS on which WILLIAM HARTLAND obteyned an Injunction who put in his Bill in Chancery and the Defendant his Answer by which it appeares that WILLIAM HARTLAND was to pay WILLIAM HARCUM in case the fellow dyed in his hands but one thousand pounds of tobacco, the Court doe order WILLIAM HARTLAND to pay to WILLIAM HARCUM one thousand pounds of tobacco and cask with costs als Execution judging the fellow in as bad a case as dead being reduced to that state as in an hosbitall

p. 187

Northumberland County Court 18th of July 1683

- MIRIAM SADLER's Comm. of Admon A Commission of Administration is granted MIRIAM SADLER of the Estate of THOMAS SADLER, her Husband, deceased, she giveing caution according to Law

- The Bond THOMAS HOBSON and RICHARD HULL standeth joyntly and severally obliged with MIRIAM SADLER in the sume of twenty thousand pounds of tobacco and cask that the said MIRIAM shall duely administer of the Decedent's Estate and doe what the Law in that case requireth

- Appraysers Ordered that DANIEL NEALE, JOHN GRAHAM, WALTER DUNNE and RICHARD LAMPREY or any three of them between this and the next Court apparyse the Estate of THOMAS SADLER, deceased, being sworne by a Justice of the Peace

- HUGHLETT agt KNIGHT Mr. GEORGE KNIGHT confesseth Judgment for the present payment of five hundred pounds of tobacco and cask unto Mr. JOHN HUGHLETT with costs als Execution

- MERCHT agt HARTLAND Ordered that WILLIAM HARTLAND forthwith discharge ELIZABETH MERCHT from all obligations that he hath of hers

- GENESIS agt HAYNIE Whereas a difference hath been long depending between EZEKIEL GENESIS in the behalf of REBECCA his Wife, one of the Orphants of JOHN SHAW, deceased, and Capt. JOHN HAYNIE, Administrator of the Estate of JOHN SHAW, about the said REBECCA her share or portion of the Estate the Court haveing examined the Accounts the said JOHN HAYNIE on his Oath did exhibite into Court doe find the ballance giveth the said HAYNIE creditt therefore ordered that the suit be dismissed and that the said HAYNIE have his quietus est from the Estate. Mr. PETER PRESLEY disenteth from this Order

- CAMMELL's Certificate Certificate is granted Mr. WILLIAM CAMMELL to the Assembly for thirteen and one half ells of Linen Cloth he haveing made Oath according to Act

- AUSTEN's Certificate Certificate is granted Mr. JAMES AUSTEN to the Assembly for twenty two and an half yards of woolen cloth he haveing made Oath according to Act

- CLOUD TULLOS freed from the Levy CLOUD TULLOS, the Sonne of CLOUD TULLOS being both deaf and dumb, it is ordered that he be released from the Levy

NORTHUMBERLAND COUNTY ORDER BOOK, 1678-1698   -5-

p. 188 Northumberland County Court 18th of July 1683

- BLEDSOE agt HARRIS &c. Whereas an Order of his Excellency and Councill dated the 23d of Aprill last was the last Court produced by Mr. GEORGE BLEDSOE wherein it was ordered that this Court should appoynt an able Jury of the Vicinage of indifferent and impartial persons noe wayes related to the Plaintiffe or Defendant who being sworne before the Court should meet on the 22d day of June following in company of Collo. THOMAS BRERETON, Capt. LEONARD HOWSON and Capt. THOMAS MATHEW or any two of them with the Surveyor mentioned in the former Order, vizt. Mr. ROBERT CHAMBERLAIN and Mr. GEORGE HAY, to survey and lay out the land of the said BLEDSOE and whereas the last Court being the 20th of June and JOHN HARRIS [then absent could not in that short time appoynt the Sheriffe to empannell] the Court swore a Jury to be there on that day did referr the businesse to this Court when it was hoped JOHN HARRIS might appeare. This Court the said HARRIS appearing, and the said BLEDSOE both declareing that they did both agree to consent that this Court should appoynt a Jury as effectually to all intents and purposes as if done as expressed in the Order and whereas most of the Inhabitants of the Neighbourhood have severally formerly served on surveys in that businesse the Court did think fitt that a Jury of understanding men of the other neighbourhoods as presumed least concerned might be empannelled and doe this Order the Sheriffe to summon the persons following to be at the house of Mr. GEORGE BLEDSOE the first Munday in 7br to be empannelled on a Jury to goe with ye Surveyors aforesaid in pursuance of the Order aforesaid

Mr. HENRY ROSSE	ROBERT SECH	JOHN GRAHAM
MR. GEORGE HUTTON	SAMUELL GERRARD	RICHARD ROGERS or any
JAMES CLAUGHTON	HENRY DAWSON	JOHN WEBB 12 of
JAMES JOHNSON	JOHN COUTANSHEW	ABRAHAM [ ] them at
WILLIAM SHOARES	THOMAS ADAMS	THOMAS HAMMONDS least
WILLIAM KEYNE	JOHN OLDAM	JOHN CORBELL

These persons being all called by name before the Plaintiffe and Defendant there was not any person to which either the Plaintiffe or Defendant did make excepted and did both consent on the day appoynted for the Jury to meet, that Capt. THOMAS MATHEW and Capt. LEONARD HOWSON should sweare the Jury and ordered that any fayling of his appearance at the day be fined two thousand pounds of tobacco

- WM. PRITCHARD Fathr to MARY CHAMBERS's bastard MARY CHAMBERS, Servant to RICHARD HULL, haveing a bastard Child did this day on her Oath declare tht Mr. WILLIAM PRITCHARD was the Father thereof

p. 189 Northumberland County Court 18th of July 1683

- Mr. HARCUM's land to be surveyed Ordered that some time between this and the next Court Capt. JOHN HAYNIE survey the land of Mr. WILLIAM HARCUM according to the expressed bounds of his Pattent

- MRS. JANE WILDEY and MRS. ELIZ: FLEET fined Whereas MRS. JANE WILDEY and MRS. ELIZABETH FLEET were both summoned to this Court to give in their Evidence in a difference depending between CHRISTOPHER KIRK and ELIZABETH WILLIAMS and not appearing, it is ordered that they be fined according to Act

- ELIZ: WMS. non suit agt KIRK Whereas CHRISTOPHER KIRK arrested ELIZABETH WILLIAMS to ths Court and not makeing out his Declaration, a non suit is granted ELIZABETH WILLIAMS against CHRISTOPHER KIRK with costs and damages according to Law als Execution

- GEO: WALKER agt GEO: KNIGHT Mr. GEORGE KNIGHT confesseth Judgment for the present payment of the sume of thirteen pounds, thirteen shillings sterling with charge of protest and damages according to Law

- THO: BARNES agt Mr. EDW: CONOWAY referred to the next Court

- JNO: OLDAM's Certificate Certificate is granted JOHN OLDAM to the Assembly for nineteen yards of Linen Woolsey to which he hath made Oath according to Law

- The Court is adjourned to tomorrow morning eight a clock

- 19th of July 1683   Present
Capt. PETER KNIGHT   Mr. NICHOLAS OWEN
Major JOHN MOTTROM   Mr. CHRISTOPHER NEALE   Justices
Capt. JOHN HAYNIE   Mr. WILLIAM ROGERS

- SAM: MAHON agt JNO: JONES Whereas SAMUELL MAHON had an Attachment awarded him against the Estate of JOHN JONES for two hundred twenty five pounds of tobacco and cask which Attachment is returned on what Estate JOHN JONES hath in the hands of Mr. JOHN SWANSON. It is ordered that the said SWANSON appear the next Court to declare what of the Estate of the said JONES he hath in his hands that accordingly the Court may proceed in that businesse

JAM: CLAUGHTON agt CLEMT. LATTIMORE referred to the next Court at the motion of the Defendant

p. 190 Northumberland County Court 19th of July 1683

- THO: TOWERS agt WALT: SIMS Thsi Cause is referred to the next Court at the motion of the Defendant

- Mr. SHAPLEIGH agt RICH: MICHAELL Whereas Mr. PHILIP SHAPLEIGH was arrested to this Court at the suit of RICHARD MICHAELL and the said MICHAELL not appearing to prosecute, a non suit is granted the said SHAPLEIGH against the said MICHAELL with costs and damages according to Law

- JOHN LAWRENCE against RICHARD PEMBERTON referred to the next Court at the motion of the Defendant

- ROGERS agt HARCUM Mr. WILLIAM ROGERS being arrested to this Court at the suit of Mr. WILLIAM HARCUM noe cause of action appearing, a non suit is granted the said ROGERS against the said HARCUM with costs and damages according to Law als Execution

- BARRATT agt HARTLAND Whereas GEORGE BARRATT was arrested to this Court at the suit of WILLIAM HARTLAND and noe cause of action appearing a non suit is granted the said BARRATT against the said HARTLAND with costs and damages according to Law als Execution

- HARTLAND agt LEWIS Whereas JOHN LEWIS was summoned to appeare this Court to give in his Evidence in the behalf of WILLIAM HARTLAND against GEORGE BARRATT and not appearing, it is ordered that he be fined according to Law

- JAM: CLAUGHTON agt PET: FLYNT Admr. of JNO: KNOTT It is ordered that this suit be dismist
- RICH: LATTIMORE agt JNO: CHAMPION referred to the next Court at the motion of the Plaintiffe
- HEN: RIDER agt RICH: HULL Whereas HENRY RIDER moved this Court [on the behalf of ANNE his Wife, Daughter of WALTER MOOR, decd], for a Child's portion out of that Estate. It is ordered that RICHARD HULL, Executor of the said MOOR, the next Court bring in an Account of what Estate the said MOOR dyed seized of and that the said HENRY in right of his Wife be possessed of the third part thereof, but whereas the said MOOR did give by his Last Will and Testament unto his Daughter, SARAH, out of his Estate if the remainder of the Estate [debts and legacies being first paid] will hold out to make two parts equall to the said SARAH her legacy that then the said HENRY have his Wife's portion out of that part of the Estate but if it should come short of it, that the whole Estate to be divided into three equall parts and that the said HENRY to have one part thereof

p. 191   Northumberland County Court 19th of July 1683
- PET: BYRAM agt DAV: FLOOKER This Cause is referred to the next Court
- EBENEZER SANDERS agt MRS. THOMAS referred to the next Court
- THO: GOLDSMYTH agt Mr. EDW. FIELDING Whereas Mr. EDWARD FIELDING, Administrator of Mr. AMBROSE FIELDING, deceased was summoned to this Court by a scire facias to shew reason why Mr. THOMAS GOLDSMYTH should not have Execution on a Judgment obteyned by him against the Estate of the said AMBROSE the 13th of May 1678 for two thousand six hundred ninety nine pounds of tobacco and cask and not shewing any reason, Judgment is granted the said GOLDSMYTH against the Estate of the said AMBROSE for the said sume with costs als Execution
- Mr. JNO: ARNER agt Mr. EDW: FIELDING Whereas Mr. EDWARD FIELDING, Administrator of Mr. AMBROSE FIELDING, deceased, was summoned to this Court by a scire facias to shew reason why Execution should not issue out against him on a Judgment obteyned by JOHN ARNER for two thousand one hundred twenty five pounds of tobacco and cask, and not shewing any reason, Judgment if granted JOHN ARNER against the said AMBROSE FIELDING for the said sume with costs als Execution
- THO: LEWIS agt JAM: BAKER Whereas an Attachment was awarded THOMAS LEWIS against the Estate of JAMES BAKER for sixteen hundred pounds of tobacco and caske, which Attachment is returned executed on a Mare now running at the Plantation of Collo. THOMAS BRERETON and whereas the said LEWIS hath this Court made his debt appeare due by Bill under the hand of the said BAKER for the said summe; Judgment is granted the said LEWIS for the said Mare attached as aforesaid [she being appraysed according to Law] with costs &c.
- TIPTON agt MOTTROM Whereas it appeares to this Court by two Bills under the hand of Major JOHN MOTTROM ye one dated ye 17th January 1679, for one thousand twenty two pounds of tobacco and cask the other dated the 14th June 1680 for eighteen hundred thirty and three pounds of tobacco and cask that the said MOTTROM is indebted to Mr. SAMUEL TIPTON two thousand eight hundred fifty

NORTHUMBERLAND COUNTY ORDER BOOK, 1678-1698

five pounds of tobacco and cask, Judgment is granted SAMUEL TIPTON against Major JOHN MOTTROM for the said sume with costs als Execution

- SAMUEL GOCH agt the Sheriffe Whereas NICHOLAS BADGER was arrested to this Court at the suit of SAMUEL GOCH for nine hundred thirty five pounds of tobacco and cask. Judgment is granted the said GOCH for the said sum with costs als Execution

p. 192 Northumberland County Court 19th of July 1683

- JAMES JONES agt ALICE PERYNE Whereas JAMES JONES was arrested to this Court at the suit of ALICE PERYNE and noe cause of action appearing, a non suit is granted the said JONES against the said PERYNE with costs and damages according to Law

- SIMPSON agt JONES Whereas it appeares to this Court that JAMES JONES standeth indebted unto JAMES SIMPSON eight hundred pounds of tobacco and cask for ten monthes service; it is ordered that the said JONES pay the said sume unto the said SIMPSON with costs als Execution and also that the said JONES deliver to the said SIMPSON his Indenture

- DRAKE and WOOLDRIDGE agt SYMPSON Whereas PHILIP DRAKE and EDWARD WOOLDRIDGE were summoned to the Court to give in their Evidence in the behalf of EDWARD WOOLDRIDGE against JAMES JONES and haveing given their attendance fower dayes in that businesse, it is ordered that the said JAMES SYMPSON pay them for their attendance according to Act with costs als Execution

- CARTER agt MOTTROM Whereas Mr. DENNIS CARTER the Assignee of ROBERT BAYLEY, the Assignee of EDWARD JONES the Executor of ROGER BAGNELL petitioned this Court for Judgment against Major JOHN MOTTROM for eight hundred and three pounds of tobacco and cask, being what remaynes to be satisfyed of two Judgments obteyned against the said MOTTROM dated March 20th 1677, the one by ROBERT BAYLEY for fower hundred seaventy five pounds of tobacco and cask, the other by ROGER BAGNELL for five hundred and fifty pounds of tobacco and cask with costs; Judgment is granted the said CARTER, Assignee as aforesaid, against the said Major MOTTROM for the sume of eight hundred and three pounds of tobacco and cask with costs als Execution

- FIELDING agt HARVEY Whereas Mr. RICHARD FIELDING was arrested to this Court at the suit of HENRY HARVEY and the said HARVEY not appearing to prosecute, a non suite is granted the said FIELDING against the said HARVEY with costs and damages according to Act als Execution

- THO: EVANS agt THO: WINTER referred to the next Court

p. 193 Northumberland County Court 19th of July 1683

- KNIGHT agt JONES Whereas Mr. GEORGE KNIGHT did exhibite an Information into this Court against Mr. THOMAS JONES, it is ordered that on the 6th of August next all the witnesses which Mr. GEORGE KNIGHT doth desire should be sworne in the businesse, be summoned to appeare at ye Courthouse and that those Magistrates that are appoynted by a dedimus potestatem to swear the Evidences of Collo. THOMAS BRERETON against Capt. PETER KNIGHT doe also sweare those witnesses which shall be summoned by Mr. GEORGE KNIGHT and

NORTHUMBERLAND COUNTY ORDER BOOK, 1678-1698 -9-

THOMAS JONES
- The next Court ye 2d Wednesday in 7ber next

- At a Court held for Northumberland County the 12th of September 1683
Present
Capt. PETER KNIGHT   Mr. PHILIP SHAPLEIGH
Mr. PETER PRESLEY   Capt. JOHN HAYNIE   Justices
Major JOHN MOTTROM   Mr. RICHARD KENNER

- MAHON agt SWANSON Whereas the last Court an Attachment was granted SAMUELL MAHON against the Estate of JOHN SWANSON, for two hundred twenty five pounds of tobacco and cask which Attachment is returned executed in the hands JOHN SWANSON, Judgment is granted the said MAHON against the said SWANSON for the said sume with costs als Execution

- JOHN FORD to have MARY MORTON Whereas ANDREW MORTON by his Will did give MARY, his Daughter, to THOMAS [   ] who being dead and the Child small, JOHN FORD who married the Aunt of the Child prayed that he might have custody of the Child, the Court considering that the said MARY a relation of the said FORD to bring up the Child and doe order that JOHN FORD in right of his Wife have the guardianship of the said MARY and that THOMAS WILLIAMS aforesaid deliver the said MARY to the said FORD

p. 194   Northumberland County Court 12th of September 1683
- Mr. WM. DOWNING's Will proved Upon the Petition of MARGARETT DOWNING, the Executrix of Mr. WILLIAM DOWNING, deceased, a Probate is granted the said MRS. MARGARETT of the Last Will and Testament of Mr. WILLIAM DOWNING, the Will being proved by th Oaths of CHRISTOPHER KIRK and WILLIAM [? POT----DELL] the witnesses to the Will

- CONWAY agt BARNES Whereas Mr. EDWARD CONWAY was arrested to this Court at the suit of THOMAS BARNES and noe cause of action appearing, a non suit is granted the said CONWAY against the said THOMAS BARNES with costs and damages according to Law

- SMYTH agt HARCUM Whereas a suit hath long depended between Mr. WILLIAM HARCUM and Mr. WILLIAM SMYTH in an action of Trespasse and it appearing that the said SMYTH hath done him noe trespasse a non suit is granted the said SMYTH against the said HARCUM with costs and damages according to Law als Execution

- LATTIMORE agt CLAUGHTON Whereas CLEMENT LATTIMORE was arrested to this Court at the suit of Mr. JAMES CLAUGHTON and noe cause of action appearing, a non suit is granted the said LATTIMORE against the said CLAUGHTON with costs and damages according to Law als Execution

- SIMS agt TOWERS Whereas WALTER SIMS was arrested to this Court at the suit of THOMAS TOWERS and noe cause of action appearing, a non suit is granted the said SIMS against the said TOWERS with costs and damages according to Law als Execution

- ROBINSON and WARD agt SIMS Whereas THOMAS ROBINSON gave attendance four dayes and JOHN WARD two dayes at the Court to give in their

Evidence in the behalf of WALTER SIMS against THOMAS TOWERS. It is ordered that the said SIMS pay THOMAS ROBINSON and JOHN WARD for their attendance as aforesaid according to Act with costs als Execution

- BAYLEY agt PARKER WILLIAM PARKER confesseth Judgment for the present payment of sixteen hundred pounds of tobacco and cask unto JOHN BAYLEY with costs als Execution

p. 195   Northumberland County Court 12th of September 1683

- LAWRENCE agt PEMBERTON Whereas RICHARD PEMBERTON did engate himselfe to cure JOHN LAWRENCE of a Malady he then lay under for which the said LAWRENCE was to pay him one thousand pounds of tobacco and caske, and if the cure was not effected then the said LAWRENCE was to pay but five hundred pounds of tobacco; and whereas it doth appear that the said PEMBERTON hath had one thousand pounds of tobacco and caske and yet the cure is not effected, it is ordered that the said PEMBERTON pay ye said LAWRENCE five hundred pounds of tobacco and caske with costs als Execution

- BYRAM agt FLUKER Whereas PETER BYRAM arrested DAVID FLUKER to this Court and noe cause of action appearing, it is ordered that the said Cause be dismist

- EVANS agt WINTER THOMAS EVANS against THOMAS WINTER referred to the next Court for want of Evidences

- SPENCER agt SHAPLEIGH Whereas the Honble. NICHOLAS SPENCER Esqr. prayed this Court for Judgment against Mr. PHILIP SHAPLEIGH for two Negroes, a man and woman, on whome an Execution was served and they delivered to THOMAS HOBSON for the use of the said NICHOLAS SPENCER Esqr. who gave the Negroes to the said SHAPLEIGH untill his Honor should demand them and whereas the said SHAPLEIGH hath deteyned the said Negroes three months since demanded and his Honor craving Judgment for the Negroes and satisfaction for the time that they have been deteyned from him according to Act, Mr. PHILIP SHAPLEIGH declaring in Court before the next Court he will deliver unto THOMAS HOBSON his Honor's Attorney good Bills with sufficient security for thirty four pounds, eighteen shillings and six pence sterling with damages according to Act, which THOMAS HOBSON in behalfe of his Honor doth accept of which for effect the said SHAPLEIGH to be discharged of that debt but if he should fayle that Judgment shall then passe against him, ye said SHAPLEIGH, according to his Honor's Petition with costs als Execution

p. 196   Northumberland County Court 12th of September 1683

- WAHOP agt KEYNE Whereas an Attachment was awarded Mr. THOMAS WAHOP against the Estate of THOMAS BEECH for twelve hundred pounds of tobacco and caske which Attachment is returned executed on eight hundred pounds of tobacco and caske in the hands of WILLIAM KEYNE, and whereas Mr. WAHOP hath this Court made his said debt appear just by a Bill under the hand and seale of THOMAS BEECH, Judgment is granted the said WAHOP against the said KEYNE for the said summe of eight hundred pounds of tobacco and caske with costs als Execution

- WADE agt KNIGHT Whereas at a Court held for this County the 20th

NORTHUMBERLAND COUNTY ORDER BOOK, 1678-1698   -11-

of August 1680 JOHN WADE obteyned Judgment against Mr. GEORGE KNIGHT for four thousand pounds of tobacco and caske, and whereas since JOHN HUGHLETT the Attorney of the said WADE, summoned the said KNIGHT by scire facias to shew reason why Execution should not issue on that Order who prayed for an Injunction to stop further proceedings at the Common Law untill he had a hearing ye next Court in Chancery, which being granted him and the last Court the said KNIGHT giving in by Note and the said HUGHLETT, Attorney as aforessid, his Answer. Mr. KNIGHT prayed time untill this Court when he said he would give in his replycation to the said WADE's Answer of which haveing fayled it is now ordered that the former Order be confirmed and ordered that the said KNIGHT forthwith pay to the said WADE the summe of four thousand pounds of tobacco and caske with costs als Execution

- JONES agt PEMBERTON JAMES JONES against RICHARD PEMBERTON referred to the next Court at the motion of the Defendant

- JOHN NICHOLS to survey his Land Upon the Petition of JOHN NICHOLS it is ordered that he survey his land according to Pattent and conveyance

p. 197   Northumberland County Court 12th of September 1683.
- MARY DOWNING Comm. of Admon with Will of WM: DOWNING A Commission of Administration with a Will annexed is granted to MARY DOWNING of the Estate of her deceased Husband, WILLIAM DOWNING, she giveing caution according to Law

- Securitie MARY DOWNING, JOHN HUGHLETT and DENNIS EYES doe bind themselves in the sum of thirty thousand pounds of tobacco that MARY shall administer of the Estate of her deceased Husband and exhibit an Inventory thereof according to Law

- Appraysers JOHN HUGHLETT, THOMAS WEBB, JOHN WORNAM and JOHN ATTKINS are appoynted this day to appryse the Estate of WILLIAM DOWNING deced. being first sworne before a Justice of the Peace

- Capt. KNIGHT discharged from his Bond Capt. PETER KNIGHT being ye last Court bound for the appearance of Mr. GEORGE KNIGHT this Court and haveing appeared, itis ordered that Capt. PETER KNIGHT be released from his Bond

- The next Court the 3d Wednesday in October

- At a Court held for Northumberland County the 17th of October 1683 Annoque Regni Regis Caroli secundi 2d, 35th &c.
                    Present
Mr. PETER PRESLEY   Capt. JOHN HAYNIE
Major JOHN MOTTROM   Mr. RICHARD KENNER   Justices
Capt. THOMAS MATHEW   Mr. WILLIAM ROGERS

- Probate of RICH: BRADLEY's Will Upon the Petition of ANNE BRADLEY Executrix of RICHARD BRADLEY, deceased, a Probate is granted her of the Last Will and Testament of the said RICHARD BRADLEY the Will being proved by the Oaths of JAMES JOHNSON and THOMAS MILLER witnesses to the Will

- Capt. JONES presented himselfe Capt. THOMAS JONES hath this day presented himselfe to the Court to answer the Information of Mr. GEORGE KNIGHT

- GEORGE HUTTON is appoynted Constable for MATTAPONY
- EVANS agt WINTER JOHN EVANS preferring an Information against THOMAS WINTER for concealing a Tythable [remainder at the bottom of the page stained]

p. 198 Northumberland County Court 17th of October 1683
- The Accts. of Mr. NUTT's Estate audited Ordered that Mr. PETER PRESLEY, SENR. and Capt. JOHN HAYNIE audite the Accounts between Mr. JOHN FARNEFOLD and Mr. WILLIAM NUTT about the Estate of Capt. WILLIAM NUTT deceased, soe far as JOHN NUTT was concerned the first Wednesday in 9br next at the Courthouse and give in their report thereof to the next Court
- ANTH: MORRIS's Estate tobe devided Whereas Capt. JOHN HAYNIE in the behalfe of JANE the heyre of ANTHONY MORRIS, deceased, and Mr. CUTHBERT SPAN [in the behalfe of DOROTHY the Relict of the said ANTHONY] petitioned this Court that a Division might be made of the Decedent's Estate between them, this Court doe order that on Munday next Mr. RICHARD FARRINGTON, JOHN WORNAM, DENNIS EYES and CLEMENT LATTIMORE doe apprayse and devide the said Estate between the said persons and deliver unto each their proper portions thereof and that they then allott unto the said Mr. CUTHBERT SPAN [in the behalfe of his Wife] the third of the land and housing, that Capt. JOHN HAYNIE take into his hands the Estate of the said JANE untill the next Court, that WILLIAM KING, Unkle to the said JANE live on her part of the land and that Mr. CUTHBERT SPAN deliver up unto DENNIS EYSE aforesaid what Pattents conveyances or other evidences he hath belonging unto the Land and that the said DENNIS EYSE have the tuition and keeping of the said JANE
- KENNER agt JEFFERSON Wheras an Attachment was awarded Mr. RICHARD KENNER against the Estate of Mr. SAMUEL JEFFERSON for twenty pounds, five shillings and four pence sterling which Attachment is returned executed on seaven hogsheads of tobacco in the hands of Mr. HENRY ROSSE and two thousand three hundred and fifty pounds of tobacco in the hands of Mr. JOHN COUTANSHEW which being by Order of Court appraysed at fourteen hundred pounds and three shillings sterling by ROBERT SECH and ROBERT BRYERY and whereas since the said RICHARD KENNER hath attached in the hands of Mr. RICHARD ROGERS five hundred thirty two pounds of tobacco and caske and three hundred pounds of tobacco in the hands of CHRISTOPHER NEALE, Judgment is granted the said KENNER against the said ROGERS and NEALE for the summes attached as aforesaid [there are three more lines but at the bottom of the page in the stain]

p. 199 Northumberland County Court 17th of October 1683
- ROBERTS agt BLAGG Mr. JOHN JULIAN, Attorney of Mr. ABRAHAM BLAGG confesseth Judgment for the present payment of one hundred fifty three pounds sterling money unto Capt. THOMAS MATHEW, substituant to Mr. EDMUND GIBBONS, the Attorney of Mr. ROBERT ROBERTS it being for Bills of Exchange protested and the damages and charges thereof with costs of suit als Execution
- WILLOUGHBY agt MOOR Whereas there appeareth due to Mr. HENRY WILLOUGHBY from the Estate of WALTER MOOR, deceased, for medicines administered to the said MOOR in the time of his sicknesse fower hundred fifty pounds

NORTHUMBERLAND COUNTY ORDER BOOK, 1678-1698   -13-

of tobacco and cask, Judgment is granted HENRY WILLOUGHBY against the Estate of WALTER MOOR, for the said sume with costs als Execution

- Cossat Exer agt LEWIS Whereas the 18th July last Judgment passed against JOHN LEWIS at the suit of WILLIAM HARTLAND for his not appearing at Court to give in his Evidence in behalf of the said HARTLAND against GEORGE BARRATT the said LEWIS declaring that he was at Court the Court before when summoned and gave in his Deposition which is lost or misplaced, a cossat exer is granted the said LEWIS untill the next Court

- HARCUM agt SMYTH Whereas it appeares to this Court that WILLIAM SMYTH standeth indebted unto Mr. WILLIAM HARCUM the sume of six hundred seaventy two pounds of tobacco and cask, Judgment is granted unto the said HARCUM against the said SMYTH for the said sume with costs als Execution unless the next Court the said SMYTH shews reason to the contrary

- HARCUM agt CHAMPION Judgment is granted Mr. WILLIAM HARCUM against JOHN CHAMPION for a Cow of his killed by the said CHAMPION unless the next Court he appeares and shews reasons to the contrary

- The Court adjourneth to the first day of the next month and ordered that on the Saturday following the Levy be layd

p. 200
- At a Court held for Northumberland County the 1st day of November 1683 Annoque Regni Regis Caroli secundi 2d. 35th &c.

Present
Lt. Collo. SAMUELL SMYTH   Mr. NICHOLAS OWEN
Mr. PETER PRESLEY   Capt. JOHN HAYNIE   Justices
Capt. LEONARD HOWSON   Mr RICHARD KENNER
Capt. THOMAS MATHEW   Mr. WILLIAM ROGERS

- THOMAS HOBSON, Sheriffe This day THOMAS HOBSON was in obediance to an Order of the Honorable the President and Councill sworne High Sheriffe of this County and JOHN TOPPING Sub Sheriffe

- Bonds THOMAS HOBSON and Lt. Collo. SAMUELL SMYTH bind themselves to our Soveraigne Lord the King in the penall summe of one hundred thousand pounds of tobacco and caske that the said THOMAS HOBSON shall duely execute ye Office of Sheriffe of this County whilst he shall he shall remayne in that place

- ANTH: MORRIS's Estate to be divided Whereas ye last Court it was ordered thAt RICHARD FARRINGTON, JOHN WORNAM, DENNIS EYES and CLEMENT LATTIMORE should meet and divide the Estate of ANTHONY MORRIS deceased between DOROTHY, the Relict, and JANE, the heir of the said MORRIS. It is ordered that the said persons before sometime between this and the next Court divide the personall Estate of the said MORRIS between the said DOROTHY and JANE [excepting one feather bedd with the furniture, one table form and small hammers] which MARTHA LANE gave unto the said JANE [as appeares by the Oath of VALENTINE MUNSLOW and GRACE his Wife] and that then they divide the land and orchards into three small lotts according to quality and quantity [into how many parcells soever it may be] and possess CUTHBERT SPANN in the behalfe of the said DOROTHY, his Wife, with such part or parts choose according to Law, that the said CUTHBERT and DOROTHY his Wife [on their Oath shew to the parties appoynted to divide the Estate as abovesaid], the full of the Estate of the said ANTHONY and that they forthwith deliver unto Capt. JOHN HAYNIE the said JANE's part who promises to take the part thereof untill the next Court if the said Capt. HAYNIE provides for those that are now on the Plantation and he be paid for his charges in providing for them out of the said Estate and that the said SPANN deliver to DENNIS EYES all the evidences belonging to the land of the said MORRIS

p. 201

Northumberland County Court 1st of November 1683

- Mr. ROGERS his Information Mr. WILLIAM ROGERS High Sheriffe the last yeare did this day give an Account unto this Court that he had received Capt. PETER KNIGHT, SYLAS DUKE and WILLIAM RENNOLLS their Levys the last yeare who were not given in in that yeare's lyst of Tythables

- THO: HUGHLETT to be allowed for keeping ARTHUR NUTWELL Ordered that THOMAS HUGHLETT be allowed four hundred pounds of tobacco for keeping ARTHUR NUTWELL a mad man foure dayes

- ARTHUR NUTWELL to be carried to LAWRENCE SYMMONS It is ordered that THOMAS HUGHLETT deliver ARTHUR NUTWELL [a mad man lately committed to Prison] to ye Constable for Cone to be by him coveyed to the Constable of CHERRY POINTE, and to be by him conveyed over to LAWRENCE SYMMONS at YEOCOMOCO POYNT and if he shall not by him be enterteyned that he be returned from Constable to Constable to ye said THOMAS HUGHLETT is to keep him in safe custody untill the next Court

- SANDERS agt THOMAS Whereas EBENEZER SANDERS brought his Information to this Court against MRS. MARY THOMAS, the Administratrix of Mr. WILLIAM THOMAS, and obteyned Judgment against her for three books with other things kept from EBENEZER SANDERS by WILLIAM THOMAS; It is ordered that the said MRS. MARY THOMAS pay unto EBENEZER SANDERS five pounds, ten shillings sterling out of the Estate of WILLIAM THOMAS for the said Books als Execution

- ELIZ: GERRARD's Comm of Admon A Commission of Administration is granted ELIZABETH GERRARD of the Estate of her Husband she giveing caution according to Law

- Bond ELIZABETH GERRARD and JAMES CLAUGHTON doe oblige themselves in Court joyntly and severally in the penall summe of thirty thousand pounds of tobacco and caske to the Justices for this County that the said ELIZABETH shall duely administer on the Estate of SAMUELL GERRARD deceased and exhibite an Inventory thereof according to Law

- Appraysers JAMES JOHNSON, WILLIAM SHOARES and GEORGE HUTTON are appoynted to apprayse the Estate of SAMUELL GERRARD, deced., being first sworn by the next Justice of the Peace

- The Court adjourneth untill tomorrow morning at eight a clock

p. 202

- Die 2nd November 1683 Annoque Regni Regis Caroli secundi 2d. 35&c.

Present

Lt. Collo. SAMUEL SMYTH	Capt. LEONARD HOWSON	
Capt. THOMAS MATHEW	Mr. RICHARD KENNER	Justices
Mr. NICHOLAS OWEN	Mr. WILLIAM ROGERS	

- **HARCUM agt CHAMPION** Whereas it appeares to this Court that JOHN CHAMPION did kill a Cow of Mr. WILLIAM HARCUM's Judgment is granted to the said HARCUM against the said CHAMPTION for five hundred pounds of tobacco and caske with costs als Execution

- **JONES agt KNIGHT** Whereas Capt. THOMAS JONES in July Court arrested Mr. GEORGE KNIGHT for Attorney's fees in a Cause he appeared for him at the Generall Court and the said KNIGHT averring that he did nothing for him on which that Cause was referred to this Court the said JONES produceing a coppy of an Account the Generall Court offered by the said JONES, Judgment is granted the said JONES against the said KNIGHT for five hundred pounds of tobacco and caske with costs als Execution

- **HOBSON agt RICE** Whereas it appeares to this Court that RICHARD RICE stands indebted unto THOMAS HOBSON for Clerk's Fees seaven hundred and twelve pounds of tobacco and two hundred fifty four pounds of tobacco for Sheriffe's Fees as he was the Attorney of JOHN ENGLISH and four hundred fifty eight pounds of tobacco owne Account; Judgment is granted the said HOBSON against the said RICE for the said summe of seaven hundred and twelve pounds of tobacco and caske with costs als Execution

- **MARY THOMAS her Accot to be audited** Whereas MRS. MARY THOMAS, the Administratrix of Mr. WILLIAM THOMAS, deceased, produced her Account of Mr. WILLIAM THOMAS his Estate and prayed that her Account might be examined and that she might have her quieta est. The Court doth order that on Munday next come fortnight Capt. LEONARD HOWSON and THOMAS HOBSON autit the Accounts of the said THOMAS

- **HOWARD, JOHNSON and PEMBERTON agt RICE** Whereas WILLIAM HOWARD, JAMES JOHNSON and RICHARD PEMBERTON were arrested to this Court at the suit of RICHARD RICE, the Attorney of EDWARD WILLIAMS, and noe cause of action appearing, a non suit is granted the said HOWARD, JOHNSON and PEMBERTON with costs and damages according to Law als Execution

p 203 Northumberland County Court 2d of November 1683

- **PITCHER agt JONES** EMANNUELL PITCHER against JAMES JONES. Referred to the next Court at the motion of the Defendant

- **HARCUM agt SMYTH** Whereas Mr. WILLIAM HARCUM had an Order granted him against Lt. Collo. SAMUEL SMYTH for sixteen hundred seaventy two pounds of tobacco and cask, unlesse this Court the said SMYTH did shew reason to the contrary, he appearing and the business fully heard, Judgment is granted the said HARCUM against the said SMYTH for ye said summe with costs als Execution

- **LEE agt CURTIS** Mr. WILLIAM LEE against Mr. JOHN CURTIS is referred to the next Court by the consent of both parties

- **JOHN LEWIS to be acquitted the Order** Whereas the last Court a cossat Exer was awarded Mr. JOHN LEWIS on an Order obteyned against him for his not appearing at July Court to give in his Evidence in his behalfe and whereas this Court the said LEWIS appearing [the left side readable, the right side too faded] it is ordered that the said LEWIS be acquitted from the said Order

- **Capt. JONES to be released from his Bond** Upon the Petition of Capt. THOMAS JONES haveing attended this Court to answer the Information of Mr.

THOMAS JONES haveing attended this Court to answer the Information of Mr. GEORGE KNIGHT and the said KNIGHT not prosecuteing his Information, it is ordered that the said Capt. THOMAS JONES be released from his Bond that he gave for his appearance

- BRYERY agt BOGGAS An Attachment is granted ROBERT BRYERY against the Estate of HENRY BOGGAS for two thousand pounds of tobacco and caske returnable to the next Court

- HULL agt RIDER Whereas RICHARD HULL did preferr a Petition against HENRY RIDER, it is ordered that the businesse be referred to the next Court it it may be hoped there may be a fuller hearing

p. 204 Northumberland County Court 2d of November 1683

- JULIAN agt BASHAW Whereas an Attachment was granted JOHN JULIAN against the Estate of GREVES GERRARD for one thousand four hundred pounds of tobacco and cask and whereas WILLIAM BASHAW did tell the said JULIAN that he had six hundred pounds of tobacco of the said GERRARD's in his hands, whereupon the said JULIAN served the Attachment on him for the said summe returnable to the next Court when the businesse being disputed the said BASHAW on his Oath did declare he had none of that Estate in his hands. The Court judging the said BASHAW to be in motion of the said JULIAN his charge doe order that the said BASHAW to pay costs

- THO: HOBSON sworne Clerk This day THOMAS HOBSON, JUNR. was sworne Clerk of this County

- TOPPING sworne Sub Sheriffe This day JOHN TOPPING was sworne Sub Sheriffe of this County

- ASHTON to be released from Levy THOMAS ASHTON a poor impotent person is ordered to be freed from the Levy

- Mr. WM: ROGERS to be allowed for one person's Levy Ordered that Mr. WILLIAM ROGERS be allowed one hundred sixty three pounds of tobacco being the last yeare overcharged for one person's Levy at his Brother, RICHARD ROGERS

- JNO: LAWRENCE to be freed from Levy Ordered that JOHN LAWRENCE be freed from paying his owne Levy this yeare

- The next Court the third Wednesday in December

p 205 - Northumberland DR

To THOMAS MORRIS for worke done at the Old Courthouse	0150
To WILLIAM YARRET for one Wolfe shot	0100
To HENRY HARTLEY for three Wolves shot	0300
To Mr. WILLIAM ROGERS one Tythable overcharged last yeare	0163
To JOHN CLAUGHTON for two Wolves in a pitt	0400
To WILLIAM HILL for two Wolves taken in a pitt	0400
To EDWARD WILLLIAMS for tending the Courthouse	0450
To JOHN WEBB for two yeares keeping the STONE MILL BRIDGE	1600
To JOHN HUGHLETT for keeping a Prisoner	0400
To the Clerk for publique businesse	1000
To Collo. THOMAS BRERETON for impannelling a Grand Inquest	0300
To Cask	0240
To Sallary	0546
	no total

NORTHUMBERLAND COUNTY ORDER BOOK, 1678-1698

- Att a Court held for Northumberland County the 19th of December 1683 Annoque Regni Regis Caroli secundi 2d, 35th &c.

Present

Mr. PETER PRESLEY	Capt. JOHN HAYNIE
Mr. NICHOLAS OWEN	Mr. PHILIP SHAPLEIGH Justices
Major JOHN MOTTROM	Mr. CHRISTOPHER NEALE

- JNO: DUKE Servt to THO: BERRY JOHN DUKE, Orphant of SYLAS DUKE, with the consent of his Mother, doth bind imselfe for to serve THOMAS BERRY untill he be one and twenty yeares of age [being seaven yeares last June] the said BERRY providing for him as is fitt for an Apprentice and att the end of the terme to pay the said JOHN one Cow and Calfe, a Mare filly and a Sow with pigg or pigg by her side

- MRS. THOMAS to have her quieta est Whereas MRS. MARY THOMAS produced her Accounts of her Husband's Estate and prayed to have her quieta est on the motion of Mr. JOSIAS [   ] ordered to be referred to the next Court

p. 206   Northumberland County Court 19th of December 1693

- ELIZ: to serve for a bastard Whereas ELIZABETH HOBSON, Servant to Lt. Collo. SAMUELL SMYTH, hath had a bastard in the time of her service. It is ordered that the said ELIZABETH serve her said Master for his charges and loss of time two yeares after the time of her service by Indenture custome or otherwise is expired and the punishment acquitted, Lt. Collo. SMYTH paying the Fine

- ALICE HUDNALL, Comm. of Admon. A Commission of Administration is granted ALICE HUDNALL of the Estate of her deceased Husband, JOHN HUDNALL she giveing caution according to Law

- Bond ALICE HUDNALL and JOHN DOWNING do oblige themselves joyntly and severally in the penall sume of thirty thousand pounds of tobacco and cask to the Justices of the Peace for this County that the said ALICE HUDNALL shall justly administer on the Estate of JOHN HUDNALL, deceased, and exhibit an Inventory thereof according to Law

- Appraysers Mr. RICHARD HULL, JOHN DONAWAY, GEORGE DAWKINS and BOYE HAMBLETON are appoynted to apprayse the Estate of JOHN HUDNALL, deceased, being sworne by the next Justice

- CURTIS agt LEE Whereas Mr. JOHN CURTIS was arrested to this Court at the suit of Mr. WILLIAM LEE and noe cause of action appearing, a non suit is ganted the said CURTIS against the said LEE with costs and damages according to Law

- JAM: AUSTEN Cert: Certificate is granted Mr. JAMES AUSTEN to the Assembly for a case of Pistolls lost in the service, Capt. COOPER, Commander of the Garrison, deposing that the Pistolls were lost

- GEO: KNIGHT to be sworne Whereas Mr. RICHARD NELMES, JUNR. brought his deceased Father's Will to this Court to be proved and Mr. GEORGE KNIGHT, one of the witnesses of the said Will, being wanting, it is ordered that some time between this and the next Court ye said KNIGHT be sworne by some Justice of the Peace for this County when he is desired to certifie the same to the next Court

- RIDER agt HULL Whereas HENRY RIDER was arrested to this Court at the suit of RICHARD HULL and noe cause of action appearing, a non suit is granted HENRY RIDER against the said HULL with costs and damages according to Law

- HOBSON agt WATERMAN THOMAS WATERMAN confesseth Judgment to THOMAS HOBSON for the present payment of two thousand pounds of tobacco and caske, and one thousand pounds of tobacco and caske the next yeare with costs als Execution

- BARNES agt CONWAY Whereas Mr. EDWIN CONWAY was arrested to this Court at the suite of THOMAS BARNES and noe cause of action appearing, it is ordred that the suit be dismissed

- The Court adjourneth till tomorrow morning at eight a clock

p. 207

Die 20th December 1683
Mr. PETER PRESLEY
Capt. THOMAS MATHEW
Capt. JOHN HAYNIE

Present
Mr. PHILIP SHAPLEIGH
Mr. CHRISTOPHER NEALE   Justices

- GEO: HAMBLETON to have GEO: HUGHS's Estate It is ordered that GEORGE HAMBLETON, Master to GEORGE HUGHS, have in his custody all the Estate of the said GEORGE HUGHS the said HAMBLETON exhibiteing to the next Court an Inventory of the Estate and giveing security to be accomptable for the same when thereto required

- Capt. JNO: HAYNIE Admr. of MORRIS's Estate Whereas the last Court it was ordered that the Estate of ANTHONY MORRIS, deceased, should be divided between JANE, the Daughter, and DOROTHY, the Relict of the said MORRIS, which accordingly being done and an Account thereof being brought into this Court by Capt. JOHN HAYNIE who is too nearly related to the said JANE, the said HAYNIE being Commissioner to the said ANTHONY, and thereby incapable to be Guardian to the said JANE, and none appearing in the behalf of the said DOROTHY, it is ordered that Capt. JOHN HAYNIE be Administrator of the Estate of the said ANTHONY MORRIS in trust for the said JANE and that he exhibite an Inventory of the same and give caution to be accomptable for it when thereto required

- HARCUM agt HARTLAND Whereas an Order the 8th of July last was granted to Mr. WILLIAM HARCUM against WILLIAM HARTLAND for one thousand pounds of tobacco and caske, whereof there was one hundred and twenty pounds of tobacco omitted; Judgment is now granted to the said HARCUM against the said HARTLAND for the said sume of one hundred and twenty pounds of tobacco and caske with costs als Execution

- SMYTH agt DAWKINS Whereas thre hath been a difference long depending between RICHARD SMYTH and GEORGE DAWKINS concerning Land, it is ordered that the suit be dismissed

- HATFIELD agt the Sheriffe Whereas GERVAS HATFIELD arrested Mr. WILLIAM HARCUM to this Court for eight hundred pounds of tobacco and caske and the said HARCUM not appearing, Judgment is granted the said HATFIELD agaisnt the Sheriffe for the said sume with costs als Execution

- HOBSON v WILDEY THOMAS HOBSON against MRS. JANE WILDEY referred to the next Court at the motion of the Defendant and ordered with the consent of the Defendant that the Evidences of the Plaintiffe be taken this Court

Northumberland County Court 20th of December 1683

p. 208

- **PEMBERTON agt GERRARD** Whereas it appeares to this Court that SAMUEL GERRARD dyed indebted unto Mr. RICHARD PEMBERTON for effecting of cure on the said GERRARD five hundred pounds of tobacco and caske, two hundred nailes and a saddle worth one hundred pounds of tobacco, Judgment is granted the said PEMBERTON against ELIZABETH, the Administratrix of the said GERRARD, for the said summe of five hundred pounds of tobacco and caske and the nailes and saddle to be paid in kind by the said ELIZABETH als Execution

- **CONSTANCE agt GERRARD** Whereas it appeares to this Court that Mr. SAMUELL GERRARD stood indebted unto PETER CONSTANCE sixteen hundred pounds of tobacco and caske, Judgment is granted the said CONSTANCE against ELIZABETH, the Administratrix of the said GERRARD for the said sum with costs als Execution

- **MATHEW agt GERRARD** Whereas Execution issued out on an Order obteyned against SAMUELL GERRARD by Capt. THOMAS MATHEW dated the 21st of February last for three thousand nine hundred ninety one pounds of tobacco and caske with the fees did amount to the sum of four thousand one hundred and eleven hundred pounds of tobacco and caske, the said GERRARD dying before the said Execution was served. It is ordered that the said Capt. MATHEW have Execution against the Estate of the said GERRARD for the said sume and that ELIZABETH, the Administratrix of the said GERRARD, doth refuse to shew the Estate that then Execution issue against her body

- **LOYD agt GERRARD** Whereas it appeares to this Court that SAMUELL GERRARD dyed indebted unto Mr. RICHARD LOYD the sum of seaventeen hundred pounds of tobacco and caske by a Bill under the hand of the sasid GERRARD dated the 19th day of July lat; Judgment is granted to the said LOYD against ELIZABETH, the Administratrix of the said GERRARD, for the said sume als Execution

- **MOOR agt GERRARD** Whereas it appears to this Court that SAMUELL GERRARD dyed indebted unto JAMES MOOR by Bill under the hand and seale of the said GERRARD six hundred pounds of tobacco and caske, Jugment is granted unto the said MOOR against ELIZABETH, the Administratrix of the said GERRARD, for the said sume als Execution

- **RICE v CLAUGHTON** Whereas RICHARD RICE was arrested to this Court at the suit of JAMES CLAUGHTON and noe cause of action appearing, a non suit is granted the said RICE against the said CLAUGHTON with costs and damages according to Law

Northumberland County Court 20th of December 1683

p. 209

- **FLYNT agt GERRARD** Whereas it appeares to this Court that SAMUELL GERRARD dyed indebted unto Mr RICHARD FLYNT the sum of nineteen hundred pounds of tobacco and caske, the said FLYNT haveing made Oath that the said debt was due; Judgment is granted to the said FLYNT against ELIZABETH, the Administratrix of the said GERRARD for the said sume als Execution

- **SHAPLEIGH agt the Sheriffe** Whereas VALENTINE MUNSLOE was arrested to this Court at the suit of Mr. PHILIP SHAPLEIGH for three hundred and fifteen pounds of tobacco and caske, and the said MUNSLOE hath fayled of his appearance, Judgment is granted the said SHAPLEIGH against the Sheriffe for the

said sume according to Law
- The next Court to be the 3d Wednesday in January

- At a Court held for Northumberland County the sixteenth day of January 1683/4 Annoque Regni Regis Caroli 2d, 35th &c.

Present
Lt. Collo. SAMUEL SMYTH   Mr. PHILIP SHAPLEIGH
Mr. PETER PRESEY   Capt. JOHN HAYNIE   Justices
Capt. THOMAS MATHEW   Mr. RICHARD KENNER

- RICE agt JOHNSON Whereas RICHARD RICE the Attorney of EDWARD WATTS arrested JAMES JOHNSON, WILLIAM HOWARD and RICHARD PEMBERTON to this Court and the Defendants praying [faded on one side readable on the other] in case the Plaintiffe be cast in this suit, Mr. JOHN HUGHLETT, SENR. doth oblige himselfe with the said RICE for the payment of all such damages as the Defendants shall receive from this suit

- HATFIELD agt HARCUM Mr. WILLIAM HARCUM confesseth Judgment for the present payment of eight hundred pounds of tobacco and caske unto Mr. GERVAS HATFIELD with costs als Execution

- PERYNE's Admon Upon the Petition of ALICE PERYNE a Commission of Administration is granted her on the Estate of her deceased Husband, THOMAS PERYNE, she giveing caution according to Law

- Bond ALICE PERYNE, JAMES CLAUGHTON and GEORGE HUTTON doe oblige themselves joyntly and severally in the penall sume of thirty thousand pounds of tobacco and caske that the said ALICE shall duly administer on the Estate of her deceased Husband and exhibite an Inventory thereof according to Law

p. 210

Northumberland County Court 16th of January 1683/4

- SANDERS on Comm. of Admon Upon the Petition of Mr. EBENEZER SANDERS and Mr. EDWARD SANDERS, the Sons of MRS. MARY THOMAS deceased, a Commission of Administrationis granted them on the Estate of their said Mother, they giveing caution according to Law

- The Bond EBENEZER SANDERS, EDWARD SANDERS, THOMAS HOBSON and EDWARD WHITE doe oblige themselves joyntly and severally in the penall sume of thirty thousand pounds of tobacco and caske that the said EBENEZER and EDWARD shall duly administer on the Estate of the said MARY and exhibite an Inventory thereof according to Law

- Appraysers Mr. WILLIAM HARCUM, THOMAS WEBB, JOHN COCKERELL and JOHN SYMMONS or any three of them are appoynted and ordered some time between this and the next Court to apprayse the Estate of MRS. MARY THOMAS, deceased, being sworne by the next Justice

- PITTS his Comm. of Admon A Commission of Administration is granted Mr. JOSIAS PITTS who married REBECCA, the Daughter of Mr. WILLIAM THOMAS, deceased, on the Estate of the said THOMAS, he giveing caution according to Law

- The Bond JOSIAS PITTS, JAMES CLAUGHTON and JAMES JOHNSON doe oblige themselves joyntly and severally in the penall sum of forty thousand pounds of tobacco and caske that JOSIAS PITTS shall duly administer on the Estate

NORTHUMBERLAND COUNTY ORDER BOOK, 1678-1698   -21-

WILLIAM THOMAS, deceased, and exhibite an Inventory thereof according to Law

- BRYERY agt BOGGAS Whereas ROBERT BRYERY moved this Court that a Division should be made of the tymber not in dispute between him and HENRY BOGGAS, it is ordered that on Munday next Mr. WILLIAM KEYNE and ABRAHAM JOYCE devide the said tymber between them

- DAWSON to build a Mill Upon the Petition of HENRY DAWSON it is ordered that the said HENRY have liberty to erect a Water Grist Mill on the head of POTOMACK CREEKE according to Act [last line lost in the stain at the bottom of the page]

p. 211 Northumberland County Court 16th of January 1683/4

- CHAMBERLAINE agt THOMAS Whereas it appeareth to this Court by a Bill under the hand of MRS. MARY THOMAS, deceased, that the said THOMAS stood indebted unto Mr. ROBERT CHAMBERLAINE the sume of one thousand pounds of tobacco and caske, Judgment is granted the said CHAMBERLAINE against the Estate of the said MRS. THOMAS for the said sume als Exection

- TOP agt BYRAM PETER BYRAM confesseth Judgment for the present payment of three hundred thirty two pounds of tobacco to THOMAS TOP with costs als Execution

- HARCUM agt DAWSON JOHN DAWSON confesseth Judgment for the present payment of the sume of five hundred pounds of tobacco and caske unto Mr. WILLIAM HARCUM with costs als Execution

- TOP agt JOHNSON JEFFERY JOHNSON confesseth Judgment for the present payment of five hundred thirty eight pounds of tobacco and caske unto THOMAS TOP with costs als Execution

- HENRY BENTLEY against JOHN WADDY referred to the next Court by consent of both parties

- JNO: DOWNING Certificate Certificate is granted JOHN DOWNING for three hundred and fifty acres of land for the importation of seaven persons into this Colony, vizt.

| JEREMIAH HARRIS, | DOROTHY HOWARD | JOHN FARIGON |
| MARY NORRIS | HENRY CHARLES | and two slaves |

- JONES agt COPPAGE Whereas it appeares to this Court by a Bill under the hand of WILLIAM COPPAGE dated the 14th of February 1681/2 that the said COPPAGE stands indebted unto Mr. THOMAS JONES ye sume of five hundred pounds of tobacco and cask, Judgment is granted the said JONES against the said COPPAGE for the said sume with costs als Execution

- LAMBERT agt JONES Whereas an Attachment was awarded WILLIAM LAMBERT against the Estate of JAMES JONES for sixteen hundred pounds of tobacco and cask, which Attachment is returned executed on one feather bed and bolster, one red rug, one blankett, two paire of canvas sheets and one little table

p. 212 Northumberland County Court 16th of January 1683/4

The Court judging the Attachment to be soe served [the said JONES being an house keeper and a Freeholder of this County and happily at this time abroad about his necessary occasion] doe order Mr. WILLIAM SHOARES being obliged with the said JONES, his Wife, for the payment of the debt in case the next Court the said JONES doe not appeare or the said goods not be secured that the Attachment may acquiese

- GENESIS agt NIPPER Whereas it appeares to this Court that JAMES NIPPER stand indebted EZEKIEL GENESIS the sume of two hundred eight pounds of tobacco and cask; Judgment is granted the said GENESIS against the said NIPPER for the said sume with costs als Execution

- SHAPLEIGH agt MUNSLOW Whereas it appeares to this Court that VALENTINE MUNSLOW standeth indebted unto Mr. PHILIP SHAPLEIGH the sume of three hundred fifteen pounds of tobacco and cask by Account to which the said SHAPLEIGH hath made Oath; Judgment is granted ye said SHAPLEIGH againt the said MUNSLOW for the said sume with costs als Execution

- AUSTEN agt WARRINGTON Whereas an Attachment was awarded Mr. JAMES AUSTEN against the Estate of RICHARD THORNE for fower hundred pounds of tobacco and cask which Attachment is returned executed on soe much in the hands of RALPH WARRINGTON, JUNR., and whereas the said AUSTEN did sweare his said debt was due and that the said WARRINGTON told him he had but three hundred pounds of tobacco of the Estate of the said THORNE to satisfy the said debt in his hands, Judgment is granted the said AUSTEN against the said WARRINGON for the sume of three hundred pounds of tobacco with costs als Execution

- BAKER agt BREWER Whereas THOMAS BAKER complayned to this Court that whereas he had bought of THOMAS BREWER fowre hundred twenty five acres of Land as by a conveyance under the hand of the said BREWER doth appeare, the said BREWER hath surveyed him out of his Orchard and Cornfield and hath thrown downe his fences and prayed for his damages against the said BREWER. It is ordered that Capt. JOHN HAYNIE lay out the land according to the bounds expressed in the said Deed of Sale that the said BAKER may know what land he hath and Mr. BARTHOLOMEW DAMERON and Mr. RALPH WARRINGTON view the damages that the said BAKER hath susteyned by the said BREWER and give in their report to the next Court

p. 213 Northumberland County Court 16th of January 1683/4

- WEEKES agt the Sheriffe Whereas MRS. ELIZABETH [the Administratrix of Mr. SAMUEL GERRARD] was arrested to this Court at the suit of THOMAS WEEKES for six thousand nine hundred thirty pounds of tobacco and cask and not appearing, Judgment is granted ye said WEEKES against the Sheriffe for the said sume according to Law

- HULL agt UPTON Whereas JOHN HULL was arrested to this Court at the suit of ELIZABETH UPTON and noe cause of action appearing, a non suit is granted the said HULL against the said UPTON with costs and damages according to Law

- SHAPLEIGH agt MATHEW Whereas PHILIP SHAPLEIGH complayned to this Court that he delivered an Execution against the body of DOMINICK RICE for sixteen hundred pounds of tobacco and cask, but Capt. THOMAS MATHEW, then High Sheriffe of this County, which was neither served nor any returne made thereof by which meanes he sayth he has lost his debt and prayed Judgment against ye said Capt. MATHEW for the said debt, the said Capt. MATHEW and Mr. RICHARD FLYNT came into Court and haveing sworne that whilst they had the said Execution in their hands, they never did serve the said RICE with the same [he being in another

County] and that the said Execution was lost, it is ordered that the suit be dismist

- Appeale Mr. PHILIP SHAPLEIGH appealeth from the Judgment to a hearing before ye Honorable the Governor and Councill the fourth day of the next Generall Court which is granted he giveing caution to prosecute his Appeale

- Bond Mr. PHILIP SHAPLEIGH and Mr. JAMES AUSTEN doe oblige themselves joyntly and severally in the sume of five thousand pounds of tobacco and cask that the said SHAPLEIGH shall appeare at his day and prosecute his said Appeale

- THOMAS agt COOPER Mr. EDWARD THOMAS the Assignee of Mr. EDWARD CHILTON, the Assignee of Mr. THOMAS RABLY against Capt. GEORGE COOPER is referred to the next Court at the motion of the Defendant

p. 214 Northumberland County Court 16th of January 1693/4

- RABLEIGH agt ROSSE Whereas Mr. EDWARD THOMAS, the Attorney of Mr. THOMAS RABLEIGH sued Mr. HENRY ROSSE for fower thousand fower hundred and ten pounds of tobacco and cask being due on ballance of a Bill dated the 27th 7ber 1679, for six thousand nine hundred and sixty pounds of tobacco and cask due from the said ROSSE unto the said RABLEIGH, Mr. ROSSE shewing to this Court severall Receipts from Mr. THOMAS GEORGE who then had the said Bill in his hands by which it appeares that the full of that debt is satisfyed, the Court doth order that the suit be dismist

- The Court adjourns till tomorrow morning nine a clock

- Die 17th January 1683/4   Present
Lt. Collo. SAMUELL SMYTH   Capt. JOHN HAYNIE
Mr. PHILIP SHAPLEIGH   Mr. RICHARD KENNER Justices

- BONOWAY agt DOWNING Whereas it appeares to this Court that JOHN HUGHLETT, JUNR. who marryed MARY, the Relict of WILLIAM DOWNING, JUNR., is indebted unto WILLIAM BONOWAY six hundred forty five pounds of tobacco and cask by Account to which he hath made Oath, Judgment is granted the said BONOWAY against the said HUGHLETT for the said sume with costs als Execution

- MAXFIELD agt HULL Whereas RICHARD HULL was arrested to this Court at the suit of PETER MAXWELL for three hundred pounds of tobacco and cask by a Note left at his house, and Attachment is awarded the said MAXFIELD against the said ULL for the said sume returnable to the next Court

- GRINSTEAD agt WEBB Whereas an Attachment was awarded WILLIAM GRINSTEAD against the Estate of JOHN LAWRENCE for one hundred pounds of tobacco and cask which Attachment is returned executed on soe much in the hands of JOHN WEBB; Judgment is granted the said GRINSTEAD against the said WEBB for the said sume with costs als Execution

- RICHARD PEMBERTON against RICHARD FLYNT referred to the next Court at the motion of the Defendant

p. 215 Northumberland County Court 17th of January 1683/4

- Appraysers of HUGHS's Estate It is ordered that Mr. JOHN HUGHLETT and JOHN PALMER apprayse the Estate of GEORGE HUGHES now in the hands of GEORGE HAMBLETON being first sworne by the next Justice of the Peace

- HAMBLETON's Bond GEORGE HAMBLETON, Mr. RICHARD HAYNIE and THOMAS HUGHLETT doe oblige themselves in the penall sume of five thousand pounds of tobacco and cask that the said HAMBLETON shall give a just Account of the Estate of GEORGE HUGHES now in his hands when thereto required

- HOBSON v WILDEY The difference between THOMAS HOBSON, SENR. Plaintiffe and MRS. JANE WILDEY, Defendant, about a Steer of the said HOBSON's that was killed by the said WILDEY at the instance of the said Defendant was tryed by a Jury whose names are underwritten, vizt

Mr. RICHARD FLYNT	ADAM YARRATT	GEORGE HAMBLETON
Mr. JOHN HARRIS	RICHARD RICE	PETER FLYNT
Mr. PETER PRESLEY, JUNR.	JOHN HUGHLETT, JUNR.	PETER MAXWELL sworne
JAMES JOHNSON	THOMAS HUGHLETT	JOHN SOUTHERLAND

- Verdict The whole Jury being agreed doth say that the Plaintiffe according to what he declares [faded] against the within Defendant, MRS. JANE WILDEY

- Verdict The Jury returned to find damages [faded] soe give for the Plaintiffe three hundred and sixty [faded] tobacco for his time expended [faded] the within mentioned Steer

RICHD: FLYNT

- Verdict The Jury returned to value the Steer for their Verdict doe say, we doe find for the Plaintiffe for the said Steer seaven hundred pounds of tobacco and cask   RICHD: FLYNT

- Judgment On the motion of THOMAS HOBSON, SENR. Plaintiffe Judgment is granted him against the Defendant according to the form of the Verdicts with his costs of suit als Execution

- PRESLEY agt ROGERS Whereas the last yeare eleven thousand pounds of tobacco and cask was ordered to be payd by Mr. WILLIAM ROGERS, then Sheriffe to Mr. WILLIAM PRESLEY out of the publique whereof haveing fayled, it is ordered that if the next Court Mr. WILLIAM ROGERS doth not appeare to shew how he hath payd the said debt that then Judgment passe againt Mr. CHRISTOPHER NEALE, Security for the said ROGERS for the said sume als Execution; always provided that the said WILLIAM ROGERS and CHRISTOPHER NEALE have timely notice of this Order

- THOMAS and ATKINS agt WILDEY Ordered that MRS. JANE WILDEY pay to ZACHARIAH THOMAS and JOHN ATKINS for their two days attendance to give in their evidence in her behalf against THOMAS HOBSON according to Act with costs als Execution

- The Court adjourned till the next month

p. 216

- At a Court held for Northumberland County the 19th of March 1683/4 Annoque Regni Regis Caroli 2d, 36th &c.

Present

Mr. PETER PRESLEY	Capt. JOHN HAYNIE
Mr. RICHARD KENNER	Mr. CHRISTOPHER NEALE Justices

- Collo. SPENCER agt Mr. SHAPLEIGH Whereas at a Court held for this County the 17th of May 1682 Judgment was granted the Honorable NICHOLAS SPENCER, Esqr. against Mr. PHILIP SHAPLEIGH for the sume of sixteen pounds, nineteen shillings and six pence sterling, it being now made appeare to this Court that the said Debt became due from the said SHAPLEIGH to his Honor aforesaid as he [the said SHAPLEIGH] was Security for Mr. THOMAS CARTER, Master of the Ketch ye "SUSANNA of BOSTON," in NEW ENGLAND, for the payment of the said sume being due for the imposition of the duties of the vessell for which the said CARTER drew Bills which were returned protested. This Court doth declare in way of explanation of the former Order that Judgment did then passe against the said SHAPLEIGH as he was Security as aforesaid and not for any proper debt of his owne

- ANNE ROYLER, Servant to WILLIAM KEYNE is by this Court adjudged to be twelve yeares of age and ordered to serve her Master according to Act of which time her Master hath in Court abated fowre yeares
- HENRY BENTLEY against JOHN WADDY referred to the next Court at the motion of the Defendant
- THOMAS JANES, Servant to DANIEL NEALE Judgment of his age is referred to the next Court DANIEL NEALE being absent
    - Present   Capt. THOMAS MATHEW
- RICHARD PEMBERTON against RICHARD FLYNT referred to the next Court at the motion of the Defendant
- PETER MAXWELL against RICHARD HULL. This suit is dismist

p. 217

Northumberland County Court 19th of March 1693/4

- Mr. CONWAY agt POTTER. Whereas it appeares to this Court by a Bill under the hand and seale of JOHN POTTER dated the 6th of March 1681/2 that the said POTTER stands indebted unto Mr. EDWIN CONAWAY the sume of eleven hundred twenty five pounds of tobacco and cask, Judgment is granted the said CONAWAY against the said POTTER for the said sume with costs als Execution Mr. CONAWAY delivering to Mr. POTTER three Rights for Land

- PETER FLYNT agt his Father's Estate. Whereas Mr. PETER FLYNT in ye behalf of himself and his Brother, THOMAS FLYNT, arrested Mr. PETER PRESLEY SENR. and THOMAS HOBSON, SENR., Executors of the Last Will and Testament of RICHARD FLYNT, deceased, their Father, to this Court that they might give in an Account of their deceased Father's Estate soe that they might know what part thereof would become their share and whereas at a Court held for this County in Xbr 1681, JOHN HAYNIE and Mr. CHRISTOPHER NEALE were appoynted to audite the Accounts of the Executors of the Estate and bringing in their report thereof, and it appearing to this Court that the Accounts were cleared and by the Account of THOMAS HOBSON brought into this Court of his disbursements about the said Estate, which was proved by receipts and his Oath, that there is due to the said HOBSON from the said Estate on ballance of all Accounts the sume of ten thousand eight hundred and eighty six pounds of tobacco and cask for which he hath Judgment and hath fairly given it in Court to THOMAS and PETER FLYNT it is ordered that the rest of the Estate of the said Mr. RICHARD FLYNT, deceased, be equally divided according to the Last Will and Testament of their deceased Father between RICHARD, THOMAS and PETER FLYNT and that Mr. PETER PRESLEY and Mr. THOMAS HOBSON, Executors as aforesaid, henceforth discharged and acquitted from their charge

- Mr. SHAPLEIGH agt Mr. FLYNT Whereas it appeares to this Court that

Mr. RICHARD FLYNT standeth indebted unto Mr. PHILIP SHAPLEIGH the sume of two thousand two hundred sixty eight pounds of tobacco and cask by Account, Judgment is granted the said Mr. SHAPLEIGH against the said Mr. FLYNT for the said sume with costs als Execution

p. 218   Northumberland County Court 19th of March 1683/4

- Collo. SPENCER agt Mr. EDW: TIPTON Whereas Mr. JOHN ENGLAND, deceased, Bills of Exchange on Mr. EDWARD JONES of Bristoll, made for the payment of eight pounds, nine shillings sterling unto the Honorable RICHARD SPENCER, Esqr.'s Order for the payment of which sume Mr. WILLIAM DOWNING became Security the Bills being returned protested. It is ordered that Mr. EDWARD TIPTON who marryed MRS. MARGARETT DOWNING, the Executrix of Mr. WILLIAM DOWNING, Security as aforesaid, pay unto the ssid NICHOLAS SPENCER Esqr, the sume of ten pounds, fowre shillings and six pence [being for the Bills protested damages and charges of protest] with costs als Execution

- PITCHER agt JONES Whereas it appeares to this Court that JOHN JONES [by his Bond under ye hand and seale of the said JONES, dated the 10th 9br 1682] standeth indebted unto EMANUELL PITCHER the sume of three thousand five hundred and sixty pounds of tobacco and caske, Judgment is granted the said PITCHER against the said JONES for the said sume with costs als Execution alwayes provided that what the said JONES shall the next Court make appeare lpayd of the said sume shall be deducted anything in this Order to the contrary notwithstanding

- MELTON agt the Sheriffe JOANE ROGERS not appearing Whereas JOANE ROGERS was arrested to this Court at the suit of MICHAEL MELTON for three hundred and five pounds of tobacco and cask and not appearing, Judgment is granted the said MELTON for the said sume against the Sheriffe according to Law

- HAYNIE agt the Sheriffe BYRAM not appearing Whereas ABRAHAM BYRAM was arrested to this Court at the suit of Mr. RICHARD HAYNIE for five hundred pounds of tobacco and cask and not appearing, Judgment is granted the said HAYNIE against the Sheriffe for the said sume according to Law

- HULL agt NESBETT Whereas it appeares to this Court that EDWARD NESBETT standeth indebted unto RICHARD HULL the sume of fowre hundred seaventeen pounds of tobacco and cask, Judgment is granted the said HULL against the said NESBETT for the said sume with costs als Execution

p. 219   Northumberland County Court 19th of March 1683/4

- The Sheriffe released from WEEKES's Order agt him Whereas the last Court Mr. THOMAS WEEKES obteyned an Order against the Sheriffe for six thousand one hundred and thirty pounds of tobacco and cask, MRS. ELIZABETH GERRARD being arrested to that Court for the said sume and appeared not; and whereas this Court Mr. RICHARD FLYNT, Attorney for the said MRS. GERRARD, apeared and the said WEEKES appeared not; It is ordered that the Sheriffe be discharged from the former and that the suit between him and the said GERRARD be dismist

- HICKMAN against BARNES, Security for WATTS Whereas EDWARD WATTS was arrested to this Court at the suit of THOMAS HICKMAN for thirteen hundred ninety and six pounds of tobacco and cask and appearing not; Judgment is granted the said THOMAS HICKMAN against the said EDWARD BARNES, Security for the said WATTS's appearance for the said sume according to Act

- WADDY agt WRIGHT Whereas an Attachment was awarded to THOMAS WADDY against the Estate of THOMAS WRIGHT for the sume of two thousand pounds of tobacco and cask and the said WADDY having to this Court proved his said debt to be due, it is ordered that before the next Court [faded] apprayse those goods which the said WRIGHT left behind him and that then the said WADDY have Judgment for soe much of them as will satisfy his said debt with costs

- Capt. MATHEW's Certificate to the Assembly Certificate is granted Capt. THOMAS MATHEW to the next Assembly for thirty five yards of serge, twenty seaven yards and an half of woolen cloth and seaventy six yards of fine linen he haveing made Oath that it was of his owne manufacture according to Act

p. 220 Northumberland County Court 19th of March 1683/4

- HULL agt NESBETT RICHARD HULL being arrested to this Court at the suit of EDWARD NESBETT in an action of defamation and noe cause of action appearing, a non suit is granted the said HULL against the said NESBETT with costs and damages according to Act

- BAKER agt BREWER Whereas the last Court THOMAS BAKER obteyned an Order against THOMAS BREWER about their Land which was not drawne up soe fully as to clear the poynt in dispute, it is ordered that THOMAS BREWER appear at the next Court and then and there shew his reasons why that Order may not be altered

- SMYTH agt GARLINGTON Whereas it appeares to this Court that CHRISTOPHER GARLINGTON standeth indebted unto Lt. Collo. SAMUELL SMYTH upon the ballance of a former Order three hundred and eighty pounds of tobacco and cask, Judgment is granted the said Lt. Collo. SMYTH against the said GARLINGTON for the said sume with costs als Execution

- Mr. ALEXANDER ATKINS against THOMAS WINTER referred to the next Court at the motion of the Defendant

- Mr. THO: MATHEW agt Mr. RICH: THOMPSON The difference between Capt. THOMAS MATHEW and Mr. RICHARD THOMPSON was referred to a Jury whose names are underwritten, vizt.

Collo. SAMUEL GRIFFIN	Mr. THOMAS [ ]	Mr. THOMAS WEEKES
Mr. JAMES HORNBY	Mr. JAMES [ ]	Mr. WILLIAM LOE
Mr. JOHN LUKE	Mr JOHN RICE	Mr. EDWIN CONWAY
Mr. ROBERT YATES	Mr. AZARCAM PARKER	Mr. THOMAS CHEWNING

- The Verdict Wee doe find for the Plaintiffe that Mr. RICHARD THOMPSON who hath made breach of the Order given him by Mr. JOHN ATTISON and Mr. THOMAS MATHEW bearing date the 30th of April 1683

SAMUELL GRIFFIN

- The Verdict The Jury being returned to inquire into the damages did returne Whereas we had a charge given us by the Gentlemen of Northumberland Court to find the damages susteyned by Capt. THOMAS MATHEW upon Mr. RICHARD THOMPSON, being Master of a Barque called "THE VINE" and employed by the said THOMAS MATHEW and Mr. JOHN ATTISON in copartnership both of the Barque and the Cargo, which Cargo amounting in the whole to one hundred and twelve pounds

fowre shillings and seaven pence half penny one eighth the moyety by Mr. THOMAS MATHEW to ye loss of Mr. JOHN ATTISON as satisfaction given by THOMAS MATHEW to the said ATTISON for ye half part of [faded] and upon breach of the abovesaid instruction made by the said RICHARD THOMPSON it is considered that he, the said THOMPSON, pay the said sume for his deficiency in not going to the port according to the said Instructions [left side readable the right side faded] on the payment of the said sume by ye said RICHARD THOMPSON to the said THOMAS MATHEW doe assigne sell and set over unto the said THOMPSON wht assurance he the said MATHEW hath from the said JOHN ATTISON for the moyety of the Barque and Cargo the said THOMPSON is now charged with
SAMUEL GRIFFIN

p. 221 Northumberland County Court 19th of March 1683/4

- The Judgment Upon the motion of Capt. THOMAS MATHEW Judgment is granted him against RICHARD THOMPSON according to the Verdict

- Appeale Mr. RICHARD THOMPSON appealeth from the the Order to a hearing before his Excellency and the Councill of State the fowrth day of the next Generall Court which is granted, the said THOMPSON giveing good caution before Munday night next to prosecute his Appeale

- The Court adjourneth untill tomorrow morning eight of the clock

- Die 20th March 1683/4   Present
Lt. Collo. SAMUEL SMYTH   Capt. JOHN HAYNIE
Mr. PETER PRESLEY   Mr. CHRISTOPHER NEALE   Justices

- PARKER agt WADDY Whereas it appeares to this Court that there is due unto Mr. AZARCUM PARKER from THOMAS WADDY the sume of thirteen shillings three pence sterling and one hundred pounds of tobacco and cask upon ballance of Accounts between them; Judgment is granted the said PARKER against the said WADDY for the money and tobacco with costs als Execution

- CLAUGHTON agt RICE Whereas JAMES CLAUGHTON prayed Judgment against Mr. JOHN RICE for fifteen hundred pounds of tobacco and cask, being due to him for a House built by him; and for the said RICE to which the Defendant alledged that the House was not finished. It is ordered that the said CLAUGHTON finish the said House [the said RICE finding materials] by the next Court which when done that he take some indifferent honest men of that neighbourhood to view the said work which if by their report to the next Court it shall appeare well done the said RICE to pay the said CLAUGHTON the sume aforesaid with costs always provided that what the said RICE shall then make appeare paid of the said debt shall be deducted any thing in this Order to the contrary notwithstanding

p. 222 Northumberland County Court 20th of March 1683/4
- Present   Mr. PHILIP SHAPLEIGH

- Collo. SMYTH's Negro freed from Levy Tony, an old Negro of Lt. Collo. SAMUEL SMYTH's being incapable to work, it is ordered that the said SMYTH for the future be acquitted from paying any Levys for him

- YEAMANS agt HAMMONDS Whereas it appeares to this Court that

NORTHUMBERLAND COUNTY ORDER BOOK, 1678-1698 -29-

THOMAS HAMMONDS standeth indebted unto BARTHOLOMEW YEAMANS the sume of seaven hundred twenty eight pounds of tobacco and cask, Judgment is granted the said YEAMANS against the said HAMMONDS for the said sume with costs als Execution

- OLDIS agt PAUL Whereas it appeares to this Court that CHARLES PAUL standeth indebted unto ROBERT OLDIS the sume of five hundred ninety three pounds of tobacco and cask on ballance of Accounts; Judgment is granted the said PAUL against the said OLDIS for the said sume with costs als Execution

- PAUL agt OLDIS Whereas CHARLES PAUL complayneth to this Court that ROBERT OLDIS doth deteyne from him his Crop which he made on the said OLDIS's land, it is ordered that the said PAUL paying unto the said OLDIS the Judgment this day obteyned against him by the said ROBERT OLDIS that he have his Crop deteyned as aforesaid delivered unto him by the said OLDIS

- GILBART and CURTIS agt OLDIS It is ordered that ROBERT OLDIS pay unto WALTER CURTIS and WILLIAM GILBART for their two dayes attendance at this Court to give in their Evidences in his behalf against CHARLES PAUL according to Act

- WILLIAMS agt JOHNSON, HOWARD & PEMBERTON Whereas EDWARD WILLIAMS arrested JAMES JOHNSON, WILLIAM HOWARD and Mr. RICHARD PEMBERTON this Court and JAMES JOHNSON not appearing, it is ordered that the next Court the first day of that Court when it may be presumed that most of the Justices may be present at the motion of the said EDWARD WILLIAMS
[the last line at the bottom of the page in stain]

p. 223 Northumberland County Court 20th of March 1683/4
' NEALE v GERRARD Whereas it appeares to this Court that ELIZABETH, Administratrix of SAMUEL GERRARD, standeth indebted unto Mr. CHRISTOPHER NEALE the Assignee of Mr. JAMES [? PREFERY] the sume of fowre hundred sixty pounds of tobacco and cask, Judgment is granted the said NEALE against the said ELIZABETH for the said sume out of the Estate of the said SAMUEL unlesse she appeares at the next Court and shews reasons to the contrary, and ordered that she have notice of ths Order

- BOND agt the Sheriffe JONES not appearing Whereas SAMUEL JONES was arrested to this Court at the suit of HENRY BOND for five hundred pounds of tobacco and cask and not appearing, Judgment is granted the said BOND against the Sheriffe for the said sume according to Law

- JONES agt the Sheriffe, BARRY not appearing Whereas WILLIAM BARRY was arrested to this Court at the suit of Capt. THOMAS JONES for fowre hundred fifty pounds of tobacco and cask and not appearing, Judgment is granted the said JONES againwt the Sheriff for the said sume according to Law

- GENESIS agt SANDERS Whereas it appeares to this Court that Mr. EBENEZER SANDERS, Administrator of MRS. MARY THOMAS, standeth indebted unto EZEKIEL GENESIS the Assignee of Mr. DENNIS CARTER eight hundred eighty fowre pounds of tobacco and cask, being due upon ballance of a former Order granted to the said CARTER against the said THOMAS; Judgment is granted the said GENESIS the Assignee of the said CARTER against the said SANDERS, Administrator of the said THOMAS for the said sume with costs als Execution

- GAYLARD agt HARTLEY HENRY HARTLEY being arrested to this Court at the suit of MRS. ANNE GAYLARD and she not appearing to prosecute, it is ordered that the suit be dismist
- Capt. THOMAS JONES against THOMAS BREWER continued till the next Court
- HULL's Acct of MOOR's Estate regulated Whereas RICHARD HULL brought an Account against the Estate of WALTER MOOR for thirteen hundred forty seaven pounds of tobacco and cask, an Account of the Crop of the said MOOR's the Court haveing regulated the said HULL's Account doe find that the said MOOR is indebted to him the ballance forty seaven pounds of tobacco
- The next Court the 3d Wednesday in the next month

p. 224
- Northumberland March the 16th 1683
- Mr. JOHN TAYLOR's Cert. for Cloth Ths day Mr. JOHN TAYLOR JUNIOR brought before us fifty six yards of linen cloth about three quarters wide he haveing taken the Oath that it was of his owne growth and manufacture
                                      PETER KNIGHT
                                      LEONARD HOWSON

- Northumberland April ye 1st 1684
- Mr. JOHN DOWNING's Cert. for cloth These are to certifie that Mr. JOHN DOWNING hath this day brought forty two yards of cloth before Collo. SAMUEL SMYTH and Mr. PETER PRESLEY and hath made Oath that it was of his owne growth and manufacture according to Act

- Northumberland County
- KEEN's Cert. for cloth These are to certifie that Mr. WILLIAM KEEN brought before us forty three yards of woolen cloth and hath given Oath of the same that is of his owne manufacture. Given under our hands this 23d of October 1683

- February ye 13th 1683;4
- KEEN's Cert. for cloth Memorandum for Mr. WILLIAM KEEN [faded] cloath of the bredth according to Act [faded] of their owne manufacture and growth [faded] the same quantity measured [faded] that it is of their owne manufacture and growth -faded]

[The next entry is readable on the left side, faded out on the right side; but is the Certificate for Mr. CHRISTOPHER NEALE three bushells and a half of something]
                                      PETER PRESLEY
                                      RICHARD KENNER

p. 225
Aprill the 1st 1684
- DUKE's Children Servants to PETER MAXWELL This day ISRAELL OAGE did before Lt. Collo. SAMUEL SMYTH and Mr. PETER PRESLEY bind her two Daughters, MARY and JANE DUKE, [MARY being judged to be ten yeares of age and JANE three yeares of age] unto PETER MAXWELL and MARY his Wife untill they shall attayne to the age of one and twenty yeares dureing which tearme the said PETER and MARY to allow MARY and JANE all things necessary for an

NORTHUMBERLAND COUNTY ORDER BOOK, 1678-1698   -31-

Apprentice and at the expiration of the said tearme or death of the said PETER and MARY each of them to have delivered to them out of the Estate one Cow with Calfe or Calfe by her side, convenient cloathing and Corne

- <u>NEALE's Cert. to the Assembly</u> These may certifie whome it may concern that wee measured for Mr. CHRISTOPHER NEALE twenty three yards of woolen cloth according to Act which he hath made Oath of was of his owne manufacture and growth; As witnesse ur hands in Northumberland County the 1st of April 1684
        PETER PRESLEY
        RICHARD KENNER

- At a Court held for Northumberland County the 4th of June 1684 Annoq Regni Regis Caroli 2d, 36th &c.
      Present

Capt. PETER KNIGHT	Mr. RICHARD KENNER
Mr. PETER PRESLEY, SENR.	Mr. PHILIP SHAPLEIGH
Mr. NICHOLAS OWEN	Mr. CHRISTOPHER NEALE Justices
Capt. JOHN HAYNIE	Mr. THOMAS BRERETON
	Mr. RICHARD ROGERS

- <u>FRAN: JONES Servt to Mr. DAN: NEALE</u> Whereas FRANCIS JONES, Servant to Mr. DANIEL NEALE, was by his said Master brought to this Court to have their Judgment of his age, the Court doe judge hm to be twelve yeares of age but being sold to DANIEL NEALE by Mr. SAMUEL HARTNELL but for seaven yeares time it is ordered that the sasid FRANCIS shall serve his said Master or his Assignes ye said tearme of seaven years and noe longer

p. 226
  <u>Northumberland County Court 4th of June 1684</u>
- <u>Sheriffe sworne</u> This day in obedience to an Order from his Excellency the Governor Generall, Mr. THOMAS HOBSON, SENR. was sworne High Sheriffe of this County and Mr. JOHN TOPPING his Under Sheriffe

- <u>Bond</u> Mr. THOMAS HOBSON and Mr. PETER PRESLEY SENR. doe oblige themselves joyntly and severally to our Soveraigne the King in the penall sume of one hundred thousand pounds of good tobacco and cask that the said HOBSON shall duely execute the Sheriffe's place this yeare

- <u>Constables</u> Ordered that THOMAS ASHTON be Constable for CHERRY POINTE NECK;
THOMAS HOPPER Constable for MATTAPONY;
WILLIAM [? SWETNAM] for Jerico and the lower Precincts of Bowtracy Parish;
RICHARD LAMPREY for the lower Precincts of Fairefield Parish;
PATRICK POLLOCK for the upper Precincts of Wicocomico Parish;
And ordered that they be forthwith sworne by the next Justice

- <u>GEO. ELLIOTT freed from the Levy</u> GEORGE ELLIOTT being poor and impotent living at Mr. WILLIAM HARCUM's at ye request of the said HARCUM it is ordered that he be freed this yeare from paying the Levy

- <u>BARNES and DAVIS ditto</u> Upon the Petition of EDWARD BARNES and THOMAS DAVIS two very aged poor and impotent persons it is ordered that they be freed from the Levy

- **EZ. GENESIS's Will proved** Upon the Petition of ALICE HUDNALL, Executrix of EZEKIEL GENESIS, deceased, a Probate is granted her of the Last Will and Testament of the said GENESIS, the Will being proved by the Oaths of JOHN HUGHLETT and EDWARD WHITE, witnesses to the Will

- **SAM: GOCHE's Will proved** Upon the Petition of the Relict and Executrix of SAMUELL GOCHE, deceased, a Probate is granted her of the Last Will and Testament of her said deceased Husband the Will being proved by the Oaths of JAMES MOOR and ELINOR REYNOLDS, witnesses to the Will

p. 227 Northumberland County Court 4th of June 1684.

- **THO: NELMES's Will proved** Upon the Petition of THOMAS THORP, he and his Wife being principall Legatees, a Probate is granted him of the Last Will and Testament of THOMAS NELMES, deceased, the Will being proved by the Oaths of ISAAC [? HESTER], MARGARET [? HESTER] and JAMES MOOR witnesses to the said Will

- **COX agt SANDERS** Whereas it appears to this Court that MRS. MARY THOMAS at the time of her decease stood indebted unto MATHEW COX the sume of fower hundred eighty pounds of tobacco and cask; Judgment is granted the said COX against EBENEZER SANDERS, Administrator of the Estate of the said MARY, for the said sume out of the Estate of the Decedent als Execution

- **ANDREW BONNER** being an aged poor man it is ordered that he be freed from the Levy

- **CLAUGHTON agt RICE** Whereas the last Court it was ordered that JAMES CLAUGHTON should finish the work tht was undone of the House which the said CLAUGHTON built for Mr. JOHN RICE which he averring he hath done and Mr. RICE that it is not done as it ought to be at the instance of the said CLAUGHTON it is ordered that THOMAS FLYNT and CLEMENT ALDRIDGE before the next Court view the said work and then give in their report tht then the Court may proceed to Judgment threon

- **The Sheriffe to be allowed out of the Levy for what overcharged on the last Lyst** It is ordered that THOMAS HOBSON, SENR. be allowed him out of the next Levy eight hundred forty eight pounds overcharged in the Lyst the last yeare

- **EDW: WMS: agt JNOSON, PEMBERTON and HOWARD** Whereas EDWARD WILLIAMS arrested JAMES JOHNSON, RICHARD PEMBERTON and WILLIAM HOWARD for a tract of land formerly belonging to ROBERT BRADSHAW and sold by the said BRADSHAW to EDWARD WILLIAMS, his Father, and the said WILLIAMS to JAMES CLAUGHTON and by the said CLAUGHTON to JOHNSON, PEMBERTON and HOWARD under the pretence of a Deed wherein the said BRADSHAW did oblige himselfe to gett a Pattent for the said land in the name of TEMPERANCE, the Mother of the first mentioned EDWARD WILLIAMS and alledged that EDWARD WILLIAMS, SENR. the Plaintiffe's Father, sold the said land

p. 228 Northumberland County Court 4th of June 1684

unto the said CLAUGHTON with the consent of the said TEMPERANCE, the Plaintiffe's Mother, in whome the right of the said land lyes and from her as her heyre in him the Plaintiffe. The Court haveing carefully assessed all the writings

NORTHUMBERLAND COUNTY ORDER BOOK, 1678-1698 -33-

relateing to thereto delivered in this Court by the Plaintiffe and Defendants and finding nothing but an ingagement from the said ROBERT BRADSHAW to procure a Pattent for the said land in the name of the said TEMPERANCE and nothing as yett offered in order thereto [though the said ingagement was acknowledged in Court] it is ordered that this suit be dismist

- RICE released from his Bond Whereas in January Court last, Mr. JOHN HUGHLETT SENR. became bound with RICHARD RICE for the payment of what damages JAMES JOHNSON RICHARD PEMBERTON and WILLIAM HOWARD should recover of him in case he should be cast in a suit depending between him and the said RICE the Attorney of Mr. EDWARD WILLIAMS Plaintiffe and they the said JOHNSON, PEMBERTON and HOWARD Defendants. This Court the suit being dismissed it is ordered that the said HUGHLETT be released from his Bond

- BAKER agt BREWER In the difference between THOMAS BAKER Plaintiffe and THOMAS BREWER, Defendant about a parcell of land, it is ordered that Capt. JOHN HAYNIE, Surveyor, with an able Jury of the Vicinage lay out the land of the said BAKER according to the Bill of Sale and such Evidences as are acquainted with the former survey being first sworne by Capt. HAYNIE

- RICH: LAMPREY Comm. of Admon Whereas RICHARD LAMPREY by his Petition did declare that BARTHOLOMEW YEAMANS was lately deceased at his House and left noe relations [that are knowne] behind him; neither made any Will and prayed that since he was at considerable charges about him he might take what small Estate of the said YEAMANS's deceased seized of into his hands; it is ordered that the said LAMPREY take the said Estate into his hands untill the time limitted by Law be expired that he bring in upon his Oath the next Court a full and perfect Inventory of the same and that he pay such debts as shall appear to this Court to be

p. 229   Northumberland County Court 4th of June 1684

justly owing by the said BARTHOLOMEW YEAMANS and recover such as shall be due to him and give in good security to this Court that he will be accomptable for the same when thereto required and within the time limitted if no other person doth appear that hath more right to the administration of the said Estate that a Commission of Administration be granted him of the said Estate he giveing caution according to Law

- The Bond RICHARD LAMPREY, JOHN DOWNING and JOHN CORBELL doe oblige themselves joyntly and severally in the sume of twenty thousand pounds of tobacco and cask to the Justices of the Peace for this County, that the said RICHARD LAMPREY shall ye next Court exhibit a full and perfect Inventory of the Estate of the said BARTHOLOMEW YEAMANS and be accomptable for the same

- Appraysers appoynted Mr. WILLIAM HARCUM, Mr. RICHARD FARRINGTON, THOMAS WEBB and JOHN WORNAM or any three of them are by the Court appoynted to apprayse the Estate of SAMUEL GOCHE, deceased, being sworne by the next Justice

- Collo. BRERETON's Will proved Whereas Mr. THOMAS BRERETON did in Court this day produce the Will and Testament of Collo. THOMAS BRERETON his deceased Father, of which he prayed a Probate might be granted, THOMAS haveing seen and read the said Will and all of them knowing the hand writing of the said Collo

THOMAS BRERETON and assured that the said Will was that of the deceased, though Mr. JOHN JENNY and Mr. PETER PLATT witnesses of the said Will are since the writing of the said Will dead, Mr. THOMAS HOBSON, SENR. upon his Oath declareing that when the said Collo. BRERETON had in his office before the said witnesses signed sealed and delivered the said Will he brought the said Will and Testament in his hands and shewing it to the said HOBSON told him that was his Last Will and Testament and asked his advice about it who then approveing of it sealed it up and gave it ye said HOBSON to keep who hath kept it by him untill a little time before the said Collo's death when he called for it and said he would alter some things in it but dyed before he effected it. The Court doe therefore grant the said Mr. THOMAS BRERETON a Probate of his said deceased Father's Will according to Law

p. 230

Die 5th June 1684   Present
Capt. PETER KNIGHT   Mr. RICHARD KENNER
Mr. PETER PRESLEY, SENR. Mr. CHRISTOPHER NEALE   Justices
Capt. JOHN HAYNIE   Mr. PETER PRESLEY, JUNR.

- WADDY agt BENTLEY Whereas JOHN WADDY was arrested to this Court at the suit of HENRY BENTLEY and noe cause of action appearing, a non suit is granted the said WADDY against the said BENTLEY with costs and damages according to Act

- ATKINS agt WINTER Whereas it appeares to this Court that THOMAS WINTER standeth indebted unto Mr. ALEXANDER ATKINS the sume of nine hundred forty pounds of tobacco and cask upon ballance of Accounts; Judgment is granted the said ATKINS against the said WINTER for the said sume with costs als Execution

- RICHARD THOMPSON against Mr. JOHN JULIAN referred to the next Court

- Mr. THOMAS CHEWNING against JOHN FARRINGTON referred to the next Court

- HARTLEY agt GAYLARD Whereas HENRY HARTLEY was arrested to this Court at the suit of MRS. ANNE GAYLARD and noe cause of action appearing, a non suit is granted HENRY HARTLEY against MRS. ANNE GAYLARD with costs and damages according to Act

- BARNES agt GEORGE Whereas THOMAS BARNES was arrested to this Court at the suit of ELIZABETH GEORGE and noe cause of action appearing, a non suit is granted the said BARNES against the said GEORGE with costs and damages according to Act

- ATKINS agt the Sheriffe Whereas Mr. RICHARD FARRINGTON was arrested to this Court at the suit of Mr. ALEXANDER ATKINS for one thousand six hundred forty pounds of tobacco and cask and hath failed of his appearance; Judgment is granted the said ATKINS for the said sume against the Sheriffe according to Law

p. 231

Northumberland County Court 5th of June 1684
- EYES agt ALLENSON Whereas DENNIS EYES complayned to this Court that whereas he bought a parcell of land of WALTER ALLENSON

being the moyety of three hundred and twenty acres of land held in joynt tenancy by the said WALTER and WILLIAM ALLENSON, his Brother, that he often desired of the said WILLIAM that a devision might be made thereof but the said WILLIAM refused it; it is ordered that the said land be devided and that the said DENNIS EYES have the full half of the said tract including the half of the ground that was cleared when the said WALTER and WILLIAM bought the land with the half of that ground that after the purchase WALTER helped to clear but the said EYES in noewise to be concerned or to have interest in such housing or other edificies or orchards which have been built or planted by the said WILLIAM without the help of the said WALTER

- PARKER agt FLYNT Whereas ELIZABETH PARKER arrested RICHARD FLYNT to this Court and complayned that the said FLYNT doth unlawfully deteyne from her her Sonne. It is ordered that if the next Court that the said FLYNT doth not appeare to shew good reasons why he deteynes the said Lad that then Judgment passe against him for the immediate delivery of him to his Mother with costs alwayes provided that the said FLYNT have due notice of this Order

- Fayrfield Parish agt JOHN BEE Whereas Mr. JOHN DOWNING and WILLIAM TIGNALL, Churchwardens of Fayrfield Parish, arrested JOHN BEE to this Court for six thousand pounds of tobacco and caske and the said BEE hath fayled of his appearance; Judgment is granted agaisnt the Sheriffe according to Law

- PET: PRESLEY JUNR's Negro boy adjudged Will Kent a Negro boy belonging to Mr. PETER PRESLEY JUNR. judged to be eight yeares of age

p. 232 Northumberland County Court 5th of November 1684

- JNO: PALMER agt the Sheriffe Whereas Mr. RICHARD FLYNT was arrested to this Court at the suit of JOHN PALMER and hath fayled of his appearance, Judgment is granted the said PALMER against the Sheriffe according to Law

- EDWARD WILLIAMS against THOMAS ADAMS referred to the next Court at the motion of the Defendant

- SIMPSON agt HUGHLETT Whereas HANNAH SIMPSON arrested JOHN HUGHLETT, JUNR. to this Court and noe cause of action appearing, a non suit is granted the said HUGHLETT against the said SIMPSON with costs and damages according to Act

- Collo. CODD agt the Sheriffe Whereas THOMAS HAMMONDS was arrested to this Court at the suit of Collo. ST. LEGER CODD for fowre hundred pounds of tobacco and caske and hath failed of his appearance, Judgment is granted the said CODD for the said sume against the Sheriffe according to Law

- BONNER to be removed out of the Parish Whereas ANDREW BONNER is lately come out of Wicocomico Parish into Fayrfield Parish and is incapable of getting his owne liveing and JOHN LEE out of another County into this and it being found that the enterteyning of such persons doth bring a great charge to the Parish where they live. It is ordered that the Churchwardens of every Parish where such persons shall come forthwith remove the said persons to the respective Parishes whence they last came

- The next Court the 3d Wednesday in July

p. 233 — Att a Court held for Northumberland County the 20th of August Anno Domini 1684 Annoque Regni Regis Caroli secundit 36th &c.

Present

Capt. PETER KNIGHT Capt. JOHN HAYNIE
Mr. NICHOLAS OWEN Mr. PETER PRESLEY, JUNR

Justices

- MARY JAMES to serve for a bastard MARY JAMES, Servant to CUTHBERT SPAN, haveing had a bastard Child in the time of her servitude, it is ordered that she serve her said Master for the said default according to Act

- THORP's Comm of Admon. Upon the Petition of THOMAS THORP a Commission of Administration is granted him of the Estate of THOMAS NELMES, deceased, he giveing caution according to Law

- Bond Capt. JOHN HAYNIE and JOHN WORNAM doe oblige themselves joyntly and severally in the penall sume of twenty thousand pounds of tobacco and cask that THOMAS THORP shall duely administer upon the said Estate and that he will exhibit an Inventory thereof to the next Court

- HARRIS p Lycence for Attorney Mr. CHARLES HARRIS declaring to this Court that he had addressed himselfe to his Honor the Secretary for a Lycence for an Attourney and that he was pleased to tell him that he should not grant any Lycence to such persons as were not before quallifyed for such imploy unless the Court where the said persons doe practice as Attourney doe recommend the said persons to his Honor. This Court doth humbly desire that his Honor would grrant the said HARRIS a Lycence of Attourney

- WMS. agt THO: ADAMS Whereas it appeares to this Court that THOMAS ADAMS stands indebted unto EDWARD WILLIAMS two barrells of Indian Corne, Judgment is granted the said WILLIAMS against the said ADAMS for the said two barrells of Corne with costs als Execution

- DYER to be allowed out of the Levy It is ordered that THOMAS DYER be allowed fifty fowre pounds of tobacco out of the publique Levy he being twice charged on the Lysts last yeare

p. 234 — Northumberland County Court 20th of August 1684

- GEORGE agt BARNES Whereas it appeares to this Court that THOMAS BARNES standeth indebted unto MRS. ELIZABETH GEORGE,, Administratrix of Mr. THOMAS GEORGE, deceased, by Bill under the hand of the said BARNES bearing date the 15th February 1681/2, the sume of four hundred pounds of tobacco and cask. Judgment is granted the said MRS. ELIZABETH GEORGE, Administratrix as aforesaid, for the said sume against the said THOMAS BARNES with costs als Execution

- GEORGE agt COX Whereas it appeares to this Court by two Bills under the hand of Mr. RICHARD COX bearing date the 23d of June 1683 that there is due to MRS. ELIZABETH GEORGE, Administratrix of Mr. THOMAS GEORGE, deced., the sume of two thousand nine hundred and fifty pounds of tobacco and cask, and whereas the said COX hath declared upon his Oath that ye said MR. GEORGE had in his life time a saddle of him for which [agreement] he was to pay him three hundred pounds of tobacco, Judgment is granted the said ELIZABETH, Administratrix as aforesaid, for two thousand six hundred and fifty pounds of tobacco and cask it being

NORTHUMBERLAND COUNTY ORDER BOOK, 1678-1698   -37-

the ballance against RICHARD COX with costs als Execution

- CODD agt HAMMOND Whereas it appeares to this Court by a Bill under the hand of THOMAS HAMMOND that the said HAMMOND standeth indebted unto Collo. ST. LEGER CODD four hundred pounds of tobacco and cask; Judgment is granted the said Collo. CODD against the said HAMMOND for the said sume with costs als Execution

- WELTHRAN BONAS's Will proved Upon the Petition of WILLIAM BEANE, a Probate is granted him of the Last Will and Testament of WELTHRAN BONAS, the Will being proved by the Oaths of SAMUELL BUCKLEY and JAMES GENN, witnesses of the said Will

- BONAS's Children to keep with whome left. Whereas WELTHRAN BONAS by her Last Will and Testament did dispose of her three Children as follows, vizt., her Sonne ROBERT BONAS to WILLIAM BEANE untill he should come of age; her Daughter, ELIZABETH, unto MRS. REBECCA MATHEW untill she should come of age, and her Daughter, ANNE BONAS, unto THOMAS MILLER untill she come of age. The Court doe order that each Child aforesaid stay with the said respective people according to their Mother's Will

p. 235

Northumberland County Court 20th of August 1684

- CARTEE agt SANDERS Whereas at a Court held for Northumberland County the 19th of March Anno 1683, EZEKIEL GENESIS [as being Assignee of Mr. DENNIS CARTEE], obteyned Judgment against Mr. EZENEZER SANDERS, Administrator of MRS. MARY THOMAS, deceased, for eight hundred eighty and one pounds of tobacco and cask it being the ballance of a former Order granted ye sd CARTEE against MRS. MARY THOMAS in her lifetime bearing date the 17th of August 1681, ALLICE HUDNALL, Executrix of ye said EZEKIEL GENESIS, doth now in Court relinquish her right in the said Order and assigne it over to the said DENNIS CARTEE

- Present   Capt. LEONARD HOWSON

- PALMER agt FLYNT The suit depending between Mr. RICHARD FLYNT and JOHN PALMER is dismist by consent of both parties

- WADDY agt WRIGHT's Estate Whereas at a Court held for Northumberland County the 17th of March 1683/4 THOMAS WADDY made it appeare that there was due to him from THOMAS WRIGHT two thousand pounds of tobacco and cask and whereas Mr. JOHN HARRIS and THOMAS WINTER were appoynted to apprayse what of the said WRIGHT's Estate which he left behind him [the said WADDY haveing before levyed an Attachment upon the said Estate] and whereas the said HARRIS and WINTER have apprayseed the Estate which amounts to seaventeen hundred pounds of tobacco, Judgment is granted the said WADDY for the whole of the said Estate amounting to seaventeen hundred pounds of tobacco als Execution

- MOOR agt BYRAM JAMES MOOR, the Attourney of JAMES [? FOULER] against PETER BYRAM as marrying the Executrix of SAMUELL GOCHE referred to the next Court at the motion of the Defendant

- SWAN agt HUDNALL Mr. ALEXANDER SWANN against ALLICE HUDNALL Administratrix of JOHN HUDNALL, referred to the next Court at the motion of the Defendant

NORTHUMBERLAND COUNTY ORDER BOOK, 1678-1693

- **WALTERS agt BYRAM als GOCHE** ROGER WALTERS against PETER BYRAM and his Wife, referred to the next Court at the motion of the Defendant

p. 236   Northumberland County Court 20th of August 1684

- **BAKER agt BREWER** Whereas the last Court it was ordered that Capt. JOHN HAYNIE with an able Jury of the Vicinage should lay out the land in dispute between THOMAS BAKER and THOMAS BREWER according to the Bill of Sale and such Evidences as were acquainted with the former survey, they being first sworn by the said Capt. HAYNIE and whereas the said Capt. HAYNIE did in pursuance of the said Order meet the Jury and Evidences and haveing first proceeded to the swearing of the, Mr. EDWIN CONWAY asserted that the said HAYNIE was in noe wise capable of administering an Oath upon which assertion then the said Capt. HAYNIE left off. The Court seriously consulting the matter are well satisfyed that the said Capt. HAYNIE is quallifyed to administer the Oath and doe order that the Jury and the Evidences be first sworne by him and that then they proceed according to the former Order

- **WALTERS agt SANDERS** Whereas it appeares to this Court by Bill under the hand of MRS. MARY THOMAS that she was in her lifetime stood indebted unto ROGER WALTERS the sume of nine hundred pounds of tobacco and cask; Judgment is granted the said WALTERS against EBENEZER SANDERS, Administrator of the said MRS. MARY THOMAS, for the said sume with costs als Execution

- **PITT agt FLOWERS** Whereas JOSIAS PITT was arrested to this Court at the suit of WILLIAM FLOWERS and noe cause of action appearing, a non suit is granted the said PITT against the said FLOWERS with costs and damages according to Law

- **SMYTH agt WARNER** Whereas it appeares to this Court that JOHN WARNER standeth indebted unto RICHARD SMYTH by Account [to which the said SMYTH hath made Oath] two hundred seaventeen pounds of tobacco and cask, Judgment is granted the said SMYTH against the said WARNER for the said sume with costs als Execution

- The next Court the Third Wednesday in ye next month and ordered that the Levy be then layd

p. 237   At a Court held for Northumberland County the 17th of 7br 1684 Annoque Regni Regis Caroli 2d. 36th &c.

Present

Capt. PETER KNIGHT   Mr. NICHOLAS OWEN
Mr. PETER PRESLEY, SENR.   Capt. JOHN HAYNIE   Justices
Capt. LEONARD HOWSON   Mr. CHRISTOPHER NEALE

- **MOOR agt GOCHE** Whereas it appeares to this Court by a Bill under the hand of SAMUEL GOCHE dated the 14th of 9br 1681, that the said GOCHE stood indebted unto JAMES MOORE, the Assignee of JAMES [? F------] the sume of five hundred eighty nine pounds of tobacco and cask; Judgment is granted the said MOOR against the said GOCHE for the said sume als Execution

- **JNO: SWANSON Will proved** Upon the Petition of MARY SWANSON a Probate is granted her of the Last Will and Testament of JOHN SWANSON her deceased Husband the Will being proved by the Oathes of SAMUEL MAHON and GEORGE BARRATT, witnesses to of the said Will,

- Comm. of Admon. of SWANSON's Estate A Commission of Administration with the Will annexed is granted to MARY, the Relict of JOHN SWANSON deceased of the Estate of the said JOHN she giveing caution according to Law
- Bond SAMUEL MAHON and JOHN [? S-----] doe oblige themselves joyntly and severally in the sume of twenty thousand pounds of tobacco and cask with the abovesaid MARY SWANSON that she shall duly administer on the Estate of JOHN SWANSON deceased and exhibite an Inventory thereof into the next Court
- Appraysers Mr. CHRISTOPHER GARLINGTON and CLEMENT LATIMORE are appoynted to appraise the Estate of JOHN SWANSON being sworne by the next Justice of the Peace
- Mr. JOHN RICE against [ ] ALLEN continued to next Court
- BRYAM agt GOCHE Whereas it appeares to this Court that the Estate of SAMUEL GOCHE standeth indebted unto PETER BYRAM by Account to which he hath made Oath for attendance in his sicknesse, charges of the doctor and funerall expences the sume of two thousand four hundred forty nine pounds of tobacco and cask; Judgment is granted the said BYRAM against the Estate of the said GOCHE for the said sume als Execution

p. 238 Northumberland County Court 17th of September 1684
- WALTERS agt BYRAM Whereas it appeares to this Court by a Bill under the hand of ANNE GOCHE [in her widowhood] dated the 10th of 9br 1683, that the said ANNE standeth indebted unto ROGER WALTERS nine hundred pounds of tobacco and cask; Judgment is granted the said WALTERS against the PETER BYRAM [who marryed the said ANNE] for the said sume als Execution
- DONOWAY to alter the Road Whereas JOHN DONOWAY by his Petition to this Court that he might include the Road where now it is to another, his Petition is granted he well clearing another Road in all things as convenient for passage as the first
- WEST agt HUDNALL Whereas Mr. ALEXANDER SWAN the Attorney of Collo. JOHN WEST, did arrest ALLICE [the Administratrix of JOHN HUDNALL, deceased] for five thousand fower hundred and thirteen pounds of tobacco and cask due to the said WEST from the said HUDNALL in his lifetime wherein it appeared that the said JOHN HUDNALL on ballance of Accounts stood indebted to the said Collo. WEST noe more than the sume of two thousand one hundred twenty seaven pounds of tobacco and cask, which Account the Plaintiffe not allowing of and the Defendant praying the benefitt of the date of Limittation, the Court doth order that the said ALLICE, Administratrix as aforesaid, pay unto the said Collo. WEST out of the Estate of the said JOHN HUDNALL two thousand one hundred twenty seaven pounds of tobacco and cask with costs als Execution
- Appeale Mr. ALEXANDER SWAN [Attorney as aforesaid] appealeth from this Order to a hearing before his Excellency the Governor and Councill the eighth day of the next Generall Court he giveing caution to prosecute his appeale
- Bond Capt. JOHN HAYNIE, Security for the said ALEXANDER SWAN bound in the penall sume of twenty thousand pounds of tobacco and cask that the said SWAN shall prosecute his appeale

- **Bond** EDWARD WHITE Security for the Defendant
- The Court adjourned to tomorrow morning at eight of the clock

p. 239

Die 18th September 1684   Present
Capt. PETER KNIGHT   Mr. NICHOLAS OWEN
Mr. PETER PRESLEY, SENR.   Capt. JOHN HAYNIE   Justices
Capt. LEONARD HOWSON   Mr. CHRISTOPHER NEALE

- **TOP agt JONES** Whereas Mr. WILLIAM JONES was arrested to this Court by a Note left at his House at the suit of THOMAS TOP for two thousand seaven hundred seaventy nine pounds of tobacco and cask and not appearing, an Attachment is awarded the said TOP against the said JONES for the said sume returnable to the next Court

- **HARRIS agt BYRAM** Mr. JOHN HARRIS assignee of DAVID WHITFORD against PETER BYRAM who marryed the Administratrix of SAMUEL GOCHE referred to the next Court at the motion of Mr. CHARLES HARRIS, the Attorney of the said BYRAM

- **BLEDSOE agt HARRIS &c.** Whereas Mr. GEORGE BLEDSOE summoned Mr. JOHN HARRIS, JOHN WADDY and THOMAS INGRAM to this Court by scire facias to shew their reasons why Execution should not issue on a Judgment obteyned against them the 10th of June 1679 for twenty thousand pounds of tobacco and cask if by the next Court they, the said HARRIS, WADDY and INGRAM, did not lay out for him, ye said BLEDSOE, eight hundred acres of land clear from all older claymes of which they fayled; this Court differing in their Judgment in this Case their votes being approbrious, Capt. PETER KNIGHT, Mr. PETER PRESLEY SENR. and Mr. NICHOLAS OWEN being of opinion that the Judgment ought to be confirmed, Capt. LEONARD HOWSON, Capt. JOHN HAYNIE and Mr. CHRISTOPHER NEALE that it ought not; it is ordered [with the consent of both parties] that the businesse be referred to a hearing before his Excellency the Governor and Councill the eighth day of the next Generall Court

- The Court adjourned to tomorrow morning eight of the clock

p. 240

- Die 19th September 1684   Present
Capt. PETER KNIGHT   Mr. CHRISTOPHER NEALE
Mr. PETER PRESLEY, SENR.   Justices
Capt. LEONARD HOWSON   Capt. JOHN HAYNIE

- **HUDNALL agt HILL & HUDNALL** Whereas EZEKIEL GENESIS by his Last Will and Testament did bequeath unto EZEKIEL HILL and PARTIN HUDNALL nine thousand pounds of tobacco and caske which ISAAC HESTER was to pay him for a tract of land sold by the said GENESIS to the said HESTER or otherwise if the said bargain went not forward for the said land they paying all such debts as were owing by the said GENESIS at the time of his decease; on the Petition of the said ALICE HUDNALL, Executrix of the said GENESIS, it is ordered that the said HILL and HUDNALL pay all such debts as were due from the said GENESIS at the time of his decease, that they enjoy the land formerly sold to the said HESTER [he haveing relinquished the said land] and that the said HESTER forthwith deliver up

NORTHUMBERLAND COUNTY ORDER BOOK, 1678-1698   -41-

to EZEKIEL HILL and PARTIN HUDNALL what Evidences he hath of the said land in his hands

- DALE agt CHAMPION Whereas JOHN CHAMPION was arrested to this Court at the suit of Mr. EDWARD DALE for fowre thousand three hundred seaventy nine pounds of tobacco and cask and the said CHAMPION fayled of his appearance, Judgment is granted the said DALE for the said sume against the Sheriffe according to Law

- TREIP agt JONES's Estate Whereas THOMAS TREIP by his Petition to this Court did declare that EZEKIEL GENESIS did by his Last Will and Testament bequeath severall things to THOMAS NELMES alias MATTOCKS and the said THOMAS NELMES alias MATTOCKS by his Last Will did bequeath the greatest part of his Estate to the said TREIP and his Wife the Mother to the said THOMAS deceased as by both the Wills relation being thereto had will more fully appeare and prayed Judgment against ALICE HUDNALL, Executrix of the said EZEKIEL GENESIS, for what was bequesthed to the said THOMAS NELMES alias MATTOCKS by the Will of the said GENESIS as aforesaid; it is ordered that ALICE HUDNALL, Executrix as aforesaid, forthwith deliver unto THOMAS TREIP, Administrator of the Estate of the said THOMAS NELMES alias MATTOCKS all such things as were bequeathed by the said GENESIS to the said THOMAS NELMES as aforesaid als Execution

p. 241   Northumberland County Court 19th of September 1684

- CHEWNING agt the Sheriffe Whereas JOHN CHAMPION was arrested to this Court at the suit of Mr. THOMAS CHEWNING for fifty shillings and the said CHAMPION appeared not, Judgment is granted the said CHEWNING against the said CHAMPION for the said sume with costs als Execution

- ELIZ: GERRARD, Admrx. of SAM: GERRARD agt EDW: WATTS this Cause is referred to the next Court at the motion of the Defendant

- ROGERS agt HUDNALL Whereas ALICE HUDNALL, Executrix of EZEKIEL GENESIS, deceased, was arrested to this Court at the suit of Mr. WILLIAM ROGERS for eight hundred sixty one pounds of tobacco and cask it appearing to this Court that the said sume is due to the said ROGERS from the said EZEKIEL GENESIS for a Judgment that Mr. THOMAS HOBSON, SENR. obteyned against the said ROGERS [when Sheriffe] for that the said GENESIS was arrested at his suit and appeared not with the charges thence growing, Judgment is granted the said ROGERS against the said HUDNALL for the said sume unlesse the next Court she shews reason to the contrary

- PEMBERTON agt ONEALE Whereas ROGER ONEALE was summoned to this Court by a scire facias to shew reason why Execution should not issue on a Judgment obteyned by RICHARD PEMBERTON against the said ONEALE for one thousand pounds of tobacco and cask, it is ordered that the Order be confirmed and that the said NEALE pay the said sume unto the said PEMBERTON with costs als Execution unlesse the next Court the said ONEALE shews reason to the contrary

- JOHN COSSENS against GEORGE BLEDSOE this Cause is referred to the next Court at the motion of the Defendant

- Lt. Collo. SAMUEL SMYTH agt CHRISTOPHER GARLINGTON referred to the next Court at the motion of the Defendant

p. 242

Northumberland County Court 19th of September 1684

- **WHITE and COTMAN agt SANDERS** Whereas EBENEZER and EDWARD SANDERS, Administrators of MRS. MARY THOMAS, were arrested to this Court at the suit of EDWARD WHITE and BENJAMIN COTMAN, Husbands to MARY and ELIZABETH, Daughters of the said MRS. MARY THOMAS for their share of the said MARY's Estate. The Defendants pleaded that they were under arrest to the Generall Court at the suit of Mr. JOSIAS PITTS, Administrator of WILLIAM THOMAS, deceased, for the whole Estate of the said THOMAS, the said PITTS haveing in this Court entered his exception; it is ordered that the next Court the difference between WHITE, COTMAN and the two SANDERS have a full hearing

- **BARNES agt CONOWAY** Whereas THOMAS BARNES exhibited his Information into this Court against Mr. EDWIN CONOWAY for that as his Excellency the Governor was pleased by his Proclamation to command that noe persons should plead in any Cause but their owne unlesse such persons to whome he should grant a Lycence of Attorney upon the perrill of incurring the penalty layd on delinquents in that case by an Act made in June 1680, yett the said CONOWAY contrary to ye Proclamation as aforesaid did appeare in severall Causes and pleaded them without haveing any such Lycence of Attorney and prayed Judgment against the said CONOWAY according to the Act aforesaid; the Court finding that that Act June [80] repealed by an Act made in September 1682 and by the 88th Act in the Printed Laws it is enacted that noe Act of Court or Proclamation shall upon any pretence whatsoever enjoyne obedience thereunto contrary to any Act of Assembly untill the reversall of that Act by a succeeding Act of Assembly doe order that this suit be dismist

- **DERMOTT agt WMS** Whereas it appeares to this Court that EDWARD WILLIAMS in consideration of his haveing on a Plantation belonging to OWEN DERMOTT in way to repayre and finish the House DERMOTT finding nayles, it is ordered that the said WILLIAMS forthwith finish the work and pay costs

- **WEBB agt GEORGE** Whereas JOHN WEBB entered his action against MRS. ELIZABETH GEORGE, the Administratrix of THOMAS GEORGE, for three hundred eighty eight pounds of tobacco and cask and the Sheriffe returning non est inventus, an Attachment is awarded Mr. JOHN WEBB againt the said GEORGE for the said sume returnable to the next Court

- The Court adjourned till the 3d Wednesay in 9br next

p. 243

Northumberland County DR. 1684

To the Publique Levy	39328
To Capt. PETER KNIGHT for ye Clerk of Assembly	00500
To JOHN WEBB for the Bridge at Cone	00800
To THOMAS DYER one Levy overcharged	00050
To the Sheriffe for 16 Levys overcharged last yeare	00348
To the Clerk	01000
To EDWARD WILLIAMS for tending the Court	00800
To JOHN NICHOLS one Wolf in a pitt	00200
To Capt. LEONARD HOWSON one Wolf shott	00100
To JOHN CLAUGHTON one Wolf in a pitt	00200
To WILLIAM HILL three Wolves in a pitt	00600
To Mr. PETER PRESLEY for Burgess charges	12145 & C.
To Capt. PETER KNIGHT for Burgess charges	11145 & C

NORTHUMBERLAND COUNTY ORDER BOOK, 1678-1698

To JOHN STANLEY for burying a Stranger	00950
To JOHN [? B------] for burying a drowned man	00200
To ye Cryer	00400
To RICHARD ROOT one Wolf shott	00100
To Cask for 24090 pounds of tobacco at 8 percent	01930
To Sallary	05870
	66572

- To be collected by the Sheriffe at eighty two pounds of tobacco per poll

- At a Court held for Northumberland County the 19th of November 1684 Annoque Regni Regis Caroli 2d, 36th &c.

Present

Capt. LEONARD HOWSON   Mr. PETER PRESLEY JUNR.
Capt. JOHN HAYNIE   Justices
Mr. RICHARD KENNER   Mr. RICHARD ROGERS

- Mr. JOHN TAVERNER against THOMAS ELLIOTT referred to the next Court by consent of both parties

- Mr. JOHN RICE agt TEAGE ALLEN In the difference between Mr. JOHN RICE and TEAGE ALLEN, it is ordered that the 6th of Xber next Mr. JOHN COUTANSHEW, Mr. RICHARD FLYNT and JAMES GINN [or any two of them] meet at the house of Mr. JOHN RICE aforesaid called "EXETOR LODGE" and audit the Accounts of the said persons and give in their report to the next Court

- ELIZ: GERRARD agt EDW: WATTS referred to the next Court and ordered that the Clark then bring in what Evidences he hath in the Office relateing to that difference

- Mr. CHARLES HARRIS Attorney of JOHN COSSENS

p. 244

Northumberland County Court 19th of November 1684

- ELINOR WALTERS's Will proved Upon the Petition of [   ] Probate is granted him of the Last Will and Testament of ELINOR WALTERS deceased, the Will being proved by the Oaths of JANE BLACKERBY and THOMAS BERRY witnesses to the said Will

- LUKE agt STRINGER An Attachment is granted Mr. JOHN LUKE against the Estate of EDMUND STRINGER for ine hundred twenty pounds of tobacco and cask returnable to the next Court

- Mr. DENNIS CARTEE Attorney of Mr. THOMAS WILKS

- PEMBERTON agt ONEALE Whereas the last Court it was ordered that ROGER ONEALE should pay one thousand pounds of tobacco and cask unto RICHARD PEMBERTON unless this Court he should shew reason to the contrary and whereas this Court the said ONEALE made appeare that he hath payd seaven hundred seaventy and six pounds of that sume, Judgment is granted the said PEMBERTON against the said ONEALE for two hundred twenty fowre pounds of tobacco and cask with costs als Execution

- WEBB against GEORGE Whereas the last Court an Attachment was awarded JOHN WEBB against the Estate of Mr. THOMAS GEORGE for three hundred eighty eight pounds of tobacco and cask returnable to this Court which Attachment is returned executed on soe much in the hands of HENRY HARTLEY and

and whereas this Court JOHN WEBB hath made his debt appeare due by a Bill under the hand of Mr. THOMAS GEORGE, Judgment is granted the said WEBB against the said HENRY HARTLEY for the said sume als Execution

- FLYNT agt WATERMAN Whereas it appeares to this Court by a Bill under the hand of THOMAS WATERMAN that the said WATERMAN is indebted unto THOMAS FLYNT the sume of two hundred eighty pounds of tobacco and cask; Judgment is granted the said FLYNT against the said WATERMAN for the said sume with costs als Execution unlesse the said WATERMAN shews reason to the contrary at the next Court
 - Mr. RICHARD HAYNE Attorney for THOMAS WATERMAN
- BUCKSTON agt SWANSON Whereas it appeares to this Court that the Estate of JOHN SWANSON standeth indebted unto SUSANNA BUCKSTON, Administratrix of JOHN JONES, ye sume of one hundred ninety pounds of tobacco and cask upon ballance of Accounts, Judgment is granted the said BUCKSTON for the said sume against the Estate of the said SWANSON als Execution
 - Capt. THOMAS JONES Attorney for SUSANNA BUCKSTON

p. 245   Northumberland County Court 19th of November 1684

- BLEDSOE agt COSSENS Whereas Mr. GEORGE BLEDSOE was arrested to this Court at the suit of JOHN COZENS and noe cause of action appearing, a non suit is granted the said BLEDSOE against the said COZENS with costs and damages according to Law als Execution

- The Honble NICH: SPENCER Esqr. agt Mr. CHRISTOPHER NEALE Whereas it appeares to this Court by a Bond under the hands and seales of Mr. PHILIP SHAPLEIGH and Mr. CHRISTOPHER NEALE that the said NEALE was Security for the said SHAPLEIGH for the payment of the sume of eighty two pounds, seaven shillings sterling unto the Honble. NICHOLAS SPENCER Esqr., in case Bills of Exchange drawne by the said SHAPLEIGH for forty one pounds, three shillings and six pence sterling payable to his Honor or order were not payd according to the tenor of the Bills and whereas it appeares that the said Bills are returned protested; Judgment is granted to the Honble NICHOLAS SPENCER Esqr. for forty seaven pounds, seaventeen shillings sterling against the said NEALE as Security aforesaid, being for the said Bills, damages and costs of protest als Execution

- LITTLEPAGE agt GOCHE Whereas it appeares to this Court by a Bill under the hand and seale of Mr. SAMUELL GOCH deceased, dated the 22d 9br 1682 that the said GOCH stood indebted unto RICHARD LITTLEPAGE the sume of twelve thousand pounds of tobacco and cask; Judgment is granted Mr. JOHN HARRIS, the Attorney of Mr. DAVID WHITFORD the Assignee of the said LITTLEPAGE against the Estate of the said GOCH for the said sume als Execution

- THO: TOP agt Mr. WM: JONES Mr. WILLIAM JONES confesseth Judgment for the present payment of two thousand seaven hundred seaventy nine pounds of tobacco and cask unto THOMAS TOP with costs als Execution

- WILKS agt KNIGHT Whereas Capt. PETER KNIGHT was summoned to this Court by a scire facias to shew his reasons why Execution should not issue out on an Order obteyned against him by Mr. THOMAS WILKS February 18th 1679 for seaven hundred pounds of tobacco and cask; it is ordered that the said Order be confirmed, that the said KNIGHT forthwith pay the said sume unto the said WILKES

NORTHUMBERLAND COUNTY ORDER BOOK, 1678-1698 -45-

with costs als Execution unlesse the next Court he shew reason to the contrary

p. 246

Northumberland County Court 19th of November 1684

- CLAUGHTON agt RICE Whereas the 4th of January lst, THOMAS FLYNT and CLEMENT ALDRIDGE were appoynted to view the work done by JAMES CLAUGHTON for Mr. JOHN RICE and give in their report to the next Court which they accordingly doing, vizt. that the House was altogether insufficient and not workman like whereon the said parties referred the said difference to Mr. RICHARD FLYNT, Mr. JAMES JOHNSON, THOMAS FLYNT and CLEMENT ALDRIDGE to arbitrate the same who did award that all Accounts between them should be ballanced nd that each should beare his owne charges; ye Court doe allow of the said award and doe order that the said JAMES CLAUGHTON pay what charges that have accrewed since the bringing of the first report

- The Court adjourned to tomorrow morning nine a clock

- Die 20th November 1684   Present
Capt. LEONARD HOWSON   Mr. PETER PRESLEY, JUNR.
Capt. JOHN HAYNIE   Justives
Mr. RICHARD KENNER   Mr. RICHARD ROGERS

- SPAN agt JAMES Whereas MARY JAMES, Servant to CUTHBERT SPAN, hath had a bastard Child in the time of her service, it is ordered that she serve her said Master according to Act, that the Sheriffe give her twenty stripes on her bare back and summon in HUMPHREY [   ] the Father of the said Child to the next Court to give security for his good behaviour and to save the Parish harmlesse from the said Child

- Mr. RICHD: FLYNT agt the Sheriffe Whereas Mr. EDMUND LUKE was arrested to this Court at the suit of Mr. RICHARD FLYNT for six hundred fifty and two pounds of tobacco and cask and fayled of her appearance, Judgment is granted the said FLYNT against the Sheriffe for the said sume according to Law

- DALE agt CHAMPION. Mr. HAYNIE Attorney for Plaintiffe Whereas it appeares to this Court that JOHN CHAMPION standeth indebted unto Mr. EDWARD DALE upon ballance of Accounts two thousand three hundred seaventy nine pounds of tobacco and cask, Judgment is granted the said DALE against the said CHAMPION for the said sume with costs als Execution

- Capt. COOPER to have the Blunder Bushers Whereas yesterday Capt. GEORGE COOPER prayed that he might have two of the Counties Blunder Bushers now out of order which are now at the house of Mr. THOMAS BRERETON. It is ordered that he take the possession in his custody and return the same fixt when there required or otherwise pay the County for them according to their full value

p. 247

Northumberland County Court 20th of November 1684

- HUDNALL agt WILKES Whereas ALICE HUDNALL, Administratrix of JOHN HUDNALL, deceased, was arrested to this Court at the suit of THOMAS WILKES and noe cause of action appearing, a non suit is granted the said HUDNALL against the said WILKES with costs and damages according to Law

- RICH: SMYTH to survey PICKERIN's Land Ordered at the instant of

RICHARD SMYTH that EDWARD PICKRIN survey his Land according to the bounds of his Pattent between this and the first of March next or otherwise the said SMYTH survey it according to the said bounds

- PINCKARD agt THOMAS Whereas the 16th August 1682 Mr. JOHN PINCKARD obteyned Judgment against MRS. MARY THOMAS for two pounds, twelve shillings sterling; Judgment is granted to the said PINCKARD against EBENEZER SANDERS, Administrator of the said THOMAS, for the said sume out of the said Estate being what in that Order was granted him for present payment als Execution

- WILKES agt BRODIE Whereas it appeares to this Court that ALEXANDER BRODIE standeth indebted unto THOMAS WILKES fowre thousand pounds of tobacco and cask, Judgment is granted the said WILKES against the said BRODIE for the said sume with costs als Execution unlesse the next Court the said BRODIE shall make satisfaction of the debt

- [The names of the persons in this entry are faded away] referred to the next Court at the motion of the said Defendant

- WILKES agt BUTLER Whereas Mr. THOMAS WILKES did in this Court produce a Note under the hand of JOHN BUTLER drawne upon Mr. THOMAS HOBSON SENR. for three barrells of Indian Corne due the said BUTLER from the said HOBSON for his Freedom Corne the said HOBSON averring that the said BUTLER has truly served him many yeares, that the last yeare he served him he kept his Mill for him, and when his time was out he often begged of the said HOBSON to buy his Freedom Corne of him, who told him he had Corne in the Mill [as he knew] and that he might there take his Corne and dispose of it and that the said BUTLER going from him he left two hogsheads of shelled Corne in the Mill which he, the said HOBSON, expecting when the said BUTLER would send for it would not dispose of it for some time [the said BUTLER haveing not left the Corne so well cleansed as he should], the Corne was spoyled with the weevely and rotted; this Court considering that the Corne was due to the said BUTLER in July 1680, the Note drawne on HOBSON in 8br of the said yeare and neither since demanded by the said WILKES of the said BUTLER nor by the said BUTLER of the said HOBSON, though he has lived severall yeares since with both of them, it is ordered that the said WILKES for his remissnesse bear the losse of the Corne and that this suit be dismist

p. 248 Northumberland County Court 20th of November 1684

- Appeale Mr. THOMAS WILKES appealeth from this Order to the eighth day of the next Generall Court which is granted him, giving caution to prosecute his said appeale

Mr. JOHN HUGHLETT, SENR. Security for the Appeallant, Mr. THOMAS HOBSON, SENR. Security for the Appellee

- CHEWNING agt CHAMPION Whereas it appeares to this Court that JOHN CHAMPION was Security for THOMAS SNELL who had drawne Bills of Exchange for forty shillings sterling payable to Mr. THOMAS CHEWNING and it appearing by the Oath of Mr. RICHARD FARRINGTON that the Bill was returned protested, Judgment is granted the said CHEWNING for fifty shillings sterling against the said CHAMPION being for the said Bill, damages and charges of the protest with costs als Execution

- **WILKES agt HUDNALL** Whereas ALICE HUDNALL, Administratrix of JOHN HUDNALL, was arrested to this Court at the suit of Mr. THOMAS WILKES and noe cause of action appearing, a non suit is granted the said HUDNALL against the said WILKES with costs and damages als Execution

- **Capt. LEONARD HOWSON against Lt. Collo. SAMUEL SMYTH** referred to the next Court

- **WATTS agt NEWHAM** Whereas it appeares to this Court that WILLIAM NEWHAM standeth indebted unto ELIZABETH WATTS the sume of three hundred pounds of tobacco and cask, Judgment is granted the said WATTS against the said NEWHAM for the said sume with costs als Execution

- **BASHAW agt HARVEY** Whereas WILLIAM BASHAW was arrested to this Court at the suit of WILLIAM HARVEY and noe cause of action appearing, a non suit is granted the said BASHAW against the said HARVEY with costs and damages according to Law

- **THOMAS ELLIOTT against Mr. MOTTROM WRIGHT** referred to the next Court at the motion of the Defendant

- **BRYAM against the Sheriffe** Whereas CLEMENT LATIMORE was arrested to this Court at the suit of PETER BYRAM for fowre hundred pounds of tobacco and caske and fayled of his appearance, Judgment is granted the said BYRAM against the Sheriffe for the said sume with costs als Execution

- **JOHN EVANS against JOHN FLOYD** referred to the next Court

p. 249

Northumberland County Court 20th of November 1684

- **JOHN REASON against WILLIAM BOURNE** referred to the next Court

- **PARRIS to keep the Children's Estate** It is ordered that on the tenth day of December JOHN ROBINSON and JOHN WORNAM meet at the house of NICHOLAS PARRIS and then devide the cattle devised by the Last Will and Testament of ELINOR WALTERS among her Grandchildren and that the said NICHOLAS PARRIS carefully look after the Cattle given to his Wife's Children and give an Account thereof when required and that he have allowed him for his paynes and charge the male increase of the said Cattle

- **SWETNAM to secure FRANCES BRITTAINE's Estate** Ordered that Mr. WILLIAM SWETNAM that liveth on the Plantation of WILLIAM CLARK preserve and secure what there is on the said Plantation belonging to the said WILLIAM CLARK and FRANCES BRITTAINE and suffer nothing to be removed of the said Plantation but by the Order of this Court

- **JOANE ROGERS to be summoned to next Court** Whereas a complaynt hath been made to this Court that JOANE ROGERS, the Relict of JOHN ROGERS, deceased, is supinely negligent both in the keeping of the said Children of her said Husband as preservation of their Estate and the Children always being in want of a due Education being neither bred like the Children of such a Father nor of a Christian and their Estate almost ruined. It is ordered that the Sheriff summon the said JOANE to the next Court to give security of the Court for the better keeping and educating of the said Children and security of the Estate or else that Mr. WILLIAM ROGERS take the Children and Estate into his hands from whome it is hoped the Children will find much better usage and their Estate more preservaton

- **COTMAN and WHITE agt SANDERS** BENJAMIN COTMAN and

EDWARD WHITE against EZENEZER and EDWARD SANDERS, Administrators of MRS. MARY THOMAS is referred to the next Court then to receive a final determination

- ROGERS's Certificate for Land Certificate is granted Mr. WILLIAM ROGERS for five hundred acres of land for the importation of ten persons into this Colony, vizt.

JOHN ALTHORP	PHILIP GAMMONDS	HENRY TAYLER
ISRAELL BERRY	ANNE SPRAG	THOMAS ECOCK
JUDITH KANNE	DANIEL DOOLY	KATHARINE BRYANT
DOMINICK RICE		

- The next Court the 3d Wednesday in January next

p. 250

- At a Court held for Northumberland County the 21st of January 1684/5 Annoque Regni Regis Caroli 2d, 36th &c.

Present
Lt. Collo. SAMUEL SMYTH   Capt. JOHN HAYNIE
Mr. NICHOLAS OWEN   Mr. RICHARD KENNER   Justices

- Severall Servants bound JAMES COX, Servant to JOHN BOWRN is judged to be ten yeares of age; JOHN CROST, Servant to PETER MAXWELL twelve yeares of age and ANTHONY COTOON, Servant to CLEMENT LATIMORE seaventeen yeares of age and all ordered to serve their respective Masters according to Act

- Mr. JOHN RICE against TEAGE ALLEN referred to the next Court with the consent of both parties

- JACOB JOHNSON released from his Bond Whereas JACOB JOHNSON became bound to our Soveraigne Lord the King in a Bond of forty pounds sterling that he would make his personall appearance at this Court and give in Evidence in the behalf of his Majesty against ROBERT OLDIS who was committed to his Maties Goale of this County for that he was by him, the said JOHNSON, suspected to have feloniously stollen out of his boat severall goods belonging to Mr. THOMAS MOUNTJOY, the said JOHNSON haveing at this Court made his appearance and ye said OLDIS haveing broke prison and made his escape it is ordered that the said JOHNSON have his bond delivered in

- WISE agt RUSSELL Whereas an Attachment was awarded SARAH WISE against the Estate of THOMAS RUSSELL for fifteen hundred sixty six pounds of tobacco and cask, which Attachment is returned executed on soe much tobacco belonging to the said RUSSELL then hanging in the house of ye said WISE and whereas this Court the said SARAH WISE hath made her debt appeare justly due, Judgment is granted the said WISE for soe much of the tobacco attached as aforesaid as will satisfye the debt with costs als Execution

- Present   Mr. CHRISTOPHER NEALE
            Mr. PETER PRESLEY, JUNR.

- TAVERNER agt ELLIOTT Whereas it appeares to this Court that THOMAS ELLIOTT standeth indebted unto Mr. JOHN TAVERNER on ballance of all Accounts the sume of one thousand pounds of tobacco and cask by Bill dated the 8th of July 1681; Judgment is granted the said TAVERNER against the said ELLIOTT for the said sume with costs als Execution

NORTHUMBERLAND COUNTY ORDER BOOK, 1678-1698

p. 251 **Northumberland County Court 21st of January 1684/5**

- MOOR agt BRYAM Whereas at a Court held for this County the 17th of 7br last, JAMES MOOR, the Assignee of JAMES FOWLER, did petition for Judgment against the Estate of SAMUEL GOCHE, deceased, for sixteen hundred sixty nine pounds of tobacco and cask, and did then produce a Bill under the hand of the said GOCHE dated the 15th of 9br 1681, for the said sume by reason of the multiplicity of businesse the Clark in entering the Order did mistake ye sume and entered the Judgment but for five hundred eighty nine pounds of tobacco and caske and in short time after the said MOOR coming to the Office to take out an Execution on the Judgment the Clark saw his mistake but durst not alter the Record. This Court doe order that PETER BYRAM, who marryed the Executrix of the said GOCHE, forthwith pay the aforesaid sume of sixteen hundred sixty nine poounds of tobacco and cask out of the Estate of the said GOCHE unto the said MOOR with costs als Execution

- TIPTON to apprayse Sloop Sayles and Rigging Whereas EDWARD TIPTON complayned to this Court that WILLIAM DOWNING and himselfe have in their possession the Sayles and Rigging belonging to a Sloop formerly left by Mr. HENRY ROACH seaven yeares and prayed that the said Sayles and Rigging might be appraysed. It is ordered that Mr. AZARCAM PARKER and Mr. GEORGE BARRATT some time between this and the next Court apprayse the same and returne the appraysment to the Court

- FLYNT agt WATERMAN THOMAS WATERMAN confesseth Judgment for the present payment of two hundred eighty pounds of tobacco and cask unto THOMAS FLYNT with costs als Execution

- HICKMAN agt WATTS Judgment is granted THOMAS HICKMAN against EDWARD WATTS for his attendance one day at Court to give in his Evidence in the behalf of the said WATTS according to Act

- GERRARD agt WATTS Whereas ELIZABETH, the Administratrix of Mr. SAMUEL GERRARD, prayed Judgment against EDWARD WATTS for twelve hundred pounds of tobacco and cask and the said WATTS made appeare that there was due to him from the said GERRARD five hundred pounds of tobacco and cask for building a tobacco house; Judgment is granted the said ELIZABETH against the said WATTS for seaven hundred pounds of tobacco and cask with costs als Execution

p. 252 **Northumberland County Court 21st of January 1694/5**

- SPICER agt COX RICHARD COX confesseth Judgment for the present payment of five hundred pounds of tobacco and cask unto Mr. ARTHUR SPICER with costs als Execution

- FLYNT agt LUKE Whereas it appeareth to this Court by a Bill under the hand of Mr. EDMUND LUKE that the said LUKE standeth indebted unto Mr. RICHARD FLYNT the sume of six hundred fifty and two pounds of tobacco and cask to which the said LUKE pleaded he had payd two hundred and fifty pounds of the said debt by ye hand of Mr. JOHN JULIAN to the said FLYNT, the Court doe order that the next Court the said LUKE make appeare that the said two hundred fifty pounds of tobacco as alledged be paid by Mr. JULIAN and that the same be deducted out of his debt to Mr. FLYNT or otherwise that he pay the full debt to the said FLYNT with costs als Execution

- DENNIS CARTEE Attorney of STEPHEN WELLS

- WADDY agt BOURNE Whereas an Attachment was awarded THOMAS WADDY against the Estate of WILLIAM BOURNE for twelve hundred pounds of tobacco and cask which Attachment is returned executed on some tools in the hands of ye said WADDY and a small parcell of tobacco in the hands of Mr. JOHN LEWIS, and some Cooper's ware in the hands of Mr. CHARLES DACRES; Judgment is granted the said WADDY for what is soe attached with costs als Execution; and whereas the rest of the debt was attached in the hands of THOMAS WILLIAMS the said WILLIAMS not being at Court and the Estate of the said BOURNE in his hands not being knowne, and he the said WILLIAM baveing an Attachment out for a debt due to him from the said BOURNE, it is ordered that the next Court the two Orders make their right appeare and that then that businesse be determined

- EDW: ALLGOOD's Will proved Upon the Petition of ELIZABETH ALGOOD Executrix of her Husband, EDWARD ALGOOD's Will, a probate is granted her of the last Will and Testament of her deceased Husband, the Will being proved by the Oaths of RICHARD SMYTH and CHARLES HARRIS witnesses to the said Will

- CONDON's Will proved Upon the Petition of ANN CONDON, Executrix of EDMUND CONDON deceased, a probate is granted her of the last Will and Testament of the said EDMUND, the Will being proved by the Oaths of DAVID LYNDSAY and WILLIAM WARWICK witnesses of the said Will

- The Court adjourned to tomorrow morning eight of the clock

p. 253

- Die 22d January 1684/5   Present
    Lt. Collo. SAMUELL SMYTH
    Capt. JOHN HAYNIE   Justices
    Mr. PETER PRESLEY, JUNR.

- There not appearing Magistrats to hold a Court doe adjourne to the 1st Wednesday in February

- February 4th 1684/5. Lt. Collo. SAMUEL SMYTH onely then appearing, adjourneth the Court to the 3d Wednesday in March

- At a Court held for Northumberland County the 18th day of March 1684/5 Annoque Regni Regis Carolin 2d, 37th &c.
        Present
Mr. PETER PRESLEY, JUNR. Mr. RICHARD KENNER
Mr. NICHOLAS OWEN   Justices
Capt. JOHN HAYNIE   Mr. RICHARD ROGERS

- NUTT's Will proved Upon the Petition of RICHARD NUTT, Executor of Mr. RICHARD NUTT, deceased, a Probate is granted him of the Last Will and Testament of the said NUTT, ye Will being proved by the Oaths of JAMES MONGOMERY, JOHN EDGAR and JOHN [   ] witnesses to the said Will

- JULIAN's Will proved Upon the Petition of Mr. NICHOLAS OWEN, Executor of Mr. JOHN JULIAN, deceased, a Probate is granted him of the last Will and Testament of the said JULIAN, the Will be proved by the Oaths of JOHN BATCHE-

NORTHUMBERLAND COUNTY ORDER BOOK, 1678-1698   -51-

LER and JOHN BAKER, witnesses to the said Will
- **PRITTS's Will proved** Upon the Petition of RICHARD RICE, Executor of the Last Will and Testament of ROBERT PRITT, deceased, the Will being proved by the Oaths of THOROUGHGOOD PATE and JEREMIAH THORNTON, witnesses to the said Will
- **BOGGAS's Will proved** Upon the Petition of RUTH BOGGESS, Executor of HENRY BOGGAS, deceased, a Probate is granted her of the Will and Testament of the said BOGGAS, ye Will being proved by the Oaths of HENRY MEDCALF, HENRY MASEY and WILLIAM PARKER witnesses
- **BREWER's Will proved** Upon the Petition of THOMAS BREWER, Executor of THOMAS BREWER, deceased, Probate is grated him of the Last Will and Testament of the said BREWER ye Will being proved by the Oaths of JOHN TURBERVILLE and JOHN SPARKES witnesses to the said Will

p. 254 **Northumberland County Court 18th of March 1684/5**
- **Severall Servants bound** HENRY HUDSON, Servant to Mr. JOHN COUTANSHEW JUNR. ordered with the consent of both parties that he serve his said Master six yeares and noe longer
JAMES MORTIMORE, Servant to Mr. JOHN COUTANSHEW, SENR. is judged to be sixteene yeares of age and ordered to serve his said Master according to Act
- **Mr. JOHN RICE against TEAGE ALLEN** referred to the next Court by consent of both parties
- **GAWLER agt KNIGHT** Mr. PETER KNIGHT by his Note to the Court confesseth Judgment for the present payment of six hundred twenty five pounds of tobacco and cask unto Mr. HENRY GAWLER with costs als Execution
- **SPICER agt KNIGHT** Mr. PETER KNIGHT by his Note to the Court confesseth Judgment for the present payment of fower hundred pounds of tobacco and cask unto Mr. ARTHUR SPICER with costs als Execution
- Present   THOMAS BRERETON
- **THOMAS HIGGINS** Servant to JOHN HULL is adjudged to be seaventeen yeares of age, ordered he serve his said Master according to Act
- **THO: SEARLE freed from Levy** THOMAS SEARLE being a poore impotent person, it is ordered that he be freed from the Levy
- **ANN GREENSTON to serve WM. YARRATT** ANNE GREENSTON, Daughter of JOHN GREENSTON, being nine yeares of age is ordered with the consent of her Father to serve WILLIAM YARRATT and JANE his Wife untill she shall be seaventeen yeares of age but not to serve any other person but them or the survivour of them
- **WILLIAM GRIMSTEAD's Children bound** THOMAS GRIMSTEAD seaven yeares old and JOHN GRIMSTEAD fowre yeares old with the consent of WILLIAM GRIMSTEAD, their Father, are ordered to serve WILLIAM TAYLER untill they be one and twenty yeares of age but if it should happen that WILLIAM TAYLER and his Wife should depart this life before the said Children attaine the age of one and twenty yeares that then they be free

p. 255 **Northumberland County Court 18th of March 1684/5**
- **BARNES agt JOYCE** Whereas THOMAS BARNES in March Court

1682/3 put in his Information against ABRAHAM JOYCE for concealing two Tythables and at the instance of some Gentlemen of the Court, the said BARNES and JOYCE came to an agreement between themselves which the said BARNES complayned to this Court the said JOYCE soe farr from complying with that he refuseth to pay him anything and prayed Judgment against the said JOYCE according to Act, Judgment is granted the said BARNES for his said Information according to Act against the said JOYCE with costs als Execution, unlesse the next Court the said JOYCE shews reason to the contrary

- ADAMS to take BENNETT's Estate in his hands. Whereas THOMAS BENNETT is lately dead at the house of THOMAS ADAMS and left noe knowne relations behind him in this Country. It is ordered that the said ADAMS exhibite a just Inventory of the Estate of the said BENNETT and exhibite it into this Court and that he secure the same nine monthes and then give a full account thereof so that the Court when if noe relations of the said BENNETT appeare, that he the said ADAMS have fuller power for the disposing thereof

- GAWLER agt BLEDSOE. GEORGE BLEDSOE confesseth Judgment for the present payment of fower thousand eight hundred sixty pounds of tobacco and cask unto Mr. HENRY GAWLER with costs als Execution

- DAWSON agt the Sheriffe. Whereas THOMAS QUICK a poor man was in the Parish Levy allowed three hundred pounds of tobacco and lately fell sick and dyed. It is ordered in consideration of the charge and trouble that WILLIAM DAWSON was at in burying of him that the Sheriffe pay the costs levyed for the said QUICK to the said DAWSON

- HULL agt STRINGER. Whereas an Attachmen was awarded RICHARD HULL against the Estate of EDMUND STRINGER for fowre hundred forty and six pounds of tobacco and cask which is returned executed on tobacco of the said STRINGER's hanging, the said HULL haveing in Court on his

p. 256 Northumberland County Court 18th of March 1684/5

Oath made his debt appeare due; Judgment is granted the said HULL against the Estate of the said STRINGER attached as aforesaid for his said debt with costs als Execution

- HULL agt STRINGER. Whereas an Attachment was awarded JOHN HULL against the Estate of EDMUND STRINGER for fowre hundred pounds of tobacco and cask which Attachment is returned executed on the tobacco of the said STRINGER's hanging and whereas this Court the said HULL did by his Oath make the said debt appeare due; Judgment is granted the said HULL against the Estate of the said STRINGER attached as aforesaid for the said debt with costs als Execution

- TEMPLAR to cleare the Road. Whereas WILLIAM TEMPLAR hath fallen many trees across the Maine Road formerly by the Surveyor of the Highways cleared and marked soe that neither Cart nor Horse can travell that way. It is ordered that the said TEMPLAR forthwith clear the way taking away the trees and make the Road as formerly fitt for travell or Neighbours to goe with horse and carts or otherwise the next Court he be punished according to Law

- PEMBERTON agt DERMOTT. Whereas RICHARD PEMBERTON complayned to this Court that OWEN DERMOTT had trespassed him in firing his tobacco house and carrying away the nayles. It is ordered that the Sheriffe take the

NORTHUMBERLAND COUNTY ORDER BOOK, 1678-1698   -53-

said DERMOTT into his custody untill he gives Bond with sufficient security for his appearance the next Court to answer the said suit

- WILLIAM NEWHAM against DAVID FLOYD This Cause was referred to a Jury whose names are underwritten, vizt

THOMAS BANKES	JOHN HUGHLETT JUNR.	CUTHBERT SPAN
JAMES JNO:SON	EBENEZER SANDERS	THOMAS HAMMON
HENRY MAYSE	EDWARD TIPTON	JOHN EVANS
JOHN EUSTACE	THOMAS ADAMS	CHRISTOPHER GARLINGTON

- Verdict We find for the Plaintiffe
- Judgment On this Verdict the Court doe order that DAVID FLOYD doe pay to WILLIAM NEWHAM three hundred pounds of tobacco and cask with costs als Execution

p. 257 Northumberland County Court 18th of March 1684/5

- JONES agt GENESIS Whereas it appeares to this Court by a condition under the hand of EZEKIEL GENESIS that the said GENESIS at the time of his decease stood indebted unto SAMUEL JONES three barrells of Indian Corne; Judgment is granted the said JONES against ALICE HUDNALL, the Executrix of EZEKIEL GENESIS [her paying thirty pounds of tobacco due from him of the Estate] for the Corne als Execution

- TIPTON to dispose of the sayles of ROACH's Sloop Whereas ye last Court it was ordered that AZARCAM PARKER and GEORGE BARRATT should prayse the rigging and sayles of a Sloop belonging to Mr. JOHN ROACH in the hands of Mr. EDWARD TIPTON which they haveing performed, and account of the same with the appraysment being by the said TIPTON exhibited into this Court, it is ordered that the said appraysment be put on the Records of this County and that the said TIPTON dispose of the same, he being accomptable for the same to the said ROACH, the Owner of them, according as appraysed when thereto required

- JONES and EUSTACE agt the Sheriffe Whereas Mr. JOHN CURTIS was arrested to this Court at the suit of Mr. WILLIAM JONES and Mr. JOHN EUSTACE and fayling of hihs appearance, Judgment is granted the said JONES and EUSTACE against the Sheriffe according to Law

- SPAN's Estate to be devided Upon the Petition of CUTHBERT SPAN that a devision of the Estate be made between him and his Brother, JOHN, it is ordered that on Wednesday next JOHN DOWNING, JOHN COLES, THOMAS WEBB and JOHN WORNAM devide the Estate and give in an account thereof to the next Court

- PEMBERTON agt LAMPERY Whereas it appeares to this Court that there is due to RICHARD PEMBERTON from the Estate of BARTHOLOMEW YEAMANS fourteen hundred pounds of tobacco and cask; Judgment is granted the said PEMBERTON against RICHARD LAMPERY, Administrator of the said YEAMANS, for the said sume with costs als Execution

p. 258 Northumberland County Court 18th of March 1684/5

- HARRIS agt LAMPERY Judgment is granted Mr. CHARLES HARRIS against RICHARD LAMPERY, Administrator of BARTHOLOMEW YEAMANS, for one hundred fifty pounds of tobacco and cask als Execution

- SMYTH agt LAMPERY Judgment is granted RICHARD SMYTH against RICHARD LAMPERY, Administrator of BARTHOLOMEW YEAMANS for seaventy pounds of tobacco and cask als Execution

- HOWSON agt SMYTH Whereas Lt. Collo. SAMUEL SMYTH was summoned to this Court at the suit of Capt. LEONARD HOWSON for fowre hundred thirty five pounds of tobacco being due for Levys and Sheriffe's fees in the year 1678; Judgment is gratned the said Capt. HOWSON against the said Lt. Collo. SMYTH for the said sume with costs als Execution unlesse the next Court Lt. Collo. SMYTH shews reasons to the contrary

- HULL agt HARRIS Mr. CHARLES HARRIS confesseth Judgment for the present payment of eighty hundred fifty pounds of tobacco and cask uto JOHN HULL with costs als Execution

- The Court adjourneth till tomorrow morning eight a clock

- Die 19th March 1684/5   Present
Mr. PETER PRESLEY, SENR.   Mr. THOMAS BRERETON
Capt. JOHN HAYNIE   Justices
Mr. RICHARD KENNER   Mr. RICHARD ROGERS

- FARMER for Feoffee for MOTTROM's Estate Whereas the Honble NICHOLAS SPENCER Esqr. did by his Letter to this Court commend Mr. WILLIAM FARMER to be Feofee in Trust for the Estate of Major JOHN MOTTROM, deceased, and did therein oblige himself that the said FARMER shall yearly give an Account thereof, this Court doe order that the said FARMER be admitted as a Feoffee in Trust into that Estate and that he take a full and just Inventory of that Estate and exhibite it into this Court and that yearly he bring in an Account thereof to the Court

p. 259 Northumberland County Court 19th of March 1684/5

- SPENCER agt MOTTROM Whereas it appeares to this Court by an Account under the hand of Mr. JOHN and ROBERT BEVERLEY that the Honble NICHOLAS SPENCER, Esqr., payed to the said BEVERLEYs for the said Major JOHN MOTTROM fower thousand pounds of tobacco and cask, being part of eight thousand pounds of tobacco due out of the publique Levy; Judgment is granted the said NICHOLAS SPENCER, Esqr. for the said sume out of the Estate of the said MOTTROM als Execution

- HOBSON agt MOTTROM Whereas Mr. THOMAS HOBSON SENR. petitioned this Court for fower thousand thirty eight pounds of tobacco and cask due to him for two yeares Levys and Quit Rents and two hundred thirty four pounds of tobacco for Clarke's fees from the Estate of Major JOHN MOTTROM deceased, to the Plaintiffe and Capt. THOMAS [   ] Attorney for the Defendant and pleads that the Clark's fees ought not to be payd the fees being due in the yeare 1678 and 1679 and produced a Law that Accounts against dead men's Estates ought to be allowed if the debts were not contracted within the yeare before ye decease of the Debtor; Judgment is therefore granted to the said HOBSON for the fowre thousand thirty eight pounds of tobacco against the said Major JOHN MOTTROM's Estate als Execution the Clark"s fees not being allowed of

- FARNEFOLD agt MOTTROM Whereas Mr. JOHN FARNEFOLD did make it appeare that a Bill under the hand of Major JOHN MOTTROM that the

NORTHUMBERLAND COUNTY ORDER BOOK, 1678-1698   -55-

MOTTROM stood indebted unto the said Mr. FARNEFOLD the sum of three thousand seaventy two pounds of tobacco and fowre hundred pounds of tobaacco more was due to him for preaching his funerall sermon; Judgment is granted the said Mr. FARNEFOLD againt the Estate of the said MOTTROM for three thousand fowre hundred seaventy two pounds of tobacco and cask als Execution

- ROGERS agt MOTTROM Whereas it appeares to this Court that there is due to Mr. WILLIAM ROGERS from the Estate of Major JOHN MOTTROM by the Oath of the said ROGERS, for Levys, Quit Rents and Secretary Fees two thousand sixty pounds of tobacco, Judgment is granted the said ROGERS against the Estate of the said MOTTROM for the said sume ale Execution

p. 260 Northumberland County Court 19th of March 1684/5

- LUKE agt MOTTROM Whereas it appeares to this Court by a Note under the hands of Major JOHN MOTTROM that the ssid MOTTROM stood indebted unto the said EDMUND LUKE the sume of three hundred pounds of tobacco and cask; Judgment is granted the said LUKE against the said MOTTROM his Estate for the said sume als Execution the Account of the said LUKE against the said MOTTROM being debt of by Act of Assembly

- HUGHES's land to be devided Whereas THOMAS HUGHES [who being at age] petitioned this Court that the land devised unto him by the Last Will and Testament of his deceased Father and his Brother, JOHN HUGHES, might be devided between them according to the tenor of the said Will, it is ordered that Capt. JOHN HAYNIE some time between this and the next Court devide the same

- HARRIS agt HARTLAND Whereas WILLIAM HARTLAND was arrested to this Court at the suit of Mr. CHARLES HARRIS for fowre hundred fifty pounds of tobacco and cask and appeared not; Judgment is granted the said HARRIS against the Sheriffe according to Law

- Attachment An Attachment is granted the Sheriffe against WILLIAM HARTLAND for fowre hundred fifty pounds of tobacco and cask with costs returnable to the next Court

- HARRIS agt KNIGHT Whereas Capt. PETER KNIGHT was summoned to this Court at the suit of Mr. CHARLES HARRIS for fowre hundred fifty pounds of tobacco and cask; Judgment is granted the said HARRIS against the said Capt. KNIGHT for the said sume with costs als Execution unless the said Capt. PETER KNIGHT appeares and shews his reasons to the contrary

- WMS: &c agt FORD Whereas THOMAS WILLIAMS and CLEMENT LATIMORE were arrested to this Court at the suit of JOHN FORD and the said FORD not appearing to prosecute, a non suit is granted the said WILLIAMS and LATIMORE against the said FORD with costs and damages according to Law

- BYRAM agt CURTIS Judgment is granted PETER BYRAM against JOHN CURTIS for five hundred thirty pounds of tobacco and cask with costs als Execution unless the next Court the said CURTIS shews reasons to the contrary

p. 261 Northumberland County Court 19th of March 1684/5

- SPENCER agt SHAPLEIGH Whereas it did appeare to this Court by two Bills under the hand of Mr. PHILIP SHAPLEIGH, the one for seaventeen thousand eight hundred pounds of tobacco and cask to the Honble NICHOLAS

SPENCER Esqr. himself the other to Mr. JOHN SEABRIGHT for two thousand pounds of tobacco and cask assigned to the Honble NICHOLAS SPENCER Esqr. and there is due from the said SHAPLEIGH to the said NICHOLAS SPENCER Esqr. nineteen thousand eight hundred pounds of tobacco and cask; Judgment is granted the said NICHOLAS SPENCER Esqr. against the said Mr. PHILIP SHAPLEIGH for the said sume with costs als Execution unless the next Court the said SHAPLEIGH shews reasons to the contrary

- <u>HARCUM agt the Sheriffe</u> Whereas CHARLES PAUL was arrested to this Court at the suit of Mr. WILLIAM HARCUM for fowre hundred pounds of tobacco and cask and appeared not, Order is granted the said HARCUM against the Sheriffe according to Law

- <u>Attachment</u> An Attachment is awarded the Sheriffe against the Estate of CHARLES PAUL for fowre hundred pounds of tobacco and cask returnable to the next Court

- <u>HARCUM agt the Sheriffe</u> Whereas CLEMENT LATIMORE was arrested to this Court at the suit of Mr. WILLIAM HARCUM for one thousand seaven pounds of tobacco and cask and appeared not, Judgment is granted the said HARCUM against the Sheriffe according to Law

- <u>Attachment</u> An Attachment is granted the Sheriffe for one thousand seaven hundred pounds of tobacco and caske retirnable to the next Court

- <u>HICKMAN agt DRAKE</u> Whereas EDWARD WATTS was arrested to this Court at the suit of THOMAS HICKMAN for nine hundred ninety fowre pounds of tobacco and cask and appeared not, Judgment is granted the said HICKMAN against PHILIP DRAKE, Security of the appearance of the said WATTS, for the said sum according to Law

- <u>Attachment</u> An Attachment is granted PHILIP DRAKE against the Estate of EDWARD WATTS returnable to the next Court for nine hundred ninety fowre pounds of tobacco and cask als Execution

p. 262 <u>Northumberland County Court 19th of March 1684/5</u>

- <u>Capt. JONES agt the Sheriffe</u> Whereas PATTRICK POLLICK was arrested to this Court at the suit of Capt. THOMAS JONES for eight hundred ninety pounds of tobacco and cask and appeared not, Judgment is granted the said JONES against the Sheriffe according to Law

- <u>Attachment</u> An Attachment is awarded the Sheriffe agaisnt the Estate of PATTRICK POLLICK for eight hundred ninety pounds of tobacco and cask returnable to the next Court

- <u>ROGERS agt NUTWELL</u> Judgment is granted Mr. WILLIAM ROGERS agaisnt ARTHUR NUTWELL for three hundred ninety seaven pounds of tobacco [being due for Levys and Quit Rents] with costs als Execution unless next Court he shews reason to the contrary

- <u>NUTWELL agt HARCUM</u> Judgment is granted ARTHUR NUTWELL agaisnt Mr. WILLIAM HARCUM for two hundred ten pounds of tobacco and cask with costs als Execution

- <u>HARRIS agt the Sheriffe</u> Whereas JOHN PALMER was arrested to this Court at the suit of Mr. JOHN HARRIS for five hundred twenty nine pounds of tobacco and cask and appeared not, Judgment is granted the said HARRIS against the Sheriffe according to Law

- Attachment An Attachment is awarded the Sheriffe against the Estate of JOHN PALMER for five hundred twenty nine pounds of tobacco and cask returnable to the next Court

- HAYNIE agt the Sheriffe Whereas WILLIAM ALLINSON was arrested to this Court at the suit of Mr. RICHARD HAYNIE for five hundred pounds of tobacco and cask and appeared not, Judgment is granted the said HAYNIE against the Sheriffe according to Law

- HARRIS agt BLACKERBY JAMES BLACKERBY confesseth Judgment for the present payment of two hundred pounds of tobacco and cask unto Mr. CHARLES HARRIS with costs als Execution

- Sheriffe agt ALLINSON An Attachment is granted the Sheriffe for five hundred pounds of tobacco and cask against the Estate of WILLIAM ALLINSON returnable to the next Court

p. 263 Northumberland County Court 19th of March 1684/5

- NUTWELL agt the Sheriffe Whereas Mr. CHARLES KER was arrested to this Court at the suit of ARTHUR NUTWELL for six hundred pounds of tobacco and cask and appeared not, Judgment is granted the said NUTWELL against the Sheriffe according to Law

- Attachment An Attachment is awarded the heriffe against the Estate of Mr. CHARLES KER for six hundred pounds of tobacco and cask returnable to the next Court

- FLOWERS agt KNIGHT Judgment is granted WILLIAM FLOWERS against Mr. PETER KNIGHT for three hundred pounds of tobacco and cask unlesse the next Court the said KNIGHT shews reason to the contrary

- SPENCER agt BRERETON Whereas the Honble NICHOLAS SPENCER Esqr. the Assignee of Capt. WILLIAM ARMAGER did arrest Mr. THOMAS BRERETON, the Executor of Collo. THOMAS BRERETON, for five thousand ounds of tobacco and cask due by Bill under the hand of the said Collo. BRERETON. Mr. THOMAS BRERETON pleaded that the greatest part of the debt was satisfyed and did produce an Account under the hand of Mr. WILLIAM FOX wherein it did appeare that two thousand seaven hundred thirty eight pounds of tobcco was paid; Judgment is granted the said NICHOLAS SPENCER, Esqr., the Assignee of Capt. AR,MAGER, against Mr. THOMAS BRERETON, the Executor of Collo. THOMAS BRERETON, for two thousand two hundred sixty two pounds of tobacco and cask, being what residue of the said debt with costs als Execution

- LUKE agt SMYTH Lt. Collo. SAMUEL SMYTH confesseth Judgment for the payment of five hundred pounds of sweet scented tobacco and cask and five hundred and fifty pounds of oronoque tobacco and cask unto Mr. EDMUND LUKE with costs als Execution

- COLES agt THOMAS Whereas an Attachment was awarded JOHN COLES against the Estate of ZACHARIAH THOMAS for fowre hundred sixty foot of planck which Attachment is returned executed on some planck in the hands of JOHN COCKERELL the said COLES haveing made his debt appear due, the planck being deducted seized by the Sheriffe for the said THOMAS's Levy, Judgment is granted the said COLES for the said planck attached as aforesaid with costs als Execution

Northumberland County Court 19th of March 1684/5

p. 264

- HARRIS agt PAUL Whereas an Attachment was awarded Mr. CHARLES HARRIS against the Estate of CHARLES PAUL for two hundred and twenty pounds of tobacco and cask which is returned executed on a beast running at the Plantation where CHARLES PAUL did live, the said HARRIS haveing by his Oath made his said debt appeare due; Judgment is granted the said HARRIS against the Estate of the said PAUL attached as aforesaid with his costs according to Law

- SMYTH agt PAUL Whereas an Attachment was awarded RICHARD SMYTH against the Estate of CHARLES PAUL which is returned executed on some Cattle running at the Plantation where the said PAUL did live, the said SMYTH haveing made his Debt appeare due by two Bills under the hand of the said PAUL; Judgment is gratned the said SMYTH against the Estate of the said Paul attached as aforesaid with costs according to Law

- LANCASTER agt PAUL An Attachment is awarded NICHOLAS LANCASTER against the Estate of CHARLES PAUL for three thousand pounds of tobacco and cask returnable to the next Court

- FARNEFOLD agt MATHEWES An Attachment is granted Mr. JOHN FARNEFOLD against the Estate of Mr. THOMAS MATHEWES for one thousand eleven pounds of tobacco and cask returnable to the next Court

- HAYNIE agt NICHOLS JOHN NICHOLS confesseth Judgment for the present payment of fowre hundred pounds of tobacco and cask unto Capt. JOHN HAYNIE with costs als Execution

- Grand Jury summoned Ordered that the Sheriffe summon in the Grand Jury to give in their Presentments and impannell another Jury to serve the next yeare

- HAYNIE agt HUDNALL Whereas ALICE HUDNALL, Executrix of EZEKIEL GENESIS, was summoned by this Court by scire facias to shew her reasons why Execution should not issue on a Judgment obteyned against EZEKIEL GENESIS by Capt. JOHN HAYNIE March the 15th 1681 for fowre hundred pounds of tobacco and cask with costs. It is ordered that the former Order be confirmed and ordered that the said ALICE HUDNALL pay the said debt unto the said Capt. HAYNIE out of the said GENESIS's Estate

Northumberland County Court 19th of March 1684/5

p. 265

- THOMAS ELLIOTT against Mr. MOTTROM WRIGHT referred to the next Court

- CONOWAY bound to his good behaviour Whereas his Excellency the Governor and the Honble Councill of State did ye last Generall Court order that this Court should take good security of Mr. EDWIN CONOWAY for his good behaviour and that he should make his personall appearance before his Excellency and Councill the 4th day of the next Generall Court, in obedience to which this Court doe order that the Sheriffe take the said CONOWAY into safe custody untill he hath given Bond with security for his performance of that Order

- FLOWERS agt HARTLAND An Attachment is awarded Mr. WILLIAM FLOWERS against the Estate of WILLIAM HARTLAND for six hundred and twelve pounds of tobacco and cask returnable to the next Court

- Lt. Collo. SAMUEL SMYTH against CHRISTOPHER GARLINGTON this

NORTHUMBERLAND COUNTY ORDER BOOK, 1678-1698

Cause in continued
- PETER BYRAM against JAMES JOHNSON This Cause is continued
- OLDIS's Estate to be Inventoryed Whereas ROBERT OLDIS was committed to the Goale for felony hath broke Prison and has made his escape, it is ordered that the Sheriffe and some of the Freeholders of the Neighbourhood take an Inventory of the Estate of ROBERT OLDIS and take care that the same be secured untill further Order
- Capt. HAYNIE to mend the Prison Whereas by Act of Assembly all County Courts are to see that all their Prisons be made sufficient and that the Rules shall be layd out and bounded. It is ordered that Capt. JOHN HAYNIE view the Prison and and get what is amisse amended and lay out and bound the Rules of the Prison between this and the next Court and that he be also allowed for his charges and trouble out of the next County Levy
- Ordered that the next Court be on the 3d Wednesday in May

p. 266 Northumberland County Court 19th of March 1684/5
- WISE agt LUKE Whereas it appeares to thsi Court that Mr. EDMUND LUKE stamdeth indebted unto SARAH WISE eight hundred fifty pounds of tobacco and cask; Judgment is granted the said WISE against the said LUKE for the said sume with costs als Execution unlesse the said LUKE gives the said WISE security for the payment of the said Debt in 8ber next

- At a Court held for Northumberland County the 20th of May 1685 Annoque Regni Regis Caroli secundi 2d, 37th &c.
                    Present
Lt. Coll. SAMUELL SMYTH   Capt. JOHN HAYNIE
Mr. PETER PRESLEY, SENR.   Mr. RICHARD KENNER
Capt. LEONARD HOWSON   Mr. THOMAS BRERETON Justices
Mr. THOMAS HOBSON   Mr. PETER PRESLEY, JUNR.
Mr. NICHOLAS OWEN   Mr. RICHARD ROGERS

- Mr. WM: LEE High Sheriffe This day in obedience to a Commission from his Excellency the Governor, Mr. WILLIAM LEE was sworne High Sheriffe of this County and Mr. JOHN TURBERVILLE Sub Sheriffe
- Bond Mr. WILLIAM LEE and Capt. LEONARD HOWSON doe oblige themselves joyntly and severally to this Worshipfull Court in the penall sume of one hundred thousand pounds of tobacco and casque that the said Mr. LEE shall well and truly collect such dues as shall be given him to discharge and duely officiate his said place according to Law
- Severall Servants bound CHARLES HOWLAND, Servant to Mr. ROBERT SECH, ia adjudged to be ten yeares of age;
ELLINOR MORELAY, Servant to JOHN CORBELL, is adjudged to be thirteen yeares of age; and ordred they serve their respective Masters according to Act
- KEEN's Will proved Upon the Petition of MRS. ELIZABETH KEENE a Probate is granted her of the Last Will and Testament of her deceased Husband, Mr. WILLIAM KEENE, the Will being proved by the Oaths of Mr. NICHOLAS OWEN, RICHARD ROGERS and Mr. JOHN CRALLE witnesses to the said Will

p. 267   Northumberland County Court 20th of May 1685

- **BRYERLY's Will proved** Upon the Petition of FRANCES, the Executrix of ROBERT BRYERLY, a Probate is granted of the Last Will and Testament of her deceased Husband the Will being proved by the Oaths of HENRY BROWNE and JOHN LAWRENCE witnesses to the said Will

- **HILL's Will proved** Upon the Petition of ANNE HILL, a Probate is granted of the Last Will and Testament of her deceased Husband, WILLIAM HILL, the Will being proved by the Oathes of RICHARD PEMBERTON, GEORGE HUTTON and JAMES MOOR witnesses to the said Will

- **QUIGG's Will proved** Upon the Petition of JOHN SMYTH a Probate is granted of the Last Will and Testament of RICHARD QUIGG deceased the Will being proved by the Oathes of Mr. WILLIAM TIGNOR, Mr. AZARCAM PARKER and [   ] witnesses to the said Will

- **NELMES Levy free** Whereas JOHN NELMES hath made his Complaint to this Court that he hath been for some time grieviously troubled and afflicted with lameness insomuch that he is incapable of helping himselfe, it is ordered that dureing the time of his lameness he be Levy free

- **Constables appoynted** It is ordered that MICHAEL VANLANDEGHAM e Constable for CHICACONE,
    JOHN LEWIS for CHERRY POYNT,
    PETER CONSTANT for MATTAPONY;
    JOSEPH PALMER for the Upper Precincts of GREAT WICOCOMICO Parish and RICHARD [L   ] for the Lower Precincts;
    GEORGE HAMBLETON appoynted for the Upper Precincts of Fayrfield Parish; HENRY RIDER for NEWMAN's NECK and HULL's CREEKE and
    Mr. CUTHBERT SPAN for the Lower parts of Fayrfield Parish and ordered that they be all sworne by the next Justice

- **Servant Indian HULL's Servant how old** Sarah, an Indian Servant to RICHARD HULL is adjudged to be twelve yeares of age

- **JAMES HADWELL freed from the Levy** It is ordered that JAMES HADWELL a poor impotent person be freed from paying Levy

- **MARGARET CRANE to serve for a bastard** Whereas MARGARET CRANE, Servant to Mr. THOMAS WILLIAMS, hath had a bastard Child, and her said Master haveing in Court engaged to pay the Fine imposed by Law, it is ordered that she be acquitted from her punishment serving her Master a halfe a yeare

p. 268   Northumberland County Court 20th of May 1685

- **GRIFFIN agt WEEKES** Whereas it appeares to this Court by a Bill under the hand of HENRY WEEKES bearing date the 6th day of March 1683/4 that the said WEEKES standeth indebted to Collo. SAMUELL GRIFFIN the sume of four hundred and forty four pounds of tobacco and cask, Judgment is granted the said Collo. GRIFFIN against the said WEEKES for the said sum with costs als Execution

- **JNO: FLOWERS's Comm. of Admon** A Commission of Administration is granted JOHN FLOWERS of the Estate of his deceased Father, WILLIAM FLOWERS, he giveing caution for his due administration according to Law

- **BOND** JOHN FLOWERS, Mr. JOHN HARRIS and Mr. EBENEZER SAN-

NORTHUMBERLAND COUNTY ORDER BOOK, 1678-1698   -61-

DERS doe oblige themselves joyntly and severally in the penall sume of thirty thousand pounds of tobacco and casque to the Justices of this County, that JOHN FLOWERS shall duely administer upon his deceased Father's Estate and exhibite an Inventory thereof according to Law

- NEALE and AUSTEN fined. Whereas Mr. DANIEL NEALE and Mr. JAMES AUSTEN, two of the Grand Jurymen for this Court were summoned to this Court by the Sheriffe to bring in their Presentments and hath fayled of their appearance, it is ordered that they be fined each of them two hundred pounds of tobacco and casque

- JONES, WINTER and HARRIS fined. It is ordered that Mr. WILLIAM JONES, Mr. THOMAS WINTER and Mr. JOHN HARRIS [who were summoned to this Court upon a Grand Jury and hath fayled of their appearance be fined three hundred pounds of tobacco amd casqie

- Lt. Collo. SAMUEL SMYTH against CHRISTOPHER GARLINGTON, referred to the next Court

- The Court adjourneth untill tomorrow morning eight of the Clock

- Die 21st May 1685   Present
Lt. Collo. SAMUELL SMYTH   Capt. JOHN HAYNIE
Mr. THOMAS HOBSON, SENR.   Mr. PETER PRESLEY, JUNR.
Mr. NICHOLAS OWEN   Mr. RICHARD ROGERS   Justices

- JNO: RICE v TEAGE ALLEN. The difference depending between Mr. JOHN RICE, Plaintiffe, and TEAGE ALLEN, Defendant, is referred to a Jury whose names are underwritten, vizt

p.   Northumberland County Court 21st of May 1685
269 Mr. JAMES AUSTEN   PETER BYRAM   JAMES JOHNSON
     JOHN GRAHAM   CLEMENT LATIMORE   STEPHEN [   ]
     JOSIAS LONG   ABRAHAM JOYCE   JOHN ROACH
     RICHARD FLYNT   PATRICK POLLICK   RICHARD RICE

Verdict. Wee being impannelled on a Jury to end the difference now depending between Mr. JOHN RICE, Plaintiffe, and TEAGE ALLEN, Defendant, on serious discussing the matter doe in full ballance of all Accounts between them to us now brought award five hundred eighty pounds of tobacco to the Plaintiffe

- Judgment. Judgment is granted Mr. JOHN RICE against TEAGE ALLEN according to the Verdict with costs als Execution

- WEBB agt NEWHAM. Whereas an Attachment was awarded Mr. THOMAS WEBB against WILLIAM NEWHAM's Estate for two hundred sixty five pounds of tobacco and casque, which Attachment is returned executed on soe much in the hands of Mr. THOMAS HOBSON, and whereas the said THOMAS WEBB hath upon Oath made his debt appeare due, Judgment is granted the said WEBB against the said HOBSON for the said sume with costs als Execution

- NEALE's Negro Levy free. Whereas Mr. CHRISTOPHER NEALE complains that he had a Negroe woman that [by reason of many yeares that afflicted her] is incapable of doeing worke; it is ordered that she be freed from the Levy

- HARRIS agt KNIGHT. Whereas last Court CHARLES HARRIS obteyned Judgment against Capt. PETER KNIGHT for four hundred fifty pounds of tobacco and casque unlesse the said KNIGHT should appear at this Court and shew reason to the contrary, and whereas the said KNIGHT hath failed of his appearance, it is ordered that that Order be confirmed with costs als Execution

- SPENCER agt SHAPLEIGH Whereas the last Court, the Honble NICHOLAS SPENCER, Esqr. obteyned Order against Mr. PHILIP SHAPLEIGH for nineteen thousand eight hundred pounds of tobacco and casque unlesse the said SHAPLEIGH should appear at this Court and shew reasons to the contrary, and the said SHAPLEIGH hath now fayled, it is ordered that that Order be confirmed with costs als Execution

p. 270 Northumberland County Court 21st of May 1685

- ROGERS agt NUTWELL Whereas Mr. WILLIAM ROGERS obteyned Judgment against ARTHUR NUTWELL last Court for three hundred ninety seaven pounds of tobacco and casque unlesse he appeared this Court and shewed reasons to the contrary, and whereas he hath now appeared but cannot make appeare any part of the debt is satisfyed; it is ordered that the said Order be confirmed with costs als Execution

- ELLIOTT agt MOTT: WRIGHT The difference depending between THOMAS ELLIOTT and Mr. MOTTROM WRIGHT is continued to the next Court and ordered that the said Mr. WRIGHT have notice to appear the said Court and that he may thereupon his Oath object what he can against the said ELLIOTT's Account [the said WRIGHT being the Defendant] otherwise that the said ELLIOTT have liberty to make Oath to his Account given in against the said WRIGHT

- [?DEBRIE agt ALLEN TEAGE ALLEN confesseth Judgment to JAMES DEBRIE for the payment of twelve hundred pounds of tobacco and casque with costs of suit als Execution

- GRAHAM agt STRINGER Whereas an Attachment was awarded Mr. JOHN GRAHAM against the Estate of EDMUND STRINGER for two hundred eighty pounds of tobacco and casque which Attachment is returned executed on a barrell of Indian Corne and a gunn in the hands of WILLIAM DRAPER who owned he had the same in his custody and whereas the said GRAHAM hath upon Oath made his said debt appeare due, Judgment is granted the said GRAHAM for the goods soe attached with costs of suit als Execution

- BARNES agt JOYCE 9ber 20th 1685. Execution issued on this Order against body of ABR: JOYCE Whereas last Court THOMAS BARNES obteyned Judgment according to Law against ABRAHAM JOYCE for concealing two Tythables unlesse the said JOYCE should this Court shew reasons to the contrary, and whereas the said JOYCE hath now appeared and answered that he did conceale them It is ordered that the former Order be confirmed with costs als Execution

- DONALDSON agt MOTTROM Whereas it appeares to this Court that the Estate of Major JOHN MOTTROM standeth indebted unto JOHN DONALDSON for taylor work by an Account [the which the said DONALDSON and WALTER GRADEY hath made Oath was contracted within a yeare of the Major's decease and that the said DONALDSON had received noe satisfaction of the said Account] the sume of seaventeen hundred ninety four pounds of tobacco and casque; Judgment is granted the said DONALDSON against the Estate of the said MOTTROM with costs als Execution

Northumberland County Court 21st of May 1685

p. 271

- **PRESLEY agt MOTTROM** Whereas Mr. PETER PRESLEY, JUNR. Heire to Mr. WILLIAM PRESLEY, deceased, brought his action into this Court against Mr. WILLIAM FARMER Feofee in Trust for the Estate of Major JOHN MOTTROM, deceased, for fifteen hundred and four pounds of tobacco and casque, due unto his said Father in part of what levyed for him in the year 1677, for Burgesses charges by an Order of this Court then held and did produce an Account drawne up by the said Major MOTTROM in his life time under his owne hand wherein it did appeare that the said sume was due from the said MOTTROM unto the said PRESLEY on ballance of the sume of nineteen thousand and ten pounds of tobacco ordered as aforesaid and also by the Oath of Mr. RICHARD FLYNT who did sweare that he did arrest Major MOTTROM at the suit of Mr. WILLIAM PRESLEY for the sume aforesaid who did owne that the said debt was justly due but thought that Capt. COOPER would have payd it; Judgment is granted the said PRESLEY against the Estate of the said MOTTROM for the said sume als Execution

- **Appeale** Capt THOMAS JONES, Attourney of Mr. WILLIAM FARMER, Feofee in Trust for the said Estate appealeth from this Order to a hearing before his Excellency the Governor and Councill the second day of the next Generall Court which is granted he giveing caution to prosecute his said appeale

- **Bond** Capt THOMAS JONES and THOMAS HOBSON, SENR. doe oblige themselves joyntly and severally in the penall sume of three thousand pounds of tobacco and casque that the said JONES shall prosecute the said appeale

- Capt. JOHN HAYNIE Security for the Appellee

- **SPENCER agt PRESLEY** Whereas it appeares to this Court by a Bill under the hand and seale of Mr. WILLIAM PRESLEY dated the 23d of December 1682 that the said WILLIAM PRESLEY stood indebted in his lifetime to the Honble NICHOLAS SPENCER, Esqr., the Assignee of Capt. WILLIAM ARMAGER the sume of three thousand eight hundred pounds of tobacco and casque, Judgment is granted the said SPENCER, Assignee as aforesaid, against the said PRESLEY for the said sume with costs als Execution

Northumberland County Court 21st of May 1685

p. 272

- **Mr. PETER PRESLEY, JUNR. against Mr. CHRISTOPHER NEALE Security of Mr. WILLIAM ROGERS** referred to the next Court at the motion of the Defendant

- **PETER BYRAM against JEFFERY JOHNSON** referred to the next Court at the motion of the Defendant

- **CRAVEN agt BENTLEY** Whereas it appeares to this Court that HENRY BENTLEY standeth indebted unto JOHN CRAVEN on full ballance from all Accounts the sume of three hundred and eighteen pounds of tobacco; Judgment is granted the said CRAVEN against the said BENTLEY for the said sume with costs als Execution

- **AUSTEN's Fine remitted** Whereas yesterday Mr. JAMES AUSTEN who was one of the Grand Jury the last yeare, was fined for his non appearance he being summoned by the Sheriffe to give in his Presentments, and whereas he hath now made appeare that he was sick which occasioned his absence it is ordered that he be acquitted from his Fine

- **SAMPSON and SWEATMER agt** Whereas WILLIAM SAMPSON and MATHEW SWEATMER hath each of them attended at Court two dayes to give in their Evidences in the behalf of JAMES [?] against WILLIAM BONAWAY, it is ordered that they be allowed according to Act

- **Tythables to whom brought** Mr. NICHOLAS OWEN and Mr. RICHARD KENNER are appoynted by the Court for to take the Lyst of Tythables in Bowtracy Parish,

Mr. PETER PRESLEY, SENR., Mr. THOMAS HOBSON SENR. and Capt. JOHN HAYNIES for Fayrfeild Parish

Capt. LEONARD HOWSON and Mr. CHARLES LEE for Wicocomico Parish; And ordered that each Tythable person in this County be given in by the Masters of the family where they reside on the 10th day of June

- The next Court the 3d Wednesday in July

p. 273 — **At a Court held for Northumberland County the 15th day of July Annoq Domini 1685** :Present

Lt. Collo. SAMUELL SMYTH	Capt. JOHN HAYNIE	
Mr. PETER PRESLEY, SENR.	Mr. RICHARD KENNE	Justives
Capt. LEONARD HOWSON	Mr. THOMAS BRERETON	
Mr. CHARLES LEE	Mr. PETER PRESLEY, JUNR.	
Mr. NICHOLAS OWEN		

- **THO: TOWERS's Will proved** Upon the Petition of DOROTHY, the Executrix of THOMAS TOWERS, late of this County deceased, a Probate is granted her of the Last Will and Testament of her Husband the Will being proved by the Oathes of EDWARD WILLIAMS, WILLIAM DAWSON, Mr. CHRISTOPHER NEALE and RICHARD PEMBERTON, witnesses to the said Will

- **RICHD: JONES's Will proved** Upon the Petition of JOHN WALTERS, Executor of RICHARD JONES, late of this County deceased, a Probate is granted the said WALTERS of the Last Will and Testament of the said JONES the Will being proved by the Oathes of JEFFERY ADDAMSON and PETER WALTERS, witnesses to the said Will

- **Appraysers appoynted** Upon the Petition of JOHN WALTERS, Executor of RICHARD JONES, it is ordered that JOHN OLDAM, HENRY DAWSON, CLOUD TULLOS and PETER FLYNT or any three of them sometime between this and the next Court meet at the House of RICHARD JONES, deceased, and make appraysment of the Decedent's Estate and exhibite an Inventory thereof to the next Court, they being first sworne by the next Justice

- **HARRIS Attourney of NEALE & TRESSRY** Mr. CHARLES HARRIS Attorney of Mr. CHRISTOPHER NEALE and Mr. JAMES TRESSRY

p. 274 Northumberland County Court 15th of July 1685

- **SMYTH agt GARLINGTON** The difference depending between Lt. Collo. SAMUELL SMYTH and Mr. CHRISTOPHER GARLINGTON is referred to a Jury whose names are underwritten, vizt.

ROBERT SECH	PATRICK POLLICK	PETER MAXWELL
THOMAS WADDY	WILLIAM DAWSON	RICHARD LATTEMORE
JAMES JOHNSON	JOSIAS LONG	JOHN FLOWERS

NORTHUMBERLAND COUNTY ORDER BOOK, 1678-1698 -65-

GEORGE DAMERON   CLEMENT LATTEMORE   ABRAHAM SHEARES

Verdict Wee whose names are here underwritten to the best of our Judgment examined and considered the matter and doe find that Mr. CHRISTOPHER GARLINGTON is indebted to Lt. Collo. SAMUELL SMYTH two monthes service ROBERT SECH &c.

- Judgment Upon this Verdict it is ordered that Mr. CHRISTOPHER GARLINGTON forthwith pay the said service unto ye said SMYTH and costs of suit als Execution

- STEWARD agt MATHEW Whereas ELIZABETH STEWARD complained to this Court that whereas one SYMON CROUCH sold her to Capt. THOMAS MATHEW for the terme of four yeares which was passed in December and she still deteyned in the said Capt. MATHEW's House as a Servant and prayes satisfaction for the time she hath been deteyned there since the expiration of her terme and whereas the said STEWARD hath produced the said CROUCH his Deposition who advised that he sold her, ye said STEWARD, unto the said Capt. MATHEW for ye said terme of four yeares and noe longer and that the said terme was expired ye last Christmas. It is ordered that she be free and that the said Capt. MATHEW pay her two hundred fifty pounds of tobacco and casque for what time she hath been there since the expiration of her time with Corne and Cloathes accustomed and cost of suit als Execution

- Appeale Mr. JOHN CRALLE, Attourney of MRS REBECCA the Attourney of Capt. THOMAS MATHEW appealeth from the said Order to a hearing before his Excellency and Councill the 6th day of the next Generall Court which is granted he giveing caution to prosecute his appeale

p. 275   Northumberland County Court 15th of July 1685

- Mr. JOHN CRALLE and Mr. CHRISTOPHER NEALE oblige themselves joyntly and severally in the penall sum of three thousand pounds of tobacco and casque that the said JOHN CRALLE shall duely prosecute his said appeale

- Bond. ABRAHAM JOYCE and ROBERT LYNSAY security for the Appellee
- Present   Mr. RICHARD ROGERS

- Mr. CHRISTOPHER NEALE against the Attourney of Mr. PHILIP SHAPLEIGH referred to the next Court at the motion of the Defendant

- [? NESTOR] RHODES a poor Child being three yeares of age in October next and given by his Mother unto JOHN FREEMAN, it is ordered that he serve the said FREEMAN untill he is one and twenty yeares old he paying the Child at the expira-tion of the said time his Corne and Cloathes

- RICE agt BRADLEY Whereas Mr. RICHARD RICE the Attourney of EDWARD WILLIAMS, Heire unto TEMPERANCE BRADSHAW, deceased, brought action into this Court against ROBERT BRADLEY who marryed ANNE the Daughter and Heire of ROBERT BRADSHAW, deceased, and prayed Judgment against the said BRADLEY for three hundred forty five acres of land produceing to the Court an Obligation under the hand of the said ROBERT BRADSHAW dated the 22d of October 1655 wherein the said ROBERT BRADSHAW did oblige himselfe to deliver unto TEMPERANCE BRADSHAW a Pattent for the said quantitie of three hundred forty five acres as by the Obligation relation thereunto being had doth more fully appeare, Judgment is granted the said RICE, Attourney of the said EDWARD

WILLIAMS, Heire to the said TEMPERANCE BRADSHAW, for the quantitie of three hundred forty five acres of land against the said ROBERT BRADLEY who marryed ANNE the Heire as abovesaid with costs als Execution

p. 276 Northumberland County Court 15th of July 1685

Mr. PETER PRESLEY, SENR. Mr. THOMAS HOBSON, SENR. Mr. RICHARD KENNER, Mr. PETER PRESLEY JUNR. and Mr. RICHARD ROGERS doe discent from thhis Order

- Appeale_ ROBERT BRADLEY who marryed ANNE the Daughter of ROBERT BRADSHAW, appealeth from this Order to a hearing before his Excellency and Councill the sixth day of the next Generall Court which is granted he giveing caution to prosecute his Appeale

- Bond_ ROBERT BRADLEY and PETER FLYNT doe oblige themselves joyntly and severally in the penall sume of thirty thousand pounds of tobacco and casque, that the said ROBERT shall duely prosecute his said Appeale

Mr. JOHN HUGHLETT, SENR. Security for the Appellee

- LEE agt JENKINS_ The difference depending betwixt Mr. CHARLES LEE, Plaintiffe, and WALTER JENKINS, Defendant referred to a Jury whose names are underwirtten, vizt.

Mr. ROBERT SECH	PATRICK POLLICK	PETER MAXWELL
THOMAS WADDY	WILLIAM DAWSON	RICHARD LATTEMORE
JAMES JOHNSON	JOSIAS LONG	JOHN FLOWERS
GEORGE DAMERON	CLEMENT LATTEMORE	ABRAHAM SHEARES

- Verdict_ The Verdict of the Jury that wee cannot find noe matter of fact for want of Evidence signed by the Foreman, ROBERT SECH., Upon this Verdict, it is ordered the suit be dismist

- BASHAW agt CANTWELL_ Whereas an Attachment was awarded WILLIAM BASHAW against the Estate of HENRY CANTWELL for nine hundred pounds of tobacco and casque which Attachment is returned executed on a loom and harnesse and a small Chest in the hands of the said BASHAW; and whereas the said BASHAW hath upon Oath made his said debt appeare due, it is ordered that the said goods be legally appraysed and if they exceed the amount of the debt ye said BASHAW be possessed with as much as will satisfie it with costs, if not that then the said BASHAW be possessed with the said goods and that the Attachment stand good against the said CANTWELL's Estate

p. 277 Northumberland County Court 15th of July 1685

- PRESLEY agt NEALE_ Whereas Mr. PETER PRESLEY, JUNR. Heire of Mr. WILLIAM PRESLEY, late of this County deceased, brought his action to this Court against Mr. CHRISTOPHER NEALE, Security of Mr. WILLIAM ROGERS for three thousand nine hundred fifty nine pounds of tobacco and casque, it being part of a greater sume due to and levyed for the said WILLIAM PRESLEY in January 1682/3, for Burgesses charges; Judgment is granted the said PRESLEY against the said NEALE the Securitie as abovesaid for the said sume with costs als Execution unlesse the said NEALE appeares at the next Court to shew reason to the contrary

- Mr. DENNIS CARTEE Attourney of Mr. THOMAS GLASCOCK

NORTHUMBERLAND COUNTY ORDER BOOK, 1678-1698   -67-

- GLASCOCK agt WHITE THOMAS WHITE confesseth Judgment unto Mr. THOMAS GLASCOCK, the Executor of Mr. ROGER WALTERS, deced., for the payment of four hundred pounds of tobacco and casque with costs als Execution

- BETTS's Estate to be devided Whereas WILLIAM BETTS by his Petition to this Court complaineth that his Father by his Last Will and Testament did give unto the said BETTS and hhis Brother, CHARLES BETTS, an Estate between them and that his said Brother had repaired the said Estate without giveing him any Account thereof and prayed that some Neighbours might be appoynted to devide the said Estate between them according to his said Father's Wil and judge of the damages [without his order] of the said Estate. It is ordered that THOMAS WEBB, CUTH-BERT SPAN, JOHN COLES and JOHN WORSHAM or any three of them sometime between this and the next Court devide the said Estate according to the Will of their said deceased Father and inquire into damages done to the Estate by the said CHARLES and give in their report to the next Court

- TOWERS for a Comm.of Admon. Upon the Petition of DOROTHY TOWERS a Commission of Administration is granted her of the Last Will and Testament of her deceased Husband, THOMAS TOWERS, she giveing caution according to Law

p. 278 Northumberland County Court 15th of July 1685

- Bond WILLIAM TAYLOR and JOHN WARD doe oblige themselves joyntly and severally with the said DOROTHY TOWERS in the penall sume of thirty thousand pounds of tobacco and casque that the said DOROTHY shall duely administer upon the said Estate and exhibite an Inventory thereof according to Law

- Appraysers appoynted It is ordered that JOHN OLDAM, HUGH STATHEM, JOHN WEBB and WILLIAM BASHAW or any three of them make an appraysment of the Estate of THOMAS TOWERS, deceased, some time between this and the next Court, they being sworne by the next Justice

- BENNETT agt CURTIS, HIGH and SHELTON Whereas Capt. ROBERT BENNETT complained to this Court that EDWARD MAXFIELD, late of this County deceased, in his life time stood indebted to him the sume of four hundred and fifty three pounds of tobacco and casque, and since his death Mr. JOHN CURTIS, THOMAS HIGH and ROBERT SHELTON have possessed themselves [without any legall course] of the Decedent's Estate whereby he is left remedilesse. The Court are of opinion that they are Executors in their owne wrong and therefore the sid BENNETT may bring his action against all or any one of them

[I cannot read the next two line entry.]

- ELLIOTT agt WRIGHT Whereas THOMAS ELLIOTT brought his action to this Court against Mr. MOTTROM WRIGHT and complained that the said Mr. WRIGHT stood indebted to him in the sume of nine pounds sterling [I cannot read the remainder of this entry being the remainder of this page, nine lines]

p. 279 Northumberland County Court 15th of July 1685

- Appeale Mr. MOTTROM WRIGHT appealeth from this Order to a hearing before his Excellency and Councill the fifth day of the next Generall Court which is granted he giveing caution to prosecute his said Appeale

- Bond Mr. MOTTROM WRIGHT and Mr. WILLIAM YARRATT doe oblige themselves joyntly and severally in the penall sume of four thousand pounds of tobacco and casque that the said Mr. MOTTROM WRIGHT shall duely prosecute his said Appeale

    RICHARD SMYTH, Securitie for the Appellee, &c.
- The Court adjourneth till tomorrow morning eight of the clock

<u>Die 16th July 1685</u>   Present
Mr. PETER PRESLEY, SENR. Mr. RICHARD KENNER
Mr. CHARLES LEE   Mr. THOMAS BRERETON   Justices
Mr. NICHOLAS OWEN   Mr. RICHARD ROGERS

- <u>GILBERT HARROLD Constable</u> Whereas PETER CONSTANT was appointed and sworne Constable in the MATTAPONY Precincts, it is ordered that GILBERT HARROLD supply his place being sworne by the next Justice
- <u>HOBSON agt BENNETT</u> The difference depending between Mr. THOMAS HOBSON, SENR. [in the behalfe of his Majestie] Plaintiffe and Capt. ROBERT BENNETT, Defendant is continued
- <u>JONES agt POLLICK</u> Whereas it appears to this Court that PATTRICK POLLICK standeth indebted unto Capt. THOMAS JONES the just sume of eight hundred pounds of tobacco and casque; Judgment is granted the said JONES against the said POLLICK for the said sume with costs als Execution
- <u>WADDY fined</u> Whereas Mr. THOMAS WADDY was yesterday impannelled on a Jury to attend the Court and hath now fayled of his appearance; it is ordered that he be fined according to Law

p. 280   Northumberland County Court 16th of July 1685
- <u>HARTNELL agt CHAMPION</u> Mr. SAMUELL HARTNELL against JOHN CHAMPION referred to the next Court at the motion of the Defendant
- <u>EVANS agt the Sheriffe</u> Whereas WILLIAM PERCIFULL was arrested to this Court at the suit of JOHN EVANS for nine hundred pounds of tobacco and casque, which action was suspended untill this Court and whereas the said PERCIFULL hath now fayled of his appearance to answer the said suit, Judgment is granted the said EVANS against Mr. THOMAS HOBSON SENR. the High Sheriffe for the said sume with costs and damages according to Law
- <u>Sheriffe's Attachment</u> An Attachment is awarded Mr. THOMAS HOBSON, SENR. against the Estate of WILLIAM PERCIFULL for nine hundred pounds of tobacco and casque returnable to the next Court
- <u>HARCUM agt PAULE</u> Whereas an Attachment was awarded Mr. WILLIAM HARCUM against the Estate of CHARLES PAULE for three hundred seaventy pounds of tobacco and casque, which Attachment is returned executed on a Mare in the hands of NICHOLAS LANKESTER and whereas the said HARCUM hath upon Oath made his said debt appeare due, it is ordered that if the said Mare [being legally brought to appraysment] exceeds the value of the said Debt with costs the said HARCUM be either possessed with the said Mare paying the said LANKESTER the surplus or that the said LANKESTER pay the said HARCUM ye said sume of three hundred and seaventy pounds of tobacco and casque with costs of suit als Execution
- <u>BENNETT agt SALLOWES</u> Whereas it appeares to this Court by a Bill

NORTHUMBERLAND COUNTY ORDER BOOK, 1678-1698

under the hand and seale of STEPHEN SALLOWES dated the 20th of March 1684/5 that the said SALLOWES is indebted unto Capt. ROBERT BENNETT the sume of twelve hundred and twenty five pounds of tobacco and casque, Judgment is granted the said BENNETT against the said SALLOWES for the said sume with costs of suit als Execution

p. 281 Northumberland County Court 16th of July 1685

- REASON agt TIGNOR JOHN REASON against WILLIAM TIGNOR referred to the next Court at the motion of the Defendant

- LONG agt BONAWAY The difference depending between JOSIAS LONG, Plaintiffe, and WILLIAM BONAWAY Defendant was referred to a Jury whose names are underwritten, vizt

Mr. ROBERT SECH	ABRAHAM SHEARES	RICHARD LATEMORE
JAMES JOHNSON	PATRICK POLLICK	JAMES AUSTEN
CLEMENT LATEMORE	JOHN FLOWERS	THOMAS BARNES
GEORGE DAMERON	WILLIAM DAWSON	WILLIAM EVES

- Verdict Wee find for the Plaintiffe one hundred and eighty pounds of tobacco and casque. ROBERT SECH.

- Juggment It is ordered that the said BONAWAY pay the said sume of one hundred and eighty pounds of tobacco and casque with costs of suit als Execution

- BRYAM v GOLDMAN Whereas PETER BYRAM was arrested to this Court at the suit of ALICE, the Administratrix of THOMAS GOLDMAN and hath fayled in her appearance to prosecute, a non suit is granted the said BRYAM against the said GOLDMAN with costs and damages according to Law

- JONES agt LUKE Whereas att a Court held for this County the 13th of January 1682/3 JOHN JONES obteyned Judgment against Mr. EDMUND LUKE for three hundred forty pounds of tobacco and casque with costs, and whereas the said JONES hath summoned the said LUKE to this Court by scire facias to shew reasons why Execution should not issue upon the Order, upon a nihil dicit it is ordered that that Order be confirmed and that the said LUKE pay the said JONES the sume of four hundred pounds of tobacco and casque it being for debt and costs with costs of this suit als Execution

- NELMES agt NEWTON Whereas RICHARD NELMES was arrested to this Court at the suit of CHRISTOPHER NEWTON and noe cause of action appearing, a non suit is granted the said NELMES against the said NEWTON with costs and damages according to Law

p. 282 Northumberland County Court 16th of July 1685

- SMYTH agt NEWTON. Ordered that RICHARD SMYTH be allowed according to Act for his two dayes attendance at Court for to give in his Evidence in the behalfe of CHRISTOPHER NEWTON against RICHARD NELMES

- REYNOLDS agt HARCUM Whereas it appeares to this Court that Mr. WILLIAM HARCUM stands indebted unto HENRY REYNOLDS upon ballance of Accounts the sume of four hundred and sixty five pounds of tobacco and casque; Judgment is granted the said REYNOLDS against the said HARCUM for the said sume with costs als Execution

- REYNOLDS agt HARCUM Whereas HENRY REYNOLDS was arrested to this Court at the suit of WILLIAM HARCUM and noe cause of action appearing a non suit is granted the said HENRY REYNOLDS against the said WILLIAM HARCUM with costs and damages according to Law

- RICE agt LUKE Whereas it appeares to this Court by a Bill under the hand of Mr. EDMUND LUKE dated the 7th day of July 1688, that the said LUKE stood indebted unto ROBERT PRITT, late of this County, deceased, three hundred and ninety pounds of tobacco and casque, Judgment is granted Mr. RICHARD RICE, the Executor of the said ROBERT PRITT, against the said LUKE for the said sume with costs of suit als Execution unlesse he shews reasons to the contrary at the next Court

- EVANS agt JONES Whereas Mr. WILLIAM JONES was arrested to this Court at the suit of JOHN EVANS for one and twenty hundred pounds of tobacco and casque and the said JONES hath fayled of his appearance to answer the said suit, Judgment is granted the said EVANS against the Sheriffe for the said sume according to Law

- Sheriffe's Attachment An Attachment is awarded the Sheriffe against the Estate of Mr. WILLIAM JONES for two thousand one hundred pounds of tobacco and casque returnable to the next Court

p. 283 Northumberland County Court 16th of July 1685

- EVANS agt EDNEE Whereas JAMES EDNEE was arrested to this Court at the suit of JOHN EVANS for five hundred pounds of tobacco and casque and hath fayled of his appearance to answer the said suit, Judgment is granted the said EVANS against the Sheriffe for the said sume according to Law

- Sheriffe's Attachment An Attachment is awarded the Sheriffe against the Estate of JAMES EDNEE for five hundred pounds of tobacco and casque returnable to the next Court

- WRIGHT agt CURTIS Whereas Mr. JOHN CURTIS was arrested to this Court at the suit of Mr. MOTTROM WRIGHT for eighteen hundred pounds of tobacco and casque and hath fayled of his appearance to answer the said suit; Judgment is granted the said WRIGHT for the said sume against the Sheriffe with costs according to Law

- Sheriffe's Attachment An Attachment is awarded the Sheriff against the Estate of JOHN CURTIS for eighteen hundred pounds of tobacco and casque returnable to the next Court

- HARCUM agt the Sheriffe Whereas Mr. PETER PRESLEY, JUNR. was arrested to this Court at the suit of Mr. WILLIAM HARCUM for two thousand eight hundred pounds of tobacco and casque which Cause was suspended untill this Court and whereas the said Mr. PRESLEY hath now fayled of his appearance to answer the said suit, Judgment is granted the said WILLIAM HARCUM against Mr. THOMAS HOBSON, the Sheriffe, with costs als Execution

- Sheriffe'S Attachment An Attachment is awarded the Sheriffe against the Estate of Mr. PETER PRESLEY, JUNR, for the said sume of two thousand eight hundred pounds of tobacco and casque returnable to the next Court

- JENKINS agt TOPP Whereas WALTER JENKINS was arrested to this Court at the suit of THOMAS TOPP who hath fayled of his appeaance to prosecute his suit, a non suit is granted the said JENKINS against the TOPP with costs and damages according to Law p., 284

Northumberland County Court 16th of July 1685

- GERRARD agt HARROLD Whereas GILBERT HARROLD was arrested to this Court at the suit of ELIZABETH, the Administratrix of SAMUELL GERRARD, the Assignee of Mr. GEORGE JONES, for four hundred and fifty pounds of tobacco and casque and hath fayled of his appearance to answer the said suit, Judgment is granted the said ELIZABETH, Administratrix of the said SAMUELL, Assignee as aforesaid, against the Sheriffe for the said sume according to Law

- Sheriffe's Attachment. An Attachment is awarded the Sheriffe against the Estate of GILBERT HARROLD for four hundred and fifty pounds of tobacco and casque returnable to the next Court

- PEMBERTON agt DERMOTT Whereas RICHARD PEMBERTON complained to this Court that OWEN DERMOTT has entered upon Bond, burned a tobacco house damaged his corn field and prayed a Writ of habere facias directed to the Sheriff which was referred to a Jury whose names are underwritten vizt

ROBERT SECH	ABRAHAM SHEARES	RICHARD LATTIMORE
JAMES JOHNSON	PATRICK POLLICK	JAMES AUSTEN
CLEMENT LATTIMORE	JOHN FLOWERS	THOMAS BARNES
GEORGE DAMERON	WILLIAM DAWSON	WILLIAM EVES

- Verdict We find for the Plaintiff three thousand pounds of tobacco and casque
ROBERT SECH

- Judgment Jugment is granted the said PEMBERTON against the said DERMOTT for the sume of three thousand pounds of tobacco and casque with costs als Execution; and ordered that the Sheriff possess the said PEMBERTON with the damages intended on by the said DERMOTT

- GLASCOCK agt REYNOLDS Whreas it appeareth to this Court by a Bill under the hand and seale of HENRY REYNOLDS dated the 20th of February 1684/5 that the said REYNOLDS stands indebted to Mr. THOMAS GLASCOCK, Executor of Mr. ROGER WALTERS, the sume of two thousand pounds of tobacco and casque, Judgment is granted to the said GLASCOCK, Executor as abovesaid for the sume with costs against the said REYNOLDS with costs als Execution

- HARRIS agt HARTLAND Whereas it appeares to this Court that WILLIAM HARTLAND standeth indebted to CHARLES HARRIS the sume of two hundred ninety pounds of tobacco and casque, Judgment is granted the said HARRIS against the said HARTLAND for the said sume with costs als Execution

p. 285

Northumberland County Court 16th of July 1685

- SMYTH agt HARRIS It is ordered that RICHARD SMYTH be allowed according to Law for one dayes attendance att Court to give in his Evidence in the behalfe of WILLIAM HARTLAND against CHARLES HARRIS

- BRYAM agt JOHNSON Whereas PETER BYRAM complained to this Court that JEFFERY JOHNSON [being Brother to himselfe] was at his [the said JEFFERY's request] permitted to stay with his Wife and Children for some small time at his House who had not been long entered but by force of armes kept possession of the House threatning him, the said BYRAM] and family to their great sorrow and prayed that a Writt of habere facias might issue to the Sheriffe him commanding for to possesse the said BYRAM with the land and premises &c., This Cause is referred to a Jury whose names are underwritten vizt.

Mr. ROBERT SECH	ABRAHAM SHEARES	RICHARD LATTIMORE
JAMES JOHNSON	PATRICK POLLICK	JAMES AUSTEN
CLEMENT LATTIMORE	JOHN FLOWERS	THOMAS BARNES
GEORGE DAMERON	HENRY DAWSON	WILLIAM EVES

- Verdict Wee find damage for the Plaintiff five hundred pounds of tobacco and casque
ROBERT SECH

- Judgment Upon the Verdict the Court doe order that the Petition of the Plaintiffe be granted against the said JOHNSON and that he pay triple damages according to the Statute of England in ye like case provided and pay the said BRYAM with costs als Execution; and that the Sheriffe possesse the said BYRAM with the Plantation so unlawfully deteyned by the said JOHNSON

- BRYAM agt MUTTOONE Whereas JOHN MUTTOONE and SARAH his Wife were summoned to this Court for to give in their Evidence in the behalfe of PETER BYRAM against JEFFERY JOHNSON and hath fayled of their appearance it is ordered that they be fined according to Law

p. 286

Northumberland County Court 16th of July 1685

- BYRAM agt LATTIMORE PETER BYRAM against CLEMENT LATTIMORE referred to the next Court at the motion of the Defendant

- GEO: KNIGHT agt THO: BURBURROUGH Whereas Mr. GEORGE KNIGHT complained to this Court that THOMAS BURBURROUGH had deteyned his Servant named WILLIAM BESOUTH als WOODAMORE, eighty nine dayes and nights from him and prayed the benefitt of the Act against the said BURBURROUGHS for enterteyning his said Servant by a Jury, and the businesse was accordingly referred to a Jury whose names are underwritten vizt.

Mr. ROBERT SECH	JOHN FLOWERS	WILLIAM EVES
JAMES JOHNSON	ABRAHAM SHEARES	RICHARD LATTIMORE
CLEMENT LATTIMORE	PATRICK POLLICK	JAMES AUSTEN
GEORGE DAMERON	WILLIAM DAWSON	THOMAS BARNES

Verdict Wee doe find that WILLIAM BESOUTH als WOODAMORE is Mr. GEORGE KNIGHT's Servant and doe find for the Plaintiffe such damages as the Law doth provide in such cases against THOMAS BURBURROUGHS, Defendant
ROBERT SECH

- Judgment Upon this Verdict the Court doe order that the said BURBURROUGHS pay the said KNIGHT the sume of two thousand six hundred and seaventy pounds of tobacco and casque with costs being what the Law in that case requires with costs als Execution

- KNIGHT agt BESOUTH Whereas Mr. GEORGE KNIGHT complained to this Court that he hyred one WILLIAM BESOUTH als WOODAMOORE for seaven hundred pounds of tobacco and casque to live with and serve him from March last untill Christmas, notwithstanding the said BESOUTH als WOODAMORE from his service did depart and absent himselfe from the said KNIGHT to the loss of his Cornfield and prayed Order against the said BESOUTH for the remaining part of his service and a Jury to inquire into the damages he hath susteyned which was accordingly referred to a Jury whose names are underwritten, vizt

p. 287

Northumberland County Court 16th of July 1685

Mr. ROBERT SECH	ABRAHAM SHEARES	RICHARD LATTIMORE

NORTHUMBERLAND COUNTY ORDER BOOK, 1678-1698   -73-

JAMES JOHNSON	PATRICK POLLICK	JAMES AUSTEN
CLEMENT LATTIMORE	JOHN FLOWERS	THOMAS BARNES
GEORGE DAMERON	WILLIAM DAWSON	WILLIAM EVES

- <u>Verdict.</u> Wee doe find that WILLIAM BESOUTH als WOODAMORE is Mr. GEORGE KNIGHT's Servant and wee doe award that the said BESOUTH als WOODAMORE serve the residue of his time and three hundred pounds of tobacco damage for the loss of the Cornfield to Mr. GEORGE KNIGHT
ROBERT SECH
- <u>Judgment.</u> Judgment is granted GEORGE KNIGHT against the said WILLIAM BESOUTH als WOODAMORE for the said service and tobacco with costs of suit als Execution
- <u>Wicocomico Vestry agt HARTLAND</u> Whereas the Vestry of Wicocomico Parish complained to this Court that whereas WILLIAM HARTLAND did in a Court held the 3d of July 1678 oblige himselfe for to finish that Parish Church [vizt] he doe all the Carpenter work that was to be done about the said Church every way workman like, but hath not complyed with the performance of any part of the said Covenant notwithstanding he had received satisfaction for the whole of what he bargained for the compleating of the said work, it is ordered that the said HARTLAND finish the said Church by Christmas next [the said Vestry finding all the materialls on their part in the said Covenant expresst] or repay the Vestry the sume of twenty five thousand five hundred pounds of tobacco and casque [it being what they had before payd him] with costs of suit als Execution

[The last two entries on this page are referrals to the next Court, but the participants being named on the margin, I cannot read through the stain]

p. 288   <u>Northumberland County Court 16th of July 1685</u>
- <u>EVANS agt SHEARES</u> Whereas it appeares to this Court that ABRAHAM SHEARES standeth indebted unto JOHN EVANS the sume of two hundred and fifty pounds of tobacco and casque, Judgment is granted the said EVANS against the said SHEARES for the said sume with costs als Execution
- <u>AUSTEN agt NEWTON</u> CHRISTOPHER NEWTON confesseth Judgment unto Mr. JAMES AUSTEN for the payment of two barrells of Indian Corne with costs of suit als Execution
- <u>HOBSON to be allowed out of the publique.</u> It is ordered that Mr. THOMAS HOBSON, SENR. who was High Sheriffe of this County in the yeare 1684 be allowed the sume of nineteen hundred thirty and six pounds of tobacco and casque out of the publique Levy it being for ten Levies overcharged in Wicocomico Parish Lyst at one hundred forty two per poll and four Levies in Fairfeild Parish at one hundred twenty nine per poll
- <u>KNIGHT and others agt KNIGHT</u> Ordred that Mr. PETER KNIGHT, LEONARD KNIGHT, WILLIAM COPPAGE, WILLIAM FISHER and WILLIAM PRICE be allowed according to Act for their two dayes attendance to give in their Evidence in the behalfe of Mr. GEORGE KNIGHT against THOMAS BURBURROUGHS
- Ordered that the next Court be the 3d Wednesday in September next and that an Orphants Court be then held and all persons that hath any businesse relatateling to Orphant's Estates to appeare at the Courthouse which is the place appointed for the said Court the said day

- Ordered that the next Court be the third Wednesday in 7br

- At a Court held for Northumberland County the 9th day of 7br 1685
        Present
Lt. Collo. SAMUEL SMYTH   Mr. THOMAS HOBSON
Mr. PETER PRESLEY, SENR   Mr. THOMAS BRERETON   Justices

- Ordered that Capt. JOHN HAYNIE as soon as the Crop is off the land procure the Courthouse [   ] and that he be allowed for the same out of the Levy [This entry at the bottom of the page is in a dark stain]

p. 289

- At a Court held for Northumberland County the 16th day of September 1685 Annoque Regni Regis James 2d, 1st &c.
        Present
Mr. THOMAS HOBSON, SENR.   Mr. RICHARD KENNER
Mr. CHARLES LEE   Mr. THOMAS BRERETON
Mr. NICHOLAS OWEN   Mr. PETER PRESLEY, JUNR.
Capt. JOHN HAYNIE   Mr. RICHARD ROGERS   Justices

- MOTT'S Will proved Upon the Petition of SAMUELL SANFORD who married ELIZABETH, Executrix of EDWARD ELLIOTT, a Probate is granted him of the Last Will and Testament of the said EDWARD ELLIOTT, the Will being proved by the Oath of FRANCIS BOONE [which was in Court produced] that the said FRANCIS did see the Testator signe seale and deliver the said Will as doth appear under the hand of WILLIAM HATTON, one of Maties Justices of the Peace for the County of ST. MARY's in the Province of MARYLAND dated the 24th of June 1685, the other witness named, WILLIAM HOOKE, being dead

- EVANS agt JONES Mr. WILLIAM JONES confesseth Judgment for the payment of fourteen hundred seaventy nine pounds of tobacco and casque to JOHN EVANS with costs of suit als Execution

- STRECHLEY agt CHAMPION Whereas it appears to this Court by a Bill under the hand of JOHN CHAMPION dated the 11th day of May 1682, that the said CHAMPION is indebted unto Mr. JOHN STRECHLEY the sume of three hundred thirty pounds of tobacco and caque; Judgment is granted the said STRECHLEY against the said CHAMPION for the said sume with costs als Execution

- STRECHLEY against WATT Whereas it appears to this Court by a Bill under the hand of ISAAC WATT dated the first day of June 1684 that the said WATT is indebted to Mr. JOHN STRECHLEY the sume of seaven hundred pounds

p. 290

Northumberland County Court 16th of September 1685

of tobacco and casque; Judgment is granted the said STRECHLEY against the said WATT for the sayd sume with costs of suit als Execution

- Mr. SAMUELL HARTNELL against Mr. JOHN CHAMPION referred to the next Court at the motion of the Defendant

- JOHN REASON agt TIGNOR Whereas JOHN REASON complained to this Court that he had upon his owne land fallen a Pine tree and made it into a Canew and that Mr. WILLIAM TIGNOR had privately taken the Canew away without his consent or knowledge and prayed reasonable satisfaction for the said Canew and the want of her some considerable time; it is ordered that the said WILLIAM TIGNOR pay the said JOHN REASON the sume of four hundred pounds of tobacco and casque it being for the Canew and damages for the want of it with costs of suit als Execution

- PETER BYRAM against CLEMENT LATTIMORE referred to the next Court

- JOHN FLOWERS agt GLASCOCK Whereas JOHN FLOWERS was arrested to this Court at the suit of Mr. THOMAS GLASCOCK and noe cause of action appearing, a non suit is granted the said FLOWERS against the said GLASCOCK with costs and damages according to Law

- HARCUM agt PRESLEY Whereas it appeares to this Court that Mr. PETER PRESLEY, JUNR. is indebted unto Mr. WILLIAM HARCUM the sume of eighteen hundred and forty pounds of tobacco and casque by Account to which the said HARCUM hath made Oath; Judgment is granted the said HARCUM against the said PRESLEY for the said sume with costs als Execution

p. 291   Northumberland County Court 16th of September 1685

- BARNES agt BEANE Whereas THOMAS BARNES brought his action to this Court against WILLIAM BEANE and complained that he had formerly put in his Information to the Court against the said BEANE for concealing one Tythable upon which some Gentlemen of the Court desired that they might conclude the difference between themselves. Whereupon THOMAS BARNES did propose what the said BEANE then freely seemed to allow of and promised to pay but when the said BEANE made his demand the said BEANE denyed to comply with his said composition and therefore prayed Judgment for his first Information according to Law; Judgment is granted the said BARNES against the said BEANE according to Act in that case made and provided with costs of suit als Execution

- MORRIS's Will proved This day the nuncupative Will of THOMAS MORRIS was proved by the Oaths of JAMES TUXBURY and JOHN MOLINAX

- CORBETT agt ALLGOOD's Estate Judgment is granted JOHN CORBETT against the Estate of EDWARD ALLGOOD, deceased for two hundred pounds of tobacco and casque for finding plank and nayles and makeing the said ALLGOOD's Coffin als Execution

- Capt. THO: JONES to prosecute Ryotters Whereas divers persons [vizt] RICHARD BRAYDON, TEAGE ALLEN, THOMAS MILLER, PATRICK DONAUGH, THOMAS BROWNE, LAWRENCE WHITE, WILLIAM LAMBERT, JOHN SALTER and CHARLES SMYTH did about the 12th day of August last past in a Cornfield near the House of MRS. ELIZABETH KEEN in this County then and there in a Riottous manner meet quarrell and fight contrary to the publique peace and in contempt of his Majestie his Crown and Dignitie and whereas such outrages committed by such indisposed persons doe requires some discreet understanding persons in his Majesties behalf to present such offenders. It is therefore ordered that Capt. THOMAS JONES a fitt person for the Presentment of the Delinquents appeare in behalf of his Majestie against them and all others within this County take care of offending untill the examinations be hereafter knowne

p. 292 Northumberland County Court 16th of September 1685

- **Riotters to give caution for their good behaviour** Upon the Petition of the Delinquents, it is ordered that they have liberty untill the next Court to traverse their indictment they giveing [in the meantime] sufficient caution for their good behaviour and their appearance at the next Court held for this County for to answer the suit of Our Soveraigne Lord the King

- **KENNER for MILLER and WHITE** Mr. RICHARD KENNER doth in Court oblige himselfe in the penall sume of forty pounds sterling that THOMAS MILLER and LAWRENCE WHITE shall be of good behaviour towards his Matie and all his leige people and make their personall appearance at the next Court held for this County then and there to answer the suit of Our Soveraigne Lord the King

- **JAMES JOHNSON Security for LAMBERT** Mr. JAMES JOHNSON doth in Court oblige himselfe in the sume of twenty pounds sterling that WILLIAM LAMBERT shall be of good behaviour towards his Matie and all his leige people and make his personall appearance at the next Court held for this County then and there to answer the suit of Our Soveraigne Lord the King

- **Mr. OWEN Security for BROWNE** Mr. NICHOLAS OWEN doth in Court oblige himselfe in the sume of twenty pounds sterling that THOMAS BROWNE shall be of good behaviour towards his Matie and all his leige people and make his personall appearance at the next Court held for this County then and there to answer the suit of Our Soveraigne Lord the King

- **COX Security for SALTER** Mr. RICHARD COX doth in Court oblige himselfe in the sume of twenty pounds sterling that JOHN SALTER shall be of good behaviour towards his Matie and all his leige people and make his personall appearance at the next Court held for this County then and there to answer the suit of Our Soveraigne Lord the King

- **TOMSON and PARKER Securities for SMYTH** RICHARD TOMSON and WILLIAM PARKER doth in Court oblige themselves joyntly and severally in the penall sume of twenty pounds that CHARLES SMYTH shall well behave himselfe towards his Matie and all his leige people and make his personall appearance at the next Court held for this County then and there to answer Our Soveraigne Lord the King

p. 293 Northumberland County Court 16th of September 1685

- **PARKER's Will proved** Upon the Petition of ELIZABETH the Relict of AZARCAM PARKER, deceased, a Probate is granted her of the Last Will and Testament of her deceased Husband, the Will being proved by the Oathes of Mr. JOHN TURBERVILLE and THOMAS BAKER, witnesses to the said Will

- **HIGH's Comm. of Admon MAXWELL's Estate** Upon the Petition of THOMAS HIGH, a Commission of Administration is granted him of the Last Will and Testament of EDWARD MAXWELL, deceased, he giveing caution according to Law

- **Bond** Mr. WILLIAM JONES and THOMAS HIGH doe oblige themselves joyntly and severally in the penall sume of ten thousand pounds of tobacco and casque to the Justices of this County that the said HIGH shall duely administer on the Estate of EDWARD MAXWELL, deceased, and exhibite an Inventory thereof according to Law

- **NEALE agt SHAPLEIGH** Whereas at a Court held for this County the

NORTHUMBERLAND COUNTY ORDER BOOK, 1678-1698

19th 9br 1684, the Honorable NICHOLAS SPENCER Esqr. obteyned a Judgment against Mr. CHRISTOPHER NEALE the Security of Mr. PHILIP SHAPLEIGH for forty seaven pounds seaventeen shillings sterling it being for Bills of Exchange drawne by the said SHAPLEIGH payable to his Honor aforesaid for forty one pounds three shillings and six pence sterling, for the payment whereof the said NEALE became Security and the said Bills were returned protested which [with the damages and charges of protest amount to the said sume of forty seaven pounds, seaventeen shillings sterling, and whereas the said NEALE hath brought his action to this Court against Mr. HANNAH, the Attourney of the said Mr. SHAPLEIGH, for the said sume and did produce a Bond under the hand and seale of the said SHAPLEIGH wherein he did oblige himselfe in the penall sume of ninety five pounds sterling for to save harmlesse the said NEALE from any damages that might arrise to the said NEALE as being his Security as aforesaid; Judgment is granted the said NEALE against the said SHAPLEIGH for the said sume of one hundred seaventeen pounds, seaventeen shillings sterling with costs of suit alias Execution

p. 294

Northumberland County Court 16th of September 1685

- **Injunction** Upon the Petition of the Defendant, an Injunction is granted him to stop all further proceedings in Common Law in the suit depending between Mr. CHRISTOPHER NEALE and himselfe untill the next Court that then he may have a hearing in Chancery
- **FARMER agt ALVERSON** The difference depending between TELEIF ALVERSON, Plaintiffe, and Mr. WILLIAM FARMER, Feoffee in Trust for the Estate of Major JOHN MOTTROM, deceased, is dismiet
- The Court adjourns till tomorrow morning eight of the clock

- **Die 17th September 1685**   Present
Mr. THOMAS HOBSON, SENR.   Capt. JOHN HAYNIE   Justices
Mr. NICHOLAS OWEN   Mr. PETER PRESLEY, JUNR.

- **BARNES agt TOMSON** Whereas THOMAS BARNES in March Court 1682/3 brought his Information against RICHARD TOMSON for concealing one Tythable and at the instance of some Gentlemen of that Court the said BARNES and TOMSON came to a Judgment between themselves which the said BARNES complained to this Court that the said TOMSON was soe farr from complying with it he would not pay him any thing and prayed Judgment against the said TOMSON according to Law. Judgment is granted the said BARNES for his Information according to Act against the said TOMSON with costs als Execution
- **RICE agt LUKE** Whereas the last Court RICHARD RICE, the Executor of ROBERT PRITT, obteyned a Judgment against Mr. EDMUND LUKE for three hundred ninety pounds of tobacco and casque unlesse the said LUKE appeared this Court and shewed reasons to the contrary; And whereas MRS. ANN LUKE did in Court averr that her Husband was sick and could not appeare, it is ordered that the former Order be confirmed with costs of sit als Execution unlesse the said LUKE appeares the next Court and shews reasons to the contrary

p. 295   Northumberland County Court 17th of September 1685

- EVANS agt PERCIFULL WILLIAM PERCIFULL confesseth Judgment unto JOHN EVANS for the payment of nine hundred pounds of tobacco and casque with costs of suit als Execution

- EVANS agt EDNEE The difference depending between JOHN EVANS and JAMES EDNEE is referred to the next Court, Mr. WILLIAM JONES in Court obliging himselfe in the penall sume of one thousand pounds of tobacco and casque that the said EDNEE shall appeare the next Court and answer the suit of the said EVANS

- Mr. RICHARD ROGERS, present

- JAMES WADDY agt TUTT Whereas JAMES WADDY complained to this Court that he did [in January Court last] have a woman named MARY TUTT for one yeare for to doe him such service as he should imploy her in but notwithstanding the Agreement she hath departed from him and been absent thirty dayes and whereas the said WADDY prayed Judgment against the said MARY for satisfaction of the said time she had absented herselfe, it is ordered that the Sheriffe take her into safe custody untill she gives security for her appearance at the next Court to be held for this County

- WRIGHT agt LEE Whereas the last Court Mr. MOTTROM WRIGHT obteyned Judgment against Mr. WILLIAM LEE, Sheriffe, for eighteen hundred pounds of tobacco and casque, Mr. JOHN CURTIS being arrested to that Court and fayled of his appearance to answer the suit of the said WRIGHT, and whereas the said CURTIS likewise now fayling of his appearance to answer the said suit, and the said WRIGHT hath made his debt appeare due by Bill under the hand and seale of the said CURTIS dated the 30th of Aprill 1684, Judgment is granted the said WRIGHT against Mr. WILLIAM LEE of the said sume and costs of suit als Execution

p. 296   Northumberland County Court 17th of September 1685

- LEE agt CURTIS Whereas ye last Court an Attachment was awarded Mr. WILLIAM LEE, Sheriffe, against the Estate of Mr. JOHN CURTIS for eighteen hundred pounds of tobacco and casque returnable to this Court; Judgment haveing passed against the said Sheriffe for the said sume at that Court, the said CURTIS not appearing at the said Court to answer the suit of Mr. MOTTROM WRIGHT which Attachment is returned executed on a Negro man of the said CURTIS's named Tony, and whereas the said CURTIS did likewise now fayle of his appearance and the said WRIGHT hath obteyned a confirmation of the said Judgment against the Sheriffe, it is ordered that the said Negro being legally brought to appraysment that the said LEE be possessed therewith paying the overplus or else that the said CURTIS release him from the aforesaid Order and costs with costs als Execution

- FARMER agt DELABREE Whereas an Attachmen was awarded Mr. WILLIAM FARMER, Trustee of the Estate of Major JOHN MOTTROM, deceased, against the Estate of JOHN DELABREE which was returned executed on a Boat and furniture and an axe, but the said FARMER being dead, it is ordered that the said Attachment continue untill further Order

- HAYNIE agt CONTANCEAN Capt. JOHN HAYNIE against JOHN CONTANCEAN referred to the next Court at the motion of the Defendant

NORTHUMBERLAND COUNTY ORDER BOOK, 1678-1698 -79-

- **WM: LIVERSAGE Levy free** It is ordered that WILLIAM LIVERSAGE [who complained to this Court that he was very impotent and incapable of doing anything or very little on his own by reason of an [   ] [in his thigh] be free from payijng any Levy this yeare

- **AUSTIN Admr. MORRIS's Estate** A Commission of Administration with a Will annexed is granted to Mr. JAMES AUSTEN of the Estate of THOMAS MORRIS, deceased he giveing caution according to Law

= **Bond** Mr. JAMES AUSTEN and Mr. RICHARD HAYNIE doe oblige themselves joyntly and severally in the sume of ten thousand pounds of tobacc and caske that the said AUSTEN shall duely administer the Estate and exhibite an Inventory thereof according to Law

p. 297   **Northumberland County Court, 17th of September 1685**

- **Collo. GRIFFIN Security for PATK: DONAUGH** Collo. SAMUELL GRIFFIN in Court doth oblige himselfe in the penall sume of twenty pounds sterling that PATRICK DONAUGH shall be of good behaviour towards his Matie and all his leige people and make his personall appearance at the next Court held for this County then and there to answer the suit of Our Soveraigne Lord the King

- **OWEN agt GEORGE** Whereas an Attachment was awarded Mr. NICHOLAS OWEN against MRS. ELIZABETH, the Administratrix of THOMAS GEORGE, deceased, for fifteen hundred pounds of tobacco and casque which Attachment was returned executed on some tobacco in the hands of Mr. RICHARD COX, who owned that he had some of it; Judgment is granted to the said OWEN against the said COX for what shall appeare to be due from the said Estate of the said Mr. GEORGE, if it doth not exceed the sume or if it doth Judgment is granted the said OWEN against the said COX for the said sume of fifteen hundred pounds of tobacco and casque als Execution unless the said MRS. GEORGE appeares the next Court and shews reasons to the contrary

- **Mr. MOOR's Estate to be divided** Upon the Petition of HENRY RIDER, who marryed ANNE, the Daughter of WALTER MOOR, deceased, it is ordered that Mr. JOHN GRAHAM and PETER MAXFIELD some time between this and the next Court make a division of the Estate of WALTER MOOR aforesaid between the said HENRY RIDER, SARAH MOOR and JOHN MOOR the said Decedent's Children and make a return thereof to the next Court

- **LYSER to have ALLGOOD's Estate** Whereas JOHN LYSER who marryed the Executrix of EDWARD ALLGOOD, deceased, complained to this Court that [haveing buryed his said Wife, the said Decedent's Executrix] he had taken care ever since her death for her Children and their Estates devised to them by their deceased Father's Will and prayed that he might have the management of the said Estates untill they come to yeares; it is ordered that the said LYSER take the Estates and Children into his custody giveing security to be accomptable for the same and exhibit an Inventory thereof to the next Court

p. 298   **Northumberland County Court 17th of September 1685**

- **Bond** JOHN LYSER, RICHARD SMYTH and THOMAS BARNES doe oblige themselves joyntly and severally in the penall sume of twenty thousand pounds of tobacco and casque that the said LYSER shall give a just account of the

Estates of EDWARD ALLGOOD, deceased, left by the said ALLGOOD to his Children when thereunto required and exhibite an Inventory thereof to the next Court

- INGRAM agt ENGLISH Whereas THOMAS INGRAM was arrested to this court at the suit of Mr. ALEXANDER ENGLISH and noe Cause of action appearing, a non suit is granted the said INGRAM agaisnt the said ENGLISH with costs and damages according to Law

- Mr. THOMAS JONES, Assignee of WILLIAM SHERWOOD against Mr. JOHN HARRIS referred to the next Court by consent of both parties

- Mr. THOMAS WINTER against Mr. WILLIAM TIGNOR referred to the next Court at the motion of the Defendant

- DENNIS CARTEE agt JOHN CURTIS Whereas Mr. JOHN CURTIS was summoned to this Court by a Note at ye suit of Mr. DENNIS CARTEE, the Attourney of JOHN FLOYD, for six hundred pounds of tobacco and casque and whereas the said CURTIS hath fayled of his appearance to answer the suit, an Attachment is awarded the said CARTEE, Attourney as aforesaid, for the said sume against the said CURTIS returnable to the next Court

- CHARLES HARRIS agt BRYANT Whereas JOHN BRYANT was arrested to this Court at the suit of CHARLES HARRIS, the Assignee of GEORGE KNIGHT, for one pound, eight shillings sterling and hath fayled of his appearance to answer the said suit, Judgment is granted the said HARRIS, Assignee as aforesaid, for the said sume against the Sheriffe with costs and damages according to Law

- Sheriffe's Attachment An Attachment is awarded Mr. WILLIAM LEE, Sheriffe, against the Estate of JOHN BRYANT for the abovesaid sume of one pound, eight shillings sterling returnable to the next Court

p. 299 Northumberland County Court, 17th of September 1685

- WM. ROGERS agt PERCIFULL WILLIAM PERCIFULL confesseth Judgment for the payment of five hundred thirty two pounds of tobacco and casque unto Mr. WILLIAM ROGERS with costs of suit als Execution

- PRESLEY agt NEALE Whereas the last Court Mr. PETER PRESLEY, JUNR. obteyned Judgment against Mr. CHRISTOPHER NEALE, the Security for Mr. WILLIAM ROGERS, for three thousand nine hundred fifty nine pounds of tobacco and casque with costs als Execution unlesse the said NEALE appeared this Court and shewed reasons to the contrary, and whereas the said NEALE hath now appeared but hath not objected anything against the said debt, it is ordered that the former Order be confirmed

- ROGERS agt the Sheriffe Whereas WILLIAM BERRY was arrested to this Court at the suit of Mr. WILLIAM ROGERS for four hundred sixty and four pounds of tobacco and casque and hath fayled of his appearance to answer the said suit, Judgment is granted the said ROGERS against Mr. WILLIAM LEE, Sheriffe, for the said sume with costs and damages according to Law

- Sheriffe's Attachment An Attachment is awarded Mr. WILLIAM LEE, Sheriffe, against the Estate of WILLIAM BERRY for the abovesaid sume of four hundred sixty and four pounds of tobacco and casque returnable to the next Curt

- ROGERS agt BLEDSOE Whereas it appeares to this Court that Mr. GEORGE BLEDSOE is indebted unto Mr. WILLIAM ROGERS the sume of fourteen hundred sixty and two pounds of tobacco and casque by a Bill under the hand of the said GEORGE BLEDSOE dated the eighth day of February 1683/4, and an Account of Secretary's fees; Judgment is granted the said ROGERS against the said BLEDSOE for the said sume with costs of suit als Execution

- FLYNT and HAYNIE BRAYDON's Security Mr. RICHARD FLYNT and Mr. RICHARD HAYNIE doth in Court oblige themselves joyntly and severally in the penall sum of twenty pounds sterling that RICHARD BRAYDON shall be of good behaviour towards his Majtie and all his leige people and make his personall appearance at the next Court to be held for this County then and there to answer the suit of Our Soveraigne Lord the King

p. 300   Northumberland County Court 17th of September 1678-1698

- SMYTH agt NELMES Whereas RICHARD SMYTH, the Overseer of JOHN NELMES, complains to this Court that RICHARD NELMES did oblige himselfe for and in consideration of a Cow and Calfe by him received of the said SMYTH to pay any Doctor for the cureing of a malady which the abovesaid Mr. JOHN NELMES had in his thigh and likewise to procure all things necessary for the said JOHN dureing the time that the cure might be effected as by an Obligation under the hands of the said NELMES might [relation being thereto had] more at large appeare which the said RICHARD NELMES was soe farr from complying with that the said JOHN [without some speedy course be taken] must perish; it is ordered that the said RICHARD NELMES procure some skilfull person at his own costs for the management of the cures and pay costs of suit

- OWEN agt JONES's Estate Whereas it appeares to this Court by a Bill under the hand of RICHARD JONES, deceased, dated the 19th 8br 1683 and an Account of the Estate that the said JONES is indebted unto Mr. NICHOLAS OWEN the Executor of Mr. JOHN [J--   ] the sume of one thousand sixty pounds of tobacco and casque, Judgment is granted the said OWEN, Executor as abovesaid, against the Estate of the said JONES for the said sume als Execution

- Collo. GRIFFIN agt JONES's Estate Whereas it appeares to this Court by a Bill under the hand of RICHARD JONES, deceased, dated the 11th of May 1684 that the Estate of the said JONES is indebted unto Collo. SAMUELL GRIFFIN the sume of eight hundred sixty five pounds of tobacco and casque; Judgment is granted the said Collo. GRIFFIN against the Estate of the said JONES for the said sume with costs als Execution

- GRIFFIN agt BEACHAM Collo. SAMUELL GRIFFIN against DANIELL BEACHAM continued till the next Court

- GRIFFIN agt the Sheriffe Whereas JOAN ROGERS was arrested to this Court at the suit of Collo. SAMUELL GRIFFIN for seaven hundred and twenty five pounds of tobacco and casque and fayled of her appearance to answer the suit, Judgment is granted the said GRIFFIN against the Sheriffe for the said sume with costs and damages according to Law

- Sheriffe's Attachment An Attachment is awarded WILLIAM LEE, Sheriffe, against the Estate of JOAN ROGERS for seaven hundred and twenty five pounds of tobacco and casque returnable to the next Court

p. 301   Northumberland County Court 17th of September 1685

- Mr. WILLIAM ALDEN against DANIELL BEACHAM contined till the next Court

- OWEN Security of TEAGUE ALLEN. Mr. NICHOLAS OWEN doth in Court oblige himselfe in the penall sume of twenty pounds sterling that TEAGUE ALLEN shall be of good behaviour towards his Majtie and all his leige people and make his personall appearance at the next Court held for the said County then and there to answer the suit of Our Soveraigne Lord the King

- The Court adjournes till tomorrow morning eight of the clock

- Die 18th of September 1685   Present
Mr. THOMAS HOBSON, SENR.   Mr. PETER PRESLEY, JUNR.
Capt. JOHN HAYNIE   Mr. RICHARD ROGERS
Mr. RICHARD KENNER   Justices

- PEMBERTON agt WALTERS Whereas Mr. RICHARD PEMBERTON the Assignee of RICHARD COX, the Administrator of GEORGE KNIGHT, deceased, arrested JOHN WALTERS to this Court for three hundred and eleven pounds of tobacco and caske and haveing made Oath that the said debt was due, Judgment is granted the said PEMBERTON, Assignee as aforesaid, against the said WALTERS for the said sume with costs of suit als Execution

- MATHEW agt the Sheriffe Whereas Mr. JAMES CLAUGHTON was arrested to this Court at the suit of Capt. THOMAS MATHEW for eight hundred ninety four pounds of tobacco and casque and hath fayled of his appearance to answer the said suit, Judgment is granted the said MATTHEWES for ye said sume against the Sheriffe according to Law

- CHANDLER agt JONES Whereas THOMAS CHANDLER was arrested to this Court at the suit of THOMAS JONES and noe cause of action appearing, a nonsuit is granted the said CHANDLER against the said JONES with costs and damages according to Law

- ASHTON agt MATHEW Whereas it appeares to this Court by a Bill under the hand of Capt. THOMAS MATHEW dated the 9th of May 1683 that the said Capt. MATTHEW is indebted to Mr. HENRY ASHTON the sume of three thousand four hundred forty and one pounds of tobacco and casque, Judgment is granted the said ASHTON against the said MATHEW for the said sume with costs als Execution

p. 302   Northumberland County Court 18th of September 1685

- STEPHEN WELLS agt PRICHARD Whereas STEPHEN WELLS was arrested to this Court at the suit of ROBERT PRICHARD and noe cause appearing, a non suit is granted the said WELLS against the said PRICHARD with costs and damages according to Law

- Collo. GRIFFIN fined. Whereas Collo. SAMUELL GRIFFIN was summoned to this Court to give in his Evidence in the difference depending between ROBERT PRICHARD and STEPHEN WELLS in the behalfe of the said PRICHARD and hath fayled of his appearance, it is ordered that he be fined according to Law with costs als Execution

- JONES agt the Sheriffe Whereas JOHN CLARK was arrested to this Court at the suit of Capt. THOMAS JONES for two hundred pounds of tobacco and casque and hath fayled of his appearance to answer the said suit, Judgment is granted the said Capt. THOMAS JONES against the Sheriffe for the said sume according to Law

- JONES agt FLEET Whereas Mr. HENRY FLEET was arrested to this Court at the suit of Capt. THOMAS JONES, the Assignee of Collo. FITZHUGH, for five pounds sterling and hath fayled of his appearance to answer the said suit, Judgment is granted the said JONES, Assignee as aforesaid, against the Sheriffe for the said sume according to Law

- Sheriffe's Attachment against CLARK An Attachment is awarded Mr. WILLIAM LEE, Sheriffe, against the Estate of JOHN CLARK for two hundred pounds of tobacco and casque returnable to the next Court

- Sheriffe's Attachment against FLEET An Attachment is awarded Mr. WILLIAM LEE, Sheriffe, against the Estate of Mr. HENRY FLEET for the sume of five pounds sterling returnable to the next Court

- JONES agt EVANS Whereas it appeares to this Court by a Bill under the hand of THOMAS EVANS dated the 19th of July 1683 that the said EVANS is indebted unto Capt. THOMAS JONES the sume of nine hundred pounds of tobacco and casque; Judgment is granted the said JONES against the said EVANS for the said sume with costs als Execution

p. 303 Northumberland County Court 18th of September 1685

- Mr. JOHN LAWRENCE agt Mr. HENRY FLEET referred to the next Court

- JONES agt HARCUM Whereas THOMAS JONES was arrested to this Court at the suit of Mr. WILLIAM HARCUM and noe cause of action appearing, a non suit is granted the said JONES against the said HARCUM with costs and damages according to Law

- FLOWERS agt LONG Whereas JOHN FLOWERS was arrested to this Court at the suit of JOSIAS LONG and noe cause of action appearing, a non suit is granted the said FLOWERS against the said LONG with costs and damages according to Law

- Appraysers FLOWERS's Estate Upon the Petition of JOHN FLOWERS, it is ordered that Mr. EBENEZER SANDERS, JOHN WORNAM, CLEMENT LATTIMORE and GEORGE BENNETT or any three of them apprayse the Estate of WILLIAM FLOWERS, deceased, being sworn by the next Justice

- ROGERS agt HARTLAND An Attachment is awarded Mr. WILLIAM ROGERS against the Estate of WILLIAM HARTLAND for five hundred sixty pounds of tobacco and casque returnable to the next Court

- WADDY's Negro Levy free Whereas JAMES WADDY complained to this Court that he had a Negro woam who was incapable of doing him any service by reason of her age; it is ordered that he be for the suture acquitted of paying any Levy for her

- ROGERS agt KNIGHT An Attachment is awarded Mr. WILLIAM ROGERS against the Estate of GEORGE KNIGHT for three hundred and seaventy nine pounds of tobacco and casque returnble to the next Court

- MATHEW agt OWEN Capt. THOMAS MATHEW against NICHOLAS OWEN is referred to the next Court

-[There is an entry of two lines in a stained part of this page I cannot read]

- The next Court the 3d Wednesday in November

p. 304

- At a Court held for Northumberland County the 18th day of November 1685 Annoque Regni Regis James 2d. 1st &c.

Present

Mr. PETER PRESLEY, SENR.	Mr. NICHOLAS OWEN	
Capt. LEONARD HOWSON	Capt. JOHN HAYNIE	Justices
Mr. CHARLES LEE	Mr. PHILIP SHAPLEIGH	

- JAMES JOHNSON, GREEN's Guardian TIMOTHY GREEN, Orphant of TIMOTHY GREEN, late of this County, deceased, hath in Court made choyce of Mr. JAMES JOHNSON for his Guardian

- Cezar, COLE's Negro how old Cezar, a Negro boy belonging to Mr. JOHN COLES, is judged to be nine yeares of age

- FOSTER to serve METCALFE JOHN FOSTER, Servant to HENRY METCALFE, is adjudged to be fourteen yeares of age and ordered that he serve his said Master according to Act

- MANDLEY to serve WILLIAMS EDMUND MANDLEY and his Wife, Servants to RICHARD HULL, haveing an Infant lately borne are willing [with the consent of their Master] that the said Child shall serve HOWELL WILLIAMS and his Wife untill she be one and twenty yeares old. It is therefore ordered that the said Child serve the said HOWELL and his Wife the said term they paying at the expiration thereof Corne and Cloathes accustomed alwayes provided that if the said HOWELL and his Wife shall dye before the end of the said terme, that then the said Child shall be free immediately after their decease

- Mr. RICHARD KENNER, Present

- Mr. SAMUELL HARTNELL against JOHN CHAMPION referred to the next Court by consent of both parties

- BIRD agt TUTT Judgment is granted JOHN BIRD against MARY TUTT according to Act for his attendance at Court to give in his Evidence on behalfe of the said TUTT against Mr. JAMES WADDY

- PARKER Comm of Admon Upon the Petition of ELIZABETH, the Relict and Widdow of AZARCAM PARKER a Commission of Administration is granted her of the Estate of her said Husband, late deceased, she giveing caution according to Law

- Bond Mr. JOHN HARRIS and THOMAS BAKER doe in Court oblige themselves joyntly and severally in the penall sume of forty thousand pounds of tobacco and casque, that the said ELIZABETH shall duely administer her deceased Husband's Estate

p. 305

Northumberland County Court 18th of November 1685

- Appraysment PARKER's Estate Ordered that Mr. JOHN NICHOLS, Mr. THOMAS WINTER, Mr. GEORGE BLEDSOE and Mr. THOMAS WADDY or any three of them meet at the house of ELIZABETH PARKER sometime between this and the next Court and apprayse the Estate of AZARCAM PARKER, deceased, they being first sworn by the next Justice

- WADDY agt TUTT Whereas the last Court Mr. JAMES WADDY obteyned

NORTHUMBERLAND COUNTY ORDER BOOK, 1685-1698

-85-

Judgment against MARY TUTT [upon a Complaint made to that Court] that the said TUTT [who hyred herselfe to him for one yeare had absented herselfe from his service some considerable time] that the Sheriffe should take the said TUTT into safe custody untill she gave Security for her appearance at this Court, which she haveing done, and it appearing that she hath absented herselfe from her said Master three months, it is ordered that the said TUTT serve the said WADDY for the said time after the expiration of her said terme by condition or otherwise and pay costs of suit als Execution

- <u>WILLIAM DOWNING's Negro how old</u> Phill, a Negro boy belonging to Mr. WILLIAM DOWNING is adjudged to be nine yeares of age

- <u>RICE agt LUKE</u> Judgment is granted RICHARD RICE against EDMUND LUKE for three hundred ninety pounds of tobacco and casque with costs als Execution, unlesse the said LUKE appeares at the next Court and shews reasons to the contrary

- <u>EVANS agt EDNEE</u> Whereas it appeares to this court by a Bill under the hand of JAMES EDNEE dated the 3d of May 1684 that the said EDNEE is indebted unto JOHN EVANS the Assignee of JOHN CRAVEN, the sume of five hundred pounds of tobacco and casque; Judgment is granted the said EVANS, Assignee as aforesaid, against the said EDNEE for the said sume with costs of suit als Execution

- <u>ORLAND agt SALLOWES</u> Whereas RICHARD ORLAND complained to this Court that whereas DAVID ORLAND, his Father, dyed Intestate and STEPHEN SALLOWES intermarrying with his Mother about ten yeares since and never administered on his deceased Father's Estate but converting it to their use and denying him a Child's part, it is ordered that the said STEPHEN SALLOWES and his Wife [haveing notice of this Order] exhibit an Inventory of the said Intestate his Estate to the next Court

p. 306

<u>Northumberland County Court 18th of November 1685</u>

- <u>WM. FARMER Trustee for Major MOTTROM's Estate</u> Whereas at a Court held for this County the 19th [stain[the Honorable NICHOLAS SPENCER Esqr. was pleased by Letter to this Court for the commendation of WILLIAM FARMER to be the Feoffee in Trust for the Estate of Major JOHN MOTTROM, deceased, and did therein oblige himselfe that the said Mr. FARMER shall regularly give in an Account thereof whereon the Court did order that the said Mr. FARMER should be admitted as Feoffee in Trust thereof for the said Estate and exhibit an Inventory thereof to the Court and being yearly accomptable for the same, but the said Mr. WILLIAM FARMER being dead, the Honorable NICHOLAS SPENCER Esqr. haveing [by his Letter to this Court] recommended that ANNE FARMER be admitted as Feoffee in Trust for the said Estate, and obligeing himselfe therein to become Securitie for her. It is ordered that she be admitted in the like nature as her said deceased Husband was she haveing exhibited an Inventory of the said Estate into the Court upon her Oath

- <u>OWEN agt COX</u> Whereas the last Court an Attachment was awarded Mr. NICHOLAS OWEN, Executor of Mr. JOHN JULIAN, against the Estate of Mr. THOMAS GEORGE for fifteen hundred pounds of tobacco and casque which Attachment was returned executed on some tobacco in the hands of RICHARD COX, quantity not knowne, whereon Judgment passed in the behalfe of the said OWEN,

Executor as aforessid, against the said Estate in the hands of the said COX unlesse MRS. ELIZABETH GEORGE, Administrator of Mr. THOMAS GEORGE should this Court appeare and shew reasons to the contrary, and the said MRS. GEORGE not appearing and Mr. NICHOLAS OWEN produced an Order of RAPPAHANNOCK County Court dated the 5th of 9br 1684 obteyned by him the said JOHN JULIAN against the Estate of the said THOMAS GEORGE for the said sume, and whereas RICHARD COX hath in Court owned that he had the full quantity of tobacco in his hands; Judgment is granted the said NICHOLAS OWEN, Executor as aforesaid, for the said sume against RICHARD COX als Execution

- DOWNING and CORBELL to have YEAMAN's Estate Whereas Mr. JOHN DOWNING and JOHN CORBELL became bound with RICHARD LAMPREY for his due administration of the Estate of BARTHOLOMEW YEAMANS and the said LAMPREY being deceased, it is ordered that they have the Estate of the said YEAMANS in their hands

- WILDEY agt JONES An Attachment is awarded MRS. JANE WILDEY against the Estate of SAMUELL JONES for eight hundred pounds of tobacco and casque returnable to the next Court

p. 307

Northumberland County Court 18th of November 1685

- HAYNIE agt COUTANCEAU The difference depending between Capt. JOHN HAYNIE in the behalfe of ANTHONY HAYNIE against JOHN COUTANCEAU is referred to a Jury whose names are underwritten, vizt

JAMES AUSTEN	JOHN EVANS	RICHARD HULL
JOHN FLOWERS	WILLIAM TIGNOR	WILLIAM TAYLOR
WILLIAM SHEARES	CLEMENT LATTIMORE	WILLIAM PARKER
WILLIAM EVES	PETER BYRAM	THOMAS BARNES

- Verduct Wee of the Jury doe find for the Plaintiffe and that the said ANTHONY HAYNIE by his false imprisonment and defamation is damnifyed a thousand pounds of tobacco with costs of suit

JAMES AUSTEN

- Judgment [May 24th 1686. Execution issued on the personall Estate of JOHN COUTANCEAU] Mr. JOHN COUTANCEAU appealeth from this Order to a hearing before his Excellency and Councill the fifth day of the next Generall Court which is granted he giveing caution to prosecute his said Appeale

- Mr. THOMAS WINTER Security for the Appellee

- GRIFFIN agt ROGERS [October ye 7th 1686. Execution issued on this Order against the body of JOAN ROGERS] Whereas it appeares to this Court by a Bill under the hand of JOAN ROGERS dated the 6th of 8br 1684 that the said JOAN ROGERS is indebted to JOHN JEFFERYES Esqr. and COMPANY the sume of seaven hundred twenty five pounds of tobacco and casque, Judgment is granted the said JOHN JEFFERYES Esqr. and COMPANY against the said ROGERS for the said sume with costs of suit als Execution

- Riotters Fined Whereas RICHARD BRAYDON, PATRICK DONAUGH, TEAGUE ALLEN, THOMA MILLER, THOMAS BROWNE, LAWRENCE WHITE, WILLIAM LAMBERT, JOHN SALTER and CHARLES SMYTH were ye last Court found guiltie by the Jury of a Ryott wherein the Court ordered that they should give Bond with sufficient securitie their good behaviour and appearance at this Court, it is ordered they they and each of them be fined one hundred pounds of

tobacco and casque and pay Attourney, Clerk and Sheriffe's fees als Execution
- The Court adjourned till tomorrow morning nine of the clock

p. 308 - Die 19th November 1685   Present
Capt. LEONARD HOWSON   Capt. JOHN HAYNIE
Mr. NICHOLAS OWEN   Mr. PHILIP SHAPLEIGH   Justices

- GRIFFIN agt COLLINS Whereas it appeares to this Court by a Bill under the hand of THOMAS COLLINS dated the 23rd of Aprill 1684 that the said COLLINS is indebted unto Collo. SAMUELL GRIFFIN, the Assignee of EDWARD WATTS, the sume of four hundred pounds of tobacco and casque, Judgment is granted the said Collo. GRIFFIN, Assignee as aforesaid, against the said COLLINS for the said sume with costs als Execution

- JONES agt HARRIS [January 21st 1685/6. Execution issued on this Order against the Estate of JOHN HARRIS] Whereas it appeares to this Court that Mr. JOHN HARRIS is indebted unto Capt. THOMAS JONES, the Assignee of Mr. WILLIAM SHERWOOD, the sume of two pounds, ten shillings sterling and likewise as he is the Assignee of Mr. MALACHY THRUSTON the sume of two pounds, ten shillings sterling by two Bills dated the 26th of 7br 1685 each of the said Bills being for two pounds, ten shillings sterling; Judgment is granted the said Capt. JONES against the said JOHN HARRIS for the said sume of five pounds sterling with cost of suit als Execution

- WEBB and TAYLER to view the Estate of BRITTAINE It is ordered that JOHN WEBB and WILLIAM TAYLER some time between this and the next Court view the damages done by WILLIAM SWETMAN unto the Estate of FRANCES, the Orphant of FRANCIS BRITTAINE and make their report to the next Court and that WILLIAM SWETMAN give good and sufficient securitie for to be acomptable for what damages they shall award that the said SWETMAN hath done to the Estate of the ssid Orphant, the viewers being sworne by the next Justice

- Mr. RICHARD KENNER, present

- Bond EDW: WILLIAMS securitie SWETMAN WILLIAM SWETMAN and EDWARD WILLIAMS doe in Court oblige themselves joyntly and severally in the penall sume of ten thousand pounds of toacco and casque that the said WILLIAM SWETMAN shall make satisfaction for the damages JOHN WEBB and WILLIAM TAYLER shall award that he has damaged the Estate of the Orphant of FRANCIS BRITTAINE and that WILLIAM SWETMAN shall make his appearance at the next Court held for this County

p. 309 Northumberland County Court 19th of November 1685
- GAYLARD agt the Sheriffe Whereas THOMAS WINTER and THOMAS INGRAM were arrested to this Court at the suit of MRS. ANNE GAYLARD, Administratrix of Mr. JAMES GAYLARD, for one thousand pounds of tobacco and casque and have fayled of their appearance to answer the said suit, Judgment is granted the said MRS. GAYLARD against the Sheriff for the said sume and costs and damages according to Law

- Sheriffe's Attachment An Attachment is awarded the Sheriffe against the Estate of Mr. THOMAS WINTER and THOMAS INGRAM for one thousand pounds of tobacco and casque returnable to the next Court

- MATHEW agt OWEN Whereas it appeares to this Court that Mr. NICHOLAS OWEN, the Executor of Mr. JOHN JULIAN, is indebted unto Capt. THOMAS MATHEW the sume of five hundred pounds of tobacco and casque by a Note drawne by Mr. JOHN JULIAN in his life time on the Honorable NICHOLAS SPENCER Esqr., for to pay the said sume which Note is by his Honor aforesaid possessed; Judgment is granted to the said MATHEW against the said OWEN for the said sume with costs als Execution

- LAWRENCE agt FLEET Mr. JOHN LAWRENCE against Mr. HENRY FLEET is referred to the next Court by consent of both parties

- HARRIS agt the Sheriffe Whereas the last Court CHARLES HARRIS, the Assignee of Mr. GEORGE KNIGHT, obteyned Judgment against Mr. WILLIAM LEE, Sheriffe, for the sume of eight and twenty shillings sterling; JOHN BRYANT being arrested to that Court and failed of his appearance to answer the said suit, And whereas the said BRYANT hath likewise now fayled of his appearance to answer the said suit of the said HARRIS, and the said HARRIS hath made appeare that there is due to him, Assignee as aforesaid, ye sume of six and twenty shillings sterling upon ballance of a Bill dated the 12th day of May 1684, Judgment is granted the said HARRIS, Assignee as abovesaid, against Mr. WILLIAM LEE, Sheriffe, for the said sume with costs of suit als Execution

- ROGERS agt the Sheriffe Whereas the last Court Mr. WILLIAM ROGERS obteyned Judgment against Mr. WILLIAM LEE, Sheriffe, for four hundred sixty four pounds of tobacco and casque WILLIAM BARRY being arrested to this Court but fayled of his appearance to answer the said suit against the said ROGERS, and whereas the said BARRY hath likewise now fayled of his appearance to answer the said suit and the said ROGERS hath made his debt appeare due by a Bill under the hand of the said BARRY dated

p. 310 Northumberland County Court 19th of November 1685

the sixth day of March 1682/3, Judgment is granted WILLIAM ROGERS against WILLIAM LEE, Sheriffe, for the said sume with costs of suit als Execution

- BRERETON agt the Sheriffe Whereas the last Court Mr. THOMAS BRERETON, Executor of Collo. THOMAS BRERETON, obteyned Judgment against the Sheriffe for thirteen hundred forty three pounds of tobacco and casque and WILLIAM BARRY being arrested to that Court at his suit and fayled of his appearance and whereas the said BARRY hath likewise now fayled of his appearance to answer the said suit, and whereas the said BRERETON hath made his debt appeare due by the ballance of a Bill bearing date the 5th of June 1680 passed by the said BARRY unto Collo. BRERETON aforesaid; Judgment is granted the said Mr. BRERETON, Executor as aforesaid, against Mr. WILLIAM LEE, Sheriffe, for the said sum with costs of suit als Execution

- Capt. JONES agt the Sheriffe Whereas the last Court Capt. THOMAS JONES obteyned Order against the Sheriffe for two hundred pounds of tobacco and casque, JOHN CLARK being arrested at his suit and fayled of his appearance, and whereas the said CLARK hatn now fayled of his appearance to answer the said suit and the said Capt. JONES hath made his debt appeare due by Bill under the hand of the said CLARK date the 12th of March 1683/4, Judgment is granted the said JONES against Mr. WILLIAM LEE, Sheriffe, for the said sume with costs of suit als Execution

- MATHEW agt CLAUGHTON [February 16th 1685/6 Execution issued against the Estate of JAMES CLAUGHTON] Whereas it appeares to this Court by a Bill under the hand of JAMES CLAUGHTON dated the 7th day of January 1683/4 that the said CLAUGHTON is indebted unto Capt. THOMAS MATHEW the sume of eight hundred ninety four pounds and casque; Judgment is granted the daid MATHEW against the said CLAUGHTON for the said sum with costs of suit als Execution

- DERMOTT agt PEMBERTON The difference depending between OWEN DERMOTT and Mr. RICHARD PEMBERTON concerning Land is referred to a Jury hereunder subscribed [vizt]

JOHN FLOWERS	PETER FLYNT	WILLIAM HARCUM
WILLIAM EVES	RICHARD FLYNT	CLEMENT LATTIMORE
JAMES AUSTEN	WILLIAM PARKER	CORNELIUS COLES
JOHN EVANS	WILLIAM TAYLER	JOHN WALTERS

- Verdict Wee give for the Plaintiffe three thousand pounds of tobacco and casque

- Judgment RICHARD PEMBERTON is to pay OWEN DERMOTT the sume of three thousand pounds of tobacco and casque with costs als Execution

p. 311 Northumberland County Court 19th of November 1685

- Appeale Mr. RICHARD PEMBERTON appeales from this Order to a hearing before his Excellency and Councill the fifth day of the next Generall Court which is granted he giveing caution to prosecute his said Appeale

- Bond Mr. RICHARD PEMBERTON and Mr. JAMES CLAUGHTON doe oblige themselves joyntly and severally in the penall sume of six thousand pounds of tobacco and casque that the said PEMBERTON shall duely prosecute his said Appeale

- OWEN DERMOTT and Mr. JOHN HARRIS doe oblige themselves joyntly and severally in the penall sume of six thousand pounds of tobacco and casque that the said DERMOTT shall answer the said Appeale

- RICE and PEMBERTON against JOHN DOWNING and JOHN CORBELL referred to the next Court at the motion of the Defendant

- JONES agt FLEET [January the 21st 1685/6 Execution issued against the body of Mr. HENRY FLEET] Whereas it appeares to this Court by a Bill under the hand of Mr. HENRY FLEET dated the 13th of December 1684 that the said FLEET is indebted unto Capt. THOMAS JONES, Assignee of Mr. WILLIAM FITZHUGH, the just sume of five pounds sterling; Judgment is granted the said JONES against the said FLEET for the said sume with costs als Execution

- HANKING agt the Sheriff THO: ELLIOTT not appearing Whereas THOMAS ELLIOTT was arrested to this Court at the suit of Mr. MARK HANKING for four hundred fifty pounds of tobacco and casque and hath fayled of his appearance to answer the suit, Judgment is granted the said HANKING against the Sheriffe according to Law

- Attachment An Attachment is awarded the Sheriffe against the Estate of THOMAS ELLIOTT for the sume of four hundred and fifty pounds of tobacco and casque returnable to the next Court

- THOMAS COPEMAN against Mr. JOHN CRALLE referred to the next Court at the motion of the Defendant; Mr. CHARLES HARRIS Attourney for the said CRALLE

- CARTEE agt CURTIS Whereas JOHN CURTIS was summoned to this Court at the suit of Mr. DENNIS CARTEE, Assignee of JOHN FLOYD, for six hundred pounds of tobacco and casque, and whereas Mr. CARTEE produced a Bill for the said debt and Mr. CURTIS being absent Capt. THOMAS JONES, his Attourney, disavowed the said Bill, it is therefore ordered that the said CURTIS appeare at the next Court and declare if the Bill be due or not so that the Court may accordingly proceed to Judgment

p. 312

Northumberland County Court 19th of November 1685

- JOHN WALTERS agt HENRY [P-----] referred to the next Court

- LAMBERT agt JONES An Attachment is awarded WILLIAM LAMBERT against the Estate of JAMES JONES for fifteen hundred pounds of tobacco and casque returnable to the next Court

- LATTIMORE agt BYRAM The reference depending between PETER BYRAM and CLEMENT LATTIMORE is referred to a Jury here subscribed, vizt

Mr. JAMES AUSTEN	Mr. RICHARD FLYNT	Mr. WILLIAM HARCUM
JOHN FLOWERS	PETER FLYNT	CLEMENT LATTIMORE
WILLIAM EVES	WILLIAM PARKER	CORNELIUS COLES
JOHN EVANS	WILLIAM TAYLER	JOHN WALTERS

- Verdict For the Defendant; JAMES AUSTEN

- Judgment A non suit is granted CLEMENT LATTEMORE against PETER BYRAM with costs and damages according to Law

- EVANS agt PARKER Whereas JOHN EVANS was arrested to this Court at the suit of ELIZABETH PARKER and noe cause of action appearing,, a non suit is granted the said EVANS against the said PARKER with costs and damages according to Law

- SHARP agt GLASCOCK Whereas JOHN SHARP hath attended at Court two dayes to give in his Evidence in the behalfe of Mr. THOMAS GLASCOCK against JOHN FLOWERS, it is ordered that he be allowed for his said attendance according to Law

- Mr. THOMAS GLASCOCK agt JOHN FLOWERS referred to the next Court

- HARCUM agt BRIDGMAN Whereas THOMAS JONES was arrested to this Court at the suit of Mr. WILLIAM HARCUM for ten thousand pounds of tobacco and casque and hath fayled of his appearance to answer the said suit, Judgment is granted the said HARCUM against THOMAS BRIDGMAN, Securitie for the said JONES, for the said sume with costs and damages according to Law

- KESTERSON agt HARCUM It is ordered that MARGRETT KESTERSON be allowed according to Act for two dayes attendance to give in her Evidence in the behalfe of Mr. WILLIAM HARCUM against THOMAS JONES

[There is a referall at the bottom of the page in the stain]

p. 313

Northumberland County Court 19th of November 1685

- TIGNOR agt WINTER Whereas Mr. WILLIAM TIGNOR was arrested to this Court at the suit of THOMAS WINTER and noe cause of action appearing, a non suit is granted the said TIGNOR against the said WINTER with costs and damages according to Law

- SHOARES, TIGNOR, HULL and BARNES fined Whereas Mr. WILLIAM SHOARES, Mr. WILLIAM TIGNOR, Mr. RICHARD HULL and THOMAS BARNES were summoned on a Jury to attend the Court and have disappeared, it is ordered that they be fined according to Act

- MORRIS's Estate to be apprayved It is ordered that JOHN BEE and RICHARD WILLIAMS some time between this and the next Court apprayse the Estate of THOMAS MORRIS, deceased, being sworne by the next Justice

- Ordered that the next Court be the 2d Wednesday in Xbr

p. 314 - At a Court held for Northumberland County the 21st of December 1685
Present
Lt. Collo. SAMUELL SMYTH   Mr. PHILIP SHAPLEIGH
Mr. PETER PRESLEY, SENR.   Mr. THOMAS BRERETON
Capt. LEONARD HOWSON   Mr. PETER PRESLEY, JUNR.
Mr. NICHOLAS OWEN   Mr. RICHARD ROGERS
Capt. JOHN HAYNIE   Justices

- WILLOUGHBY's Will proved Upon the Petition of Mr. RICHARD HULL a Probate is granted him of the Last Will and Testament of Mr. HENRY WILLOUGHBY deceased, the Will being proved by the Oaths of Mr. CHARLES HARRIS and EDWARD NESBITT who did sweare that the Testator did owne the said Will but dyed before signing thereof

- HAYNIE agt KING Judgment is granted Capt. JOHN HAYNIE against the Estate of WILLIAM KING for five hundred pounds of tobacco and casque in the hands of ALEXANDER WEATHERSTONE unlesse the said WEATHERSTONE appeares the next Court amd shews reasons to the contrary

- Servants bound THOMAS WHEELER, Servant to THOMAS BREWER is adjuged to be fourteen yeares of age; ROBERT WILKS, Servant to JOHN BOWIN is adjudged to be ten years of age and ordered that the said Servants serve their Masters according to Law

- ROGERS agt HARTLAND Whereas the last Court an Attachment was awarded Mr. WILLIAM ROGERS against the Estate of WILLIAM HARTLAND for five hundred sixty and four pounds of tobacco and casque which Attachment was returned executed on one hogshead of tobacco in the hands RICHARD LATTEMORE quantitie unknowne and whereas the said Mr. ROGERS hath produced a Bill under the hand of the said HARTLAND dated the 21st day of March 1682/3 for the debt due to him, Judgment is granted the said ROGERS for the Estate attached in the hands of RICHARD LATTEMORE with costs als Execution; and ordered that the Attachment be continued against the Estate of WILLIAM HARTLAND to the next Court

p. 315 Northumberland County Court 21st of December 1685
- ROGERS ast PARSONS Whereas an Attachment was awarded Mr. RICHARD ROGERS against the Estate of EMANUELL PARSONS for three hundred thirty eight pounds of tobacco and casque and this yeare's Levy, which Attachment was returned executed on soe much in his owne hands and whereas he

hath made his said debt appeare due by Bill under the hand and seale of the said EMANUELL PARSONS dated the 20th of November 1684, Judgment is granted RICHARD ROGERS against the Estate for the said Bill and Levy as alsoe reasonable satisfaction for striping and packing and casque for the same with costs of suit als Execution

- Procession when to be made and Law Books sent for Whereas there is an Act of Assembly which doth provide that every four yeares there shall be by the Court appoynted to procession, and whereas there is another Act of Assembly which doth enjoyne every respective County Court to provide such Land Books ye aforessaid Act appoynts and requires, the Court doth therefore order that upon Easter Monday next the Inhabitants of this County doe commence and begin the said procession and renew the marks and boundaries of each freeholder's land within this County and that the Vestry of each Parish in this County doe order the severall precincts of the neighbourhoods and the dayes of perambulation and that the next Court to be held for this County take course that such Books be sent for as the Law nominates to the intent they may be here produced the next ensueing shipping

- WALTERS RICHARD JONES's Guardian RICHARD JONES did this day in Court make choyce of JOHN WALTERS for his Guardian

- BENNETT agt HOBSON The difference depending between Mr. THOMAS HOBSON, Plaintiffe, in behalfe of his Majesty and Capt. ROBERT BENNETT Defendant is referred to a Jury here subscribed, [vizt]

Mr. GEORGE HUTTON	THOMAS [B]	ALEXANDER WEATHERSTONE
THOMAS WINTER	PETER MAXWELL	JOHN BRYANT
RICHARD LATTEMORE	JAMES EDNEE	ALEXANDER BRODIE
EDWARD TIPTON	WILLIAM PARKER	RICHARD HULL

Verdict Wee find for the Defendant

p. 316

Northumberland County Court, 21st of December 1685

- HARROLD to appeare at next Court It is ordered that GILBERT HARROLD appeare at the next Court [he haveing notice hereof] and answer the Complaint of Mr. JAMES JOHNSON, the Guardian of TIMOTHY GREEN

- HUTCHINS agt PARSONS and DUKE Whereas an Attachment was awarded to Mr. MATHEW HUTCHINS against the Estate of EMANUELL PARSONS for two hundred and nineteen pounds of tobacco and casque, and against the Estate of JOHN DUKE for two hundred and three pounds of tobacco and casque which Attachment was returned executed on soe much in the hands of Mr. RICHARD ROGERS, Judgment is granted the said HUTCHINS against the said ROGERS for the said sumes amounting to four hundred twenty two pounds of tobacco and casque with costs als Execution

- The Court adjourns till tomorrow morning eight of the clock

- Die 22nd December 1685   Present

Mr. PETER PRESLEY, SENR.	Mr. PHILIP SHAPLEIGH
Capt. LEONARD HOWSON	Mr. PETER PRESLEY, JUNR.
Mr. NICHOLAS OWEN	Mr. RICHARD ROGERS
Capt. JOHN HAYNIE	Justices

- PRESLEY and SECH's wenches to come to the next Court Whereas

Mr. PETER PRESLEY, JUNR. and Mr. ROBERT SECH had information exhibited against them into this Court by the Grand Jury of Inquest for their wenches haveing bastard Children. It is ordered that the said persons bring their said wenches to the next Court

- NEWTON and JACKMAN to appeare at the next Court. Whereas the Grand Jury of Inquest exhibited an Information into this Court againt CHRISTOPHER NEWTON and TABTHY JACKMAN for lacivious living and they not appearing, it is ordered that the Sheriffe take them into safe custody untill they give caution for teir good behaviour and their appearance at the next Court

p. 317

Northumberland County Court 22d of December 1685

- Sheriffe agt CLARK Whereas at a Court held for this County the 18th day 7br 1685 an Attachment was awarded Mr. WILLIAM LEE, Sheriffe, against the Estate of JOHN CLARK for two hundred pounds of tobacco and casque. Judgment haveing then passed against the said Mr. LEE for the sume at the suit of Capt. THOMAS JONES, and whereas at a Court held the 19th of November 1685 the said Capt. JONES obteyned a confirmation against the said Sheriffe and whereas the said Attachment is now returned executed on tobacco hanging in the tobacco house at the Plantation where PATRICK DONAUGH lived, Judgment is granted the said Mr. LEE against the Estate of the said CLARK soe attached for the said sume with costs als Execution

- LEE agt BARRY Whereas at a Court held for this County the 17th 7br 1685, an Attachment was awarded Mr. WILLIAM LEE, Sheriffe, against the Estate of WILLIAM BARRY for four hundred sixty and four pounds of tobacco and casque, Judgment haveing that Court passed against the said Sheriffe for the said sume the said BARRY not appearing to answer the suit of Mr. WILLIAM ROGERS, and whereas at a Court held the 19th of 9br 1685 the said BARRY not appearing the said ROGERS obteyned confirmation of the said Order against the Sheriffe for the said sume and costs and whereas the said Attachment is returned executed on a hogshead of tobacco in the hands of the said BARRY, Judgment is granted the said LEE against the said BARRY for the hogshead of tobacco soe attached and that which shall appeare due besides the said tobacco als Execution

- OWEN agt WMS. Whereas an Attachment was awarded Mr. NICHOLAS OWEN against the Estate of ROGER WILLIAMS for two hundred twenty pounds of tobacco and casque which Attachment was returned executed on soe much in the hands of Mr. ROBERT LYNDSAY and whereas the said Mr. OWEN hath made his debt appeare due by Bill under the hand of the said ROGER WILLIAMS dated the last day of March 1678, Judgment is granted the said Mr. OWEN against the said LYNDSAY for the said sume with costs als Execution

- Vestry agt COX Ordered that RICHARD COX make his appearance at the next Court to be held for this County to answer the Complaint of the Vestry of Bowtracy Parish he haveing notice of this Order

p. 318

Northumberland County Court 22d of December 1685

- WINTER agt GRACTON Whereas an Attachment was awarded Mr. THOMAS WINTER against the Estate of THOMAS GRACTON for seaventeen hundred seaventy eight pounds of tobacco and casque which Attachment was returned executed on some tobacco hanging on the Plantation of the said THOMAS WINTER and whereas the said WINTER hath produced two Bills one assigned from JAMES YOUNG for the sume of one hundred ninety and three pounds of tobacco dated the 28th of January 1683/4, and the other for the sume of two hundred fifty pounds of tobacco and casque dated the 26th 7br 1684, which said Bills with an Account [to which the said WINTER hath made Oath] amounts to the abovesaid sumes of seaventeen hundred seaventy and eight pounds of tobacco and casque; Judgment is granted the said WINTER against the Estate of the said GRACTON for as much of the Estate soe attached as will sattisfie the said debt and costs als Execution but if the Debt exceeds ye quantitie of tobacco attached, then the Attachment to continue good against the said GRACTON's Estate

- <u>KEELY agt DIAMOND</u> Whereas JOHN KEELY was arrested to this Court at the suit of NICHOLAS DIAMOND and noe cause of action appearing, a non suit is granted the said KEELY against the said DIAMOND with costs and damages according to Law

- <u>COPEMAN agt CRALLE [March the 10th 1685/6 Execution issued against the body of Mr. JOHN CRALLE]</u> Whereas it appeares unto this Court that Mr. JOHN CRALLE is indebted unto THOMAS COPEMAN in the sume of four hundred sixty and four pounds of tobacco and cask; Judgment is granted the said COPEMAN against the said CRALLE for the said sume with costs als Execution

- <u>CRALLE agt OWEN</u> Whereas an Attachment was awarded Mr. JOHN CRALLE against the Estate of THOMAS BROWN for three hundred pounds of tobacco and casque, and whereas JAMES GENN did upon Oath declare that the said Debt was due, Judgment is granted the said CRALLE against the Estate of the said BROWNE in the hands of Mr. NICHOLAS OWEN unlesse the said Mr. OWEN appeares at next Court and shews reasons to the contrary

- Mr. CHARLES HARRIS the Attourney of Mr. JOHN CRALLE

p. 319

Northumberland County Court 22d of December 1685
- Northumberland County DR 1685

To Capt. PETER KNIGHT for Burgess charges	11000	& casque
To Mr. CHRISTOPHER NEALE for Burgess charges	11000	& casque
To Mr. JOHN COUTANCEAU two Wolfe's heads in pitt	00400	
To Mr. WILLIAM LEE one Wolf shot	00100	
To Mr. CHRISTOPHR GARLINGTON one Wolf shot	00100	
To Mr. JOHN NICKLESS one Wolf in a pitt	00200	
To Mr. RICHARD PEMBERTON one Wolf in a pitt	00200	
To ABRAHAM SHEARES one Wolf shot	00100	
To JOHN TAYLOR, JUNR. one Wolf shot	00100	
To RICHARD LATTEMORE one Wolf shot	00100	
To Mr. GEORGE BLEDSOE one Wolf shot	00100	
To JOHN ROBINSON one Wolf shot	00100	
To THOMAS BARNES one Wolf shot	00100	
To JOHN GREENSTED two Wolves in a pitt	00400	
To WILLIAM TAYLOR five Wolves in a pitt	01000	
To JOHN [---DRILL] one Wolf shot	00100	
To WILLIAM PERCIFULL one Wolf shot	00100	
To ye Cryer	00400	
To ye Clerk for publique business	01000	
To JOHN WEBB for Cone Bridge	00800	

NORTHUMBERLAND COUNTY ORDER BOOK, 1678-1698   -95-

To EDWARD WILLIAMS for tending the Court	00800	
To THOMAS BERRY for tending and burying a poor man	00400	
To THOMAS HOBSON for Order of the Court	11936	
To Capt. JOHN HAYNIE for covering the Courthouse and nayles	03777	& casque
To Capt. JOHN HAYNIE for work done on the Prison	00200	& casque
To Capt. JOHN HAYNIE for laying out the Prison Rules	00400	& casque
To Capt. JOHN HAYNIE for a Jury of Inquest	00266	& casque
To Casque for 26643 pounds of tobacco	02131	
To Sallary	03761	

- Ordered that the Sheriffe collect it at forty nine pounds of tobacco per poll

p. 320

- At a Court held for Northumberland County the 22d of January 1685/6 Annoque Regni Regis James 2d, 1st &c.

Present

Mr. PETER PRESLEY, SENR.   Mr. NICHOLAS OWEN
Capt. LEONARD HOWSON   Mr. RICHARD KENNER   Justices
Mr. CHARLES LEE   Mr. THOMAS BRERETON
                             Mr. PETER PRESLEY, JUNR.

- JANE SHIRLEY to serve for a bastard JANE SHIRLEY, Servant to Mr. PETER PRESLEY, JUNR. haveing had a bastard Child in the time of her service, it is ordered that she serve her said Master for her said offence according to Act and her punishment remitted her said Master paying her Fine and alsoe ordered that the said Mr. PRESLEY bring JOSEPH WALKER [who ye said wench hath sworne is the Father of the said Child] to the next Court

- Capt. JOHN HAYNIE, Present

- RICE agt LUKE Whereas in November Court last past RICHARD RICE, the Executor of ROBERT PRITT, obteyned Judgment against Mr. EDMUND LUKE for the sume of three hundred ninety pounds of tobacco and casque unlesse the said LUKE should appeare and shew reasons to the contrary, and whereas the said LUKE hath fayled of his appearance and the said RICE hath produced a Bill for the sume dated the 7th of July 1683, Judgment is granted the said RICE, Executor as abovesaid, for the said sume against the said LUKE with costs als Execution

- PEMBERTON agt DOWNING & CORBELL Whereas RICHARD PEMBERTON brought his action into this Court against Mr. JOHN DOWNING and JOHN CORBELL, Securities of RICHARD LAMPREY, the Administrator of BARTHOLOMEW YEAMANS, for the sume of fourteen hundred pounds of tobacco and casque and did produce an Order of this Court dated the 21st of January 1684/5 which the said PEMBERTON obteyned against the Estate of the said YEAMANS in the hands of the said LAMPREY, Administrator as abovesaid, for the said sume, Judgment is granted the said PEMBERTON against the said DOWNING and CORBELL, Securities as abovesaid, for the said sume als Execution

- WMS agt COX The difference depending between THOMAS WILLIAMS on behalfe of his Majestie and MATHEW COX is put to a Jury [vizt]

JAMES AUSTEN	GILBERT HARROLD	THOMAS FLYNT
WILLIAM DAWSON	JOHN HUGHLETT, SENR.	WALTER SIMS
JAMES JOHNSON	JOHN LYSER	HENRY [ ]
GEORGE HAMBLETON	WILLIAM PARKER	RALPH WADDINGTON JUNR

[The Verdict severall words I cannot read. signed by JOHN AUSTEN]

p. 321   Northumberland County Court 22d of January 1685/6

- WILLIAM HARCUM against JOHN LAWRENCE referred to the next Court at the motion of the Defendant

- HANKING agt BRODIE Whereas the last Court Mr. MARK HANKING obteyned Oder against the Sheriffe for four hundred fifty pounds of tobacco and casque, THOMAS ELLIOTT being arrested to that Court and fayled of his appearance to answer the said suit and whereas Mr. ALEXANDER BRODIE, the Securitie of the said ELLIOTT hath appeared and it doth appeare that the said ELLIOTT is indebted to the said HANKING the sume of four hundred and fifty pounds of tobacco and casque due by Account and the said HANKING hath made Oath before Mr. THOMAS HOBSON, SENR. one of his Majties Justices of the Peace for this County, Judgment is confirmed against the said ALEXANDER BRODIE, Securitie as abovesaid, for the said sume with costs of suit als Execution

- Mr. WILLIAM BOGLE against WILLIAM SWETMAN referred to the next Court at the motion of the Defendant

- Mr. WILLIAM HARCUM against WALTER SIMS This suit is dismist

- NEALE agt GRAHAM Whereas DANIELL NEALE was arrested to this Court at the suit of Mr. JOHN GRAHAM and hath fayled of his appearance to prosecute, a non suit is granted the said NEALE against the said GRAHAM with costs and damages according to Law

- HAYNIE agt BADGER Whereas it appeares to this court that NICHOLAS BADGER is indebted to Mr. RICHARD HAYNIE the sume of four hundred fifty pounds of tobacco and casque by Bill under the hand of the said BADGER dated the 3d of June 1684; Judgment is granted to the said HAYNIE against the said BADGER for the said sume with costs als Execution

- ALEXANDER WEATHERSTON against Mr. PHILIP SHAPLEIGH referred to the next Court at the motion of the Defendant

- ANTHONY BENNETT against JAMES EDNEE This suit is dismist CHARLES HARRIS Attourney for ANTHONY BENNETT

- TRESSRY agt SHIRLEY Whereas it appeares to this Court that FRANCES SHIRLEY is indebted to Mr. JAMES TRESSRY the sume of eight hundred sixty six pounds of tobacco and casque by Bill under the hand of the said SHIRLEY dated the 24th of December 1684, Judgment is granted the said TRESSRY against the said SHIRLEY for the said sume with costs of suit als Execution

p. 322   Northumberland County Court 22d of January 1685/6

- Injunction Upon the Petition of FRANCES SHIRLEY, Defendant, an Injunction is granted her for to stop all further proceedings in Common Law untill she have a hearing in Chancery

- RICHARD PEMBERTON against ELIZABETH KEEN Referred to the next Court at the motion of the Defendant

- TRESSRY against CLAUGHTON Whereas JAMES CLAUGHTON was summoned to this Court by a Note left at the suit of Mr. JAMES TRESSRY and hath fayled of his attendance to answer the said suit, an Attachment is award the said TRESSRY against the said CLAUGHTON for twelve hundred pounds of tobacco and casque with costs returnable to the next Court

- LAMBERT agt JONES Judgment is granted WILLIAM LAMBERT

against JAMES JONES for sixteen hundred pounds of tobacco and casque with costs als Execution unlesse the said JONES appeares at the next Court and shews reasons to the contrary

- JEFFERYES Esqr. & COMPA. agt THO: DYER Whereas it appeares to this Court that THOMAS DYER is indebted unto JOHN JEFFERYES Esqr. and COMPANY the sume of four hundred twenty and four pounds of tobacco and casque by a Bill under the hand of the said DYER dated the 31st of July 1685, Judgment is granted the said JOHN JEFFERYES Esqr. against the said DYER for the said sume with costs of suit als Execution

- PEMBERTON agt GREENSTED Whereas it appeares to this Court that WILLIAM GREENSTED is indebted to RICHARD PEMBERTON the sume of four hundred pounds of tobacco and casque by Bill under the hand of the said GREENSTED dated the 21st of May 1685; Judgment is granted the said PEMBERTON against the said GREENSTED for the said sume with costs als Execution

- COPEMAN agt MATHEW. HARRIS Attor: of MATHEW Whereas THOMAS COPEMAN was arrested to this Court at the suit of Capt. THOMAS MATHEW and the said MATHEW hath fayled in due time to file his Declaration, a non suit is granted the said COPEMAN against the said MATHEW with costs and damages according to Law

- JOHNSON agt ALVERSON Whereas JAMES JOHNSON brought his action to this Court against TELEIF ALVERSON for seaventeen hundred and sixty eight pounds of tobacco and casque, and the said ALVERSON hath fayled in his appearance, an Attachment is awarded the said JOHNSON against the Estate of the said ALVERSON returnable to the next Court

p, 323

Northumberland County Court 22d of January 1685/6

- DOROTHY JACKMAN to be brought to Court Whereas the last Court it was ordered that the Sheriffe should take DOROTHY JACKMAN into his custody untill she should give good caution for her appearance this Court and her good behaviour, and whereas the said DOROTHY doth obstinately refuse to comply with the said Order notwithstanding she hath been often requested, it is ordered that MICHAELL VANLANDEGHAM, Constable for the Precinct where the said DOROTHY liveth, take her into safe custody and bring her to the Courthouse tomorrow morning by ten of the clock

- GLASCOCK agt FLOWERS Judgment is granted Mr. THOMAS GLASCOCK against JOHN FLOWERS for the sume of four hundred and fifty pounds of tobacco and casque unlesse the said FLOWERS appeares at the next Court and shews reasons to the contrary

- HARRIS agt THOMAS Whereas HUGH HARRIS brought his action to this Court against the Estate of CHRISTOPHER THOMAS for the sume of eleaven hundred pounds of tobacco and casque, and whereas the said CHRISTOPHER was returned non est inventus an Attachment is granted the said HARRIS against the Estate of the said THOMAS for the said sume with costs als Execution

- BONOWAY agt HUGHLETT Whereas JOHN HUGHLETT, JUNR. who marryed MARY, the Relict of WILLIAM DOWNING, was summoned to this Court by scire facias to shew reasons why Execution shold not issue on a Judgment obteyned against him the 17th day of January 1683/4 by WILLIAM BONOWAY for the sume of six hundred forty and five pounds of tobacco and casque, upon nihil dicit it is ordered that the said former Order be confirmed and that the said HUGHLETT pay ye sume unto the said BONOWAY with costs of suit als Execution

p. 324 Northumberland County Court 22d of January 1685/6

- FLYNT agt CURTIS Whereas THOMAS FLYNT, the Assignee of RICHARD FLYNT, hath brought his action to this Court against Mr. JOHN CURTIS for the sume of twelve hundred pounds of tobaccco and casque, and the said Mr. CURTIS being returned non est inventus upon the Dockett, an Attachment is awarded the said FLYNT against the said CURTIS for the said sume with costs returnable to the next Court

- JOHN LATHERAM against HENRY MAIZE referred to the next Court at the motion of the Defendant RICHARD HAYNIE Attourney for JOHN LATHERAM

- Capt. THO: JONES agt MRS. ELIZABETH, Administrx. of AZRICAM PARKER referred to the next Court

- Ordered that what actions Capt. THOMAS JONES is concerned with be suspended untill the next Court he being sick and not able to come to Court

- Mr. RICHARD ROGERS, present

- HOWSON agt LAWRENCE Whereas an Attachment was awarded Capt. LEONARD HOWSON against the Estate of THOMAS LAWRENCE for five hundred fifteen pounds of tobacco and casque which Attachment is returned executed on a hogshead of tobacco in the hands of Mr. CHARLES LEE, and whereas the said Capt. HOWSON hath made Oath that there is due to him upon the ballance of an Account the sume of four hundred thirty and five pounds of tobacco and casque, Judgment is granted the said Capt. HOWSON against the said LEE for the said hogshead of tobacco als Execution and the said Attachment to continue good against the Estate of the said LAWRENCE for what shall be due besides the said hogshead of tobacco for the satisfaction of the said debt and costs

- PARKER and HARROLD's Fines remitted Whereas WILLIAM PARKER and GILBERT HARROLD were this day fined according to Act being summoned on a Jury to attend the Court and fayled of their appearance, and whereas the said GILBERT HARROLD hath appeared and shewed sufficient reasons for his absence, it is ordered that his Fine be remitted, And whereas the Court hath taken into consideration that the said PARKER hath severall Courts successively attended as a Juror, it is ordered that his Fine be remitted alsoe

- BRODY agt JACKMAN Ordered that DAVID BRODIE be allowed according to Act for three dayes attendance to give in his Evidence in the behalfe of CHARLES JACKMAN against THOMAS DYER

p. 325 Northumberland County Court 22d of January 1685/6

JACKMAN agt DYER The difference depending between CHARLES JACKMAN and THOMAS DYER is referred to a Jury here under written, vizt.

Mr. JAMES AUSTEN	JOHN LYSER	THOMAS HUGHLETT
WILLIAM DAWSON	THOMAS FLYNT	HENRY FLEET
JAMES JOHNSON	RALPH WADDINGTON, JUNR.	THOMAS WEBB
GEORGE HAMBLETON	JOHN HUGHLETT, JUNR.	JOHN HUGHLETT, SENR.

- Verdict The whole Jury agreed and wee doe find for the Plaintiffe that THOMAS DYER hath killed a Cow of CHARLES JACKMAN belonging to the Estate of

THOMAS FLOWERS without the consent of the CHARLES JACKMAN but with the consent of his Wife   JAMES AUSTEN

- <u>Judgment</u> Ordered upon this Verdict that THOMAS DYER return in consideration of the said Cow and Calfe by the last of Aprill and pay costs of suit als Execution

- <u>THO: DYER to execute Bond for his good behaviour</u> CHARLES JACKMAN haveing in Court sworne that he goeth in feare of his life of THOMAS DYER, it is ordered that the Sheriffe take the said DYER into safe custody untill he gives good caution for his good behaviour

- Ordered that the next Court be the 3d Wednesday in February

p. 326

- <u>At a Court held for Northumberland County the 24th day of February 1685/6</u>   Present

Mr. PETER PRESLEY, SENR.   Mr. THOMAS BRERETON
Mr. NICHOLAS OWEN   Mr. PETER PRESLEY, JUNR.   Justices
Capt. JOHN HAYNIE   Mr. RICHARD ROGERS
Mr. RICHARD KENNER

- <u>HOBSON to officiate in the Clerk's place</u> Whereas THOMAS HOBSON, JUNR., Clerk of this Court, is sick whereby he is forced to be absent, it is ordered that Mr. GERVASE HATTFIELD [who is now sworne] officiate the said place for this present Court

- <u>MARGT. SMYTH has bastard Child</u> Whereas MARGARETT SMYTH, Servant to Mr. ROBERT SECH, was brought to this Court for haveing a bastard Child and has sworne that it was gotten at sea by LYMON PICKMORE, Chirurgeon, and whereas the said SECH hath in Court assumed to pay the Fine, it is ordered that her punishment be remitted

- <u>PRESLEY agt OWEN</u> Whereas Mr. NICHOLAS OWEN the Executor of Mr. JOHN JULIAN, Chirurgeon, brought his action to this Court against Mr. PETER PRESLEY, JUNR. and produced an account wherein he makeing the said PRESLEY debtor the sume of twelve hundred pounds and casque, and the Defendant pleading the Act of Limittations declaring Chirurgeon Accounts not pleadable six months after the decease or the recovery of the person to whome the medicines are administered, it is ordered that the suit be dismist with costs. RICHARD HAYNIE Attourney for Mr. PETER PRESLEY, JUNR. .

- <u>MARMADUKE agt FARMER als MOTTROM</u> Whereas it appears to this Court by a Bill under the hand and seale of Major JOHN MOTTROM dated the 29th of November 1683 that the said Major MOTTROM in his lifetime stood indebted to MILES MARMADUKE the sume of ten pounds sterling, and one pound, four shillings sterling by Account to which the said MILES hath made Oath and that he had received noe part of sattisfaction for the said Bill as alsoe four hundred fifty pounds of tobacco and casque as appeares by the Oath of ROBERT LAWSON; Judgment is granted the said MILES MARMADUKE against MRS. ANNE FARMER Trustee for the said Estate for the sume of eleaven pounds, four shillings sterling and four hundred fifty pounds of tobacco with costs als Execution

Northumberland County Court 24th of February 1685/6

p. 327

- **PEMBERTON agt KEEN** Whereas it appeares to this Court that MRS. ELIZABETH KEEN is indebted unto Mr. RICHARD PEMBERTON the sume of three hundred fifty pounds of tobacco and casque by Account to which the said PEMBERTON hath made Oath; Judgment is granted the said PEMBERTON against MRS. KEEN for the said sume with costs of suit als Execution

- **GLASCOCK agt FLOWERS** Whereas it appeares to this Court by Bill under the hand of JOHN FLOWERS dated the 19th of 8br 1684 that the said FLOWERS is indebted unto Mr. THOMAS GLASCOCK, the Executor of Mr. ROGER WALTERS, the sume of four hundred fifty pounds of tobacco and casque, Judgment is granted the said GLASCOCK, Executor as abovesaid, against the said FLOWERS for the said sume with costs als Execution

November the 17th 1686 Execution issue on this Order against the body of JOHN FLOWERS

- **LATHERAM agt MAIZE RICHARD HAYNIE Attourney of JOHN LATHERAM** Whereas it appeares to this Court that Mr. HENRY MAIZE standeth indebted unto JOHN LATHERAM in the just quantitie of four hundred seaventeen pounds of tobacco and casque; Judgment is granted the said LATHERAM against the said MAIZE for the said sume with costs als Execution

- **JONES agt PARKER** Whereas it appeares to this Court that ELIZABETH the Administratrix of AZRIKAM PARKER is indebted unto Capt. THOMAS JONES the sume of nine hundred pounds of tobacco and casque the said JONES haveing in Court produced an Account of fees amounting to the said sume to which he hath made Oath and alsoe two Warrants of Attourney impowering him to appeare in all causes for him in the County Court of Northumberland and LANCASTER. Judgment is granted the said JONES against the said ELIZABETH, Administratrix as abovesaid, for the said sume out of the Estate of the said AZRIKAM als Execution

Northumberland County Court 24th of February 1685/6

p. 328

- **HARCUM agt LAWRENCE** The difference depending between Mr. WILLIAM HARCUM and JOHN LAWRENCE concerning Land is referred to a Jury whose names are here subscribed, [vizt]

Mr. THOMAS FERNE	Mr. DENNIS EYES	Mr. JOHN SOUTHERLAND
Mr. THOMAS WEBB	Mr. JOHN CORBELL	Mr. WALTER SIMS
Mr. ROBERT SECH	Mr. JOHN LYSER	Mr. JOHN EVANS
Mr. JOHN WEBB	Mr. JOHN WALTERS	Mr. WILLIAM CAMELL

- **Verdict** Wee of the Jury are agreed and doe find for the Defenant
THOMAS FERNE

- **Judgment** A non suit is granted JOHN LAWRENCE against Mr. WILLIAM HARCUM with costs and damages according to Law
CHARLES HARRIS the Attourney of Mr. WILLIAM HARCUM

- **HARCUM agt BRIDGMAN, Securitie of JONES** The difference between Mr. WILLIAM HARCUM and THOMAS BRIDGMAN, the Securitie of THOMAS JONES, concerning a Negro pretended by the said HARCUM to be killed by the said JONES, is refered to the underwritten Jury Mr. THOMAS FERNE &c.

- **Verdict** Wee of the Jury are all agreed and cannot find that the Negro within mentioned dyed by the blows given by THOMAS JONES
THOMAS FERNE

NORTHUMBERLAND COUNTY ORDER BOOK, 1678-1698 -101-

- <u>Judgment</u> A non suit is granted THOMAS BRIDGMAN, the Securitie of THOMAS JONES, against Mr. WILLIAM HARCUM with costs and damages according to Law
    - RICHARD HAYNIE Attourney for THOMAS BRIDGMAN
    - CHARLES HARRIS, Attourney for Mr. WILLIAM HARCUM
    - <u>MRS. ANNE GAYLARD against THOMAS WINTERS and THOMAS WILLIAMS</u> referred to the next Court at the motion of the Defendants

p. 329 <u>Northumberland County Court 24th of February 1685/6</u>
- <u>MELTON agt JACKMAN</u> Whereas it appeares to this Court by Bill under the hand of THOMAS TOWERS dated the 19th of May 1682 and an Account [to which MICHAELL MELTON hath made Oath] that the said TOWERS in his lifetime stood indebted unto the said MELTON the sume of four hundred twenty pounds of tobacco and casque; the said MELTON haveing sworne that he had never received any part of sattisfaction for the said debt; and alsoe THOMAS DYER haveing upon Oath declared that he heard THOMAS TOWERS [in his lifetime] desire his Wife to pay that debt to the said MELTON, Judgment is granted the said MELTON against CHARLES JACKMAN, who marryed the Relict and Widdow of THOMAS TOWERS for the said sume out of the said TOWERS's Estate als Execution
    - <u>CRALLE agt CROUCH</u> Whereas an Attachment was awarded Mr. JOHN CRALLE against the Estate of SIMON CROUCH for the sume of one hundred seaventy pounds of tobacco and casque which Attachment was returned executed on soe much in the hands of JAMES GENN, and whereas the said CRALLE hath made his said debt appeare due, Judgment is granted him against the said GENN for the said tobacco soe attached als Execution
    - <u>WORMLEY agt KNIGHT</u> Whereas CHRISTOPHER WORMLEY Esqr. brought his action to this Court against Mr. PETER KNIGHT for the sume of fourteen hundred pounds of tobacco and casque and the said KNIGHT being returned by a Note left and fayling of his appearance to answer the said suit, an Attachment is awared the said CHRISTOPHER WORMLEY, Esqr., against the Estate of the said KNIGHT with costs of suit returnable to the next Court

p. 330 <u>Northumberland County Court 24th of February 1685/6</u>
- <u>MATHEW agt KNIGHT</u> Whereas Capt. THOMAS MATHEW brought his action to this Court against Mr. PETER KNIGHT for the sume of four hundred pounds of tobacco and casque, who haveing fayled of his appearance to answer the said suit, and being returned upon the Dockett by a Note left, an Attachment is awarded the said MATHEW against the said KNIGHT's Estate with costs returnable to the next Court CHARLES HARRIS Attourney for Capt. MATHEW
    - The Court adjournes untill tomorrow morning at eight o'clock

- <u>Die the 25th February 1685/6</u> Present
Mr. PETER PRESLEY, SENR.   Mr. RICHARD KENNER
Capt. LEONARD HOWSON   Mr. PETER PRESLEY, JUNR.
Capt. JOHN HAYNIE   Justices

- **LAMBERT agt JONES** Whereas last Court WILLIAM LAMBERT obteyed Judgment against JAMES JONES for the sume of sixteen hundred pounds of tobacco and casque with costs als Execution unlesse the said JONES this Court should appeare and shew reasons to the contrary, and whereas the said JONES hath now fayled of his appearance and the said LAMBERT hath proved the said debt by Bill under the hand of the said JONES bearing date the 28th of December 1682, It is ordered that the former Order be confirmed with costs als Execution

March ye 1st 1685/6 Execution issued on this Order against the said JAMES JONES

- **SPAN agt CHAMPION** Whereas JOHN CHAMPION was summoned to Court by a Note left at the suit of Mr. CUTHBERT SPAN for the sume of four hundred ninety pounds of tobacco and casque, and the said CHAMPION haveing fayled of his appearance to answer, an Attachment is awarded the said Mr. SPAN against the said CHAMPION's Estate with costs returnable to the next Court

p. 331 **Northumberland County Court, 25th of February 1685/6**

- **WADDING & POPE agt the Sheriffe** Whereas PETER BYRAM was arrested to this Court at the suit of THOMAS WADDING, JOHN HOCKLEY and [   ] POPE for the sume of eight hundred twenty pounds of tobacco and casque and the said BYRAM haveing fayled of his appearance to answer the said suit Judgment is granted the said WADDING, HOCKLEY and POPE against Mr. WILLIAM LEE, Sheriffe, for the said sume with costs and damages according to Law

- **LAWRENCE agt FLEET** Judgment is granted Mr. JOHN LAWRENCE against Mr. HENRY FLEET for the sume of nine hundred thirty and six pounds of tobacco and casque with costs als Execution unlesse the said FLEET appeares at next Court and shews reasons to the contrary

- **CARTEE agt CURTIS** Whereas it appeares to this Court by Bill under the hand of JOHN CURTIS dated the 10th of July 1684, that the said CURTIS is indebted unto Mr. DENNIS CARTEE, Assignee of JOHN FLOYD, the sume of six hundred pounds of tobacco and casque, Judgment is granted the said CARTEE against the said CURTIS for the said sume with costs als Execution

- **Mr. ALEXANDER ENGLISH Attourney of Mr. JAMES MARSHALL against THOMAS INGRAM** referred to the next Court

- **MRS. ELIZABETH PARKER, Administratrix of Mr. AZRIKAM PARKER against JOHN EVANS** referred to the next Court at the motion of the Defendant

- **ROBERT PRICHARD against STEPHEN WELLS** referred to the next Court

- **HOBSON agt FLEET** An Attachment is awarded THOMAS HOBSON, SENR. against the Estate of Mr. HENRY FLEET for the sume of eight hundred forty six pounds of tobacco and casque with costs returnable to the next Court

p. 332 **Northumberland County Court, 25th of February 1685/6**

- **HOBSON agt FLOWERS** Whereas THOMAS HOBSON, SENR. brought his action to this Court against JOHN FLOWERS for nine hundred ninety seaven pounds of tobacco and casque and whereas the said FLOWERS hath fayled of his appearance to answer the said suit, being returned a Note left upon the Dockett, an Attachment is awarded the said HOBSON against the Estate of the said

NORTHUMBERLAND COUNTY ORDER BOOK, 1678-1698   -103-

JOHN FLOWERS for the said sume with costs returnable to the next Court

- HAYNIE agt WEATHERSTONE Whereas Capt. JOHN HAYNIE brought his action to this Court against ALEXANDER WEATHERSTONE for the sume of two thousand thirty nine pounds of tobacco and casque and whereas the said WEATHERSTONE was returned by a Note left upon the Dockett and hath fayled of his appearance to answer the said suit, an Attachment is awarded the said HAYNIE against the said WEATHERSTONE's Estate for the said sume with costs returnable to the next Court

- JONES agt the Sheriffe Whereas Mr. GEORGE BLEDSOE was arrested to this Court at the suit of Mr. THOMAS JONES for the sume of two thousand pounds of tobacco and casque and hath fayled of his appearance to answer the said suit, Judgment is granted the said JONES against Mr. WILLIAM LEE, Sheriffe, for the said sume with costs and damages according to LAW

- Mr. CHRISTOPHER NEALE against Mr. CHARLES JACKMAN referred to the next Court

- HARRIS agt KNIGHT [May 3d 1686 Execution issued on this Order against Mr. KNIGHT's Estate] Whereas Mr. PETER KNIGHT was summoned to this Court by scire facias to shew reasons why Execution should not issue on a Judgment obteyned against him at the suit of Mr. JOHN HARRIS for the sume of nine hundred ninety eight pounds of tobacco and casque dated the 18th of June 1679 upon a nihil dicit, it is ordered that the said Judgment be renewed against the said Mr. KNIGHT for the sume of four hundred ninety pounds of tobacco and casque it being what remaines due to the said HARRIS out of the said Judgment with costs als Execution

- Mr. WILLIAM HARCUM on the behalfe of HANNAH, his Wife against THOMAS SMYTH referred to the next Court at the motion of the Defendant

p. 333 Northumberland County Court 25th of February 1685/6

- RICHARD NELMES agt JOSIAS LONG referred to the next Court at the motion of the Defendant

- CORBELL agt FLYNT Whereas it appeares to this Court by a Bill under the hand of RICHARD FLYNT dated the 11th of January 1684/5 that the said FLYNT is indebted unto JOHN CORBELL the sume of five hundred eighty seaven pounds of tobacco and casque; Judgment is granted the said CORBELL against the said FLYNT for the said sume with costs als Execution

- Mr. CHRISTOPHER NEALE against EDWARD WHITE referred to the next Court

- HAYNIE agt SMYTH Whereas it appeares to this Court by Bill under the hand of RICHARD SMYTH dated the 9th of March 1684/5 that the said SMYTH is indebted unto Capt. JOHN HAYNIE the sume of four hundred thirty three pounds of tobacco and casque, Judgment is granted the said HAYNIE against the said SMYTH for the said sume with costs als Execution

- NEALE agt DYER THOMAS DYER confesseth Judgment for the payment of four hundred sixty pounds of tobacco and casque unto Mr. CHRISTOPHER NEALE with costs of suit als Execution

- CLARK to give caution for his appearance at next Court Ordered that WILLIAM CLARK give good caution for his appearance at the next Court and answer what shall be objected to against him concerning the Estate of FRANCES, Orphant of FRANCIS BRITTAINE, deceased, and be accomptable for the same

- EATON Securitie for CLARK RICHARD EATON obligeth himselfe in the penall sume of tenn thousand pounds of tobacco and casque that the abovesaid WILLIAM CLARK shall make his personall appearance at the next Court held for this County and give an Account of the Estate of FRANCES BRITTAINE

- MATHEW agt COPEMAN Ordered that THOMAS COPEMAN be arrested he makeing his appearance at the next Court and answer the suit of Capt. THOMAS MATHEW

p. 334 Northumberland County Court 25th of February 1685/6

- DYER and Others to appeare at next Court Ordered that the Sheriffe take THOMAS DYER, CHRISTOPHER NEWTON and DOROTHY JACKMAN into his safe custdy untill they give good caution for their appearance at the next Court to answer what shall be there objected against them and stand to and abide the award of the Court

- Mr. THOMAS HOBSON against MRS. JANE WILDEY referred to the next Court

- Mr. THOMAS JONES against WILLIAM BROWN referred to the next Court

- DYER to give caution for good behaviour Whereas the last Court CHARLES JACKMAN swore the peace against THOMAS DYER whereon it was ordered that the Sheriff should take him into safe custody untill he gave caution for his good behaviour which the said DYER accordingly did untill the next Court and noe longer, it is therefore ordered that he find further securitie on the said behalfe in the penall sume of twenty pounds sterling payable to Our Soveraigne Lord the King and that the Sheriffe have him in custody untill he performes the same

- Ordered the the Court be the 3d Wednesday in March

- Att a Court held for Northumberland County the 17th of March 1685/6
        Present
Mr. NICHOLAS OWEN   Mr. RICHARD KENNER
Capt. JOHN HAYNIE   Mr. PETER PRESLEY JUNR. Justices

- There not appearing Magistrates to hold a Court soe adjourned to the 1st Wednesday in Aprill

- Att a Court held for Northumberland County the 7th of Aprill 1686
        Present
Mr. THOMAS HOBSON, SENR.   Mr. PHILIP SHAPLEIGH
Mr. NICHOLAS OWEN   Mr. PETER PRESLEY JUNR.
Capt. JOHN HAYNIE   Justices

- JAMES YOUNG Levy free Upon the Petition of JAMES YOUNG an old decreped person it is ordered that he be freed from paying the County Levys

NORTHUMBERLAND COUNTY ORDER BOOK, 1678-1698 -105-

p. 335   Northumberland County Court 7th of April 1686

- **Severall Servant judged** MARY AUBOURNE, Servant to MRS. ANNE FARMER is adjudged to be eleaven yeares of age; ELIZABETH PRICE, Servant to THOMAS FLYNT is adjuged to be seaven yeares of age; ROBERT PHILLIPS, Servant to Mr. JOHN CRALLE is adjudged to be eight yeares of age; DAVID ROBERTS, Servant to WILLIAM and JOHN KEEN is adjuged to be fifteen yeares of age; JOHN [? A---] Servant to PETER COUTANCEAU is adjudged to be thirteen yeares of age and all ordered to serve their respective Masters according to Act

- **SHAPLEIGH agt BLYGHT** Whereas Mr. PHILIP SHAPLEIGH had an Attachment awarded him against the Estate of Mr. JAMES BLIGHT for the sume of four hundred forty and four pounds of tobacco and casque, which Attachment was returned executed on a hogshead of tobacco in the hands of Mr. JOHN NICKLES, and whereas the said SHAPLEIGH hath produced an Account amounting to the said sume to which he hath made Oath, Judgment is granted the said SHAPLEIGH for the hogshead of tobacco attached against the said NICKLES als Execution

- **WADDY's Will proved** Upon the Petition of JAMES WADDY a Probate is granted him of the Last Will and Testament of his deceased Father, JOHN WADDY, the Will being proved by the Oath of ELIZABETH [? ELPHANT] one of the witnesses of the said Will, the other witness being dead

- **DAVIS's Certificate to the Assembly** Certificate is granted JOHN DAVIS to the Assembly for two hundred acres of Land for the transportation of four persons into this Collony [vizt]

JOHN DAVIS SENR.   HESTER DAVIS
JOHN DAVIS JUNR.   MATHEW DAVIS   in all four

- **SHAPLEIGH's Certificate to the Assembly** Certificate is granted Mr. PHILIP SHAPLEIGH for three hundred acres of land for the transportation of six persons into this Collony, [vizt]

MATHEW BENHAM   STEPHEN CLARKERETT   LAWRENCE OKEANE
KATHERINE LONGHAM   DANIELL LEHEGE   HUMPHREY VEALE

p. 336   Northumberland County Court 7th of April 1686

- ANNE GAYLARD against THOMAS WINTER referred to the next Court

- **KETTLE agt COUTANCEAU** Whereas SUSANNA KETTLE, Servant to Mr. JOHN COUTANCEAU, petitioned this Court that she might be free she haveing served her full time out, it being four yeares and whereas RICHARD TIDWELL did upon Oath in Court declare that he heard Mr. MICHAELL CHIN [who was the person that sold the said SUSANNA unto the said COUTANCEAU] says that the said SUSANNA had but four yeares to serve, and RACHELL YARRET haveing likewise upon Oath declared that she heard Mr. THOMAS FRIEND say that the said SUSANNA had but four yeares to serve, it is ordered that the said SUSANNA be free and that the said COUTANCEAU forthwith pay her Corne and Cloathes accustomed with costs of suit als Execution. May the 21st 1686, Execution issued on this Order against the body of JOHN COUTANCEAU

- **Grand Jury convened** Whereas this day the Grand Jury of Inquest are by Act of Assembly appointed to appear at the Court and give in their Presentments and seaven of them being absent [vizt] JOHN COLES, RICHARD PEMBERTON, CHRISTOPHER GARLINGTON, JOHN NICKLES, JOHN CLAUGHTON

ABRAHAM JOYCE and EDMUND BASYE, upon the Petition of Mr. THOMAS JONES, the King's Attourney, it is ordered that PATRICK POLLICK, EDWARD TIPTON, JOHN BRYANT, JOSIAS LONG and JOHN LAWRENCE being all summoned and sworn in Court supply their vacancy

- DYER to give Bond for good behaviour Ordered that the Sheriffe forthwith take THOMAS DYER into safe custody untill he gives Bond in the sume of forty pounds sterling with sufficient caution for his further good behaviour and in the mean time to abstaine from the company of DOROTHY, the Wife of CHARLES JACKMAN

- DOROTHY JACKMAN to goe to JAMES CITTIE Whereas the Grand Jury of Inquest for this County found two Bills of Indictment against DOROTHY JACKMAN, one for her treason, the other for petty larcency, it is ordered that the Sheriffe forthwith convey her to JAMES CITTIE and take care she appeare at the fourth day of the next Generall Court and

p. 337 Northumberland County Court 7th of April 1686
that the witnesses that were sworne in this Court appeare there the said day and give in their Evidence in the behalfe of his Majtie and whereas the Generall Court is soe neare that a Writt of habere facias cannot possibly be timely issued for the summoning a Jury of the Vicinage, it is ordered that six persons of the Neighbourhood [vist] HENRY DAWSON, RICHARD TAYLOR, WILLIAM GREENSTED, RICHARD COX, HUGH STATHEM and CLOUD TULLOS goe with the said DOROTHY to the said Generall Court

- The Court adjourned to the 3d Wednesday in May

[Northumberland County Order Book 1678-1698 will continue in another book, beginning on page 337 with the Court held the 19th day of May 1686]

INDEX, NORTHUMBERLAND ORDERS 1683-1686

ADAMS.
   Thomas -5, 35, 36, 52, 53,
ADDAMSON.
   Jeffery -54,
ALDEN.
   William 81,
ALDRIDGE.
   Clement -32, 45,
ALGOOD.
   Edward, deced. [Will proved -50], 75, 79, 80,
   Elizabeth, Exrx. of Edward, deced. -50, [m. John Lyser-79],
ALLEN.
   39,
   Teage -39, 48, 51, 61, 62, [Rioter -75], 82, 86,
ALLENSON.
   Walter 34, 35,
   William 35, 57,
ALTHORP
   John [imported -48],
ALVERSON.
   Teleif -77, 97,
ARMAGER.
   William, Capt. -57, 63,
ARNER.
   John -7,
ASHTON.
   Henry -82,
   Thomas, [Levy free -16],
   Thomas [appt. Constable -31],
ATKINS.
   Alexander -27, 34,
   John -1, 11, 24,
ATTISON.
   John -27, 28,
AUBOURNE.
   Mary, Servant to Mrs. Anne Farmer 105,
AUSTEN.
   James [Cert. for woolen cloth -4], [Cert. for Pistolls lost -17], 22, 23, 61, 63, 69, 71-73, 86, 89, 90, 95, 98, 99,
   James, Admr. of Thomas Morris, deced. -79,

BADGER.
   Nicholas 8, 95,
BAGNELL.
   Roger, deced. -8,
BAKER.
   James -7,
   John -51,
   Thomas -22, 27, 33, 38, 76, 84,
BANKES.
   Thomas 53,
BARNES.
   Edward -27, [Levy free -31],
   Thomas -6, 9, 18, 34, 36, 42, 51, 52, 62, 69, 71-73, 75, 77, 79, 86, 91, 94,
BARRATT.
   George -6, 13, 39, 49, 53,
BARRY
   William -29, 88, 93,

BASHAW.
   William 16, 47, 66, 67,
BATCHELER.
   John 50,
BASYE.
   Edmund -106.
BAYLES.
   Christopher [apptd. Constable -1],
BAYLEY.
   John -10,
   Robert -8,
BEACHAM.
   Daniel 81,
BEANE.
   William -76,
   William, Exr. Welthran Bonas, deced -37,
BEE,
   John -35, 91,
BEECH.
   Thomas -2, 10,
BENHAM.
   Mathew [imported -105],
BENNETT.
   Anthony -96,
   George -83,
   Robert, Capt. -67-69, 92,
   Thomas, deced. 52,
BENTLEY.
   Henry -21, 25, 34, 63,
BERRY.
   Israell [imported -47],
   Thomas -17, 43, 95,
   William -80,
BESOUTH als WOODAMORE
   William, Servant to George Knight -72, 73,
BETTS
   Charles, Brother of William -67,
   William -67,
BEVERLEY.
   John -54,
   Robert -54,
BIRD.
   John -84,
BLACKERBY.
   James 57,
   Jane -43,
BLACKSTON
   Susanna, Admr. of John Jones, deced. -44,
BLAGG.
   Abraham -12,
BLEDSOE,
   George -5, 40, 41, 44, 52, 80, 81, 84, 94, 103,
BLIGHT.
   James -105,
BOGGAS
   Henry [apptd. Constable -1], 16, 21,
   Henry, deced. [Will proved -51],
   Ruth, Exrx. of Henry, deced. -51,
BOGLE.
   William -96,
BONAS.
   Anne, Dau. of Welthran, deced. -37,

BONAS [contd.]
  Elizabeth, Dau. of Welthran, deced. -27,
  Robert, Son of Welthran deced. -37,
  Welthran, deced. [Will proved -37],
BOND.
  Henry -29,
BONNER.
  Andrew [Levy free -32], 35,
BONOWAY.
  William -23, 69, 97, 98,
BOONE.
  Francis -74,
BOURNE.
  John -48,
  William -47, 50,
BOWIN.
  John -91,
BOWYER.
  Thomas, Servant to John Nichols -2,
BRADLEY.
  Anne, Exrx. of Richard, deced. 11,
  Anne, Wife of Robert, Dau of Robert Bradshaw deced. -65, 66,
  Richard [apptd. Constable -1],
  Richard, deced. [Will proved -11],
  Robert [m. Anne Dau. of Robert Bradshaw, deced. -65], 66.
BRADSHAW.
  Robert 32, 33, 66.
  Temperance, deced. -65, 66.
BRAYDON.
  Richard [Rioter -75, 81, 86],
BRERETON.
  Thomas 45, 57,
  Thomas, Gent. [Justice -51],
  Thomas, Son & Exr. of Collo. Thomas deced. -33, 34, 88,
  Thomas, Collo. -2, 3, 5, 7, 8, 16,
  Thomas, Collo. deced [Will proved -33, 34, 57, 88,
BREWER.
  Thomas -22, 27, 30, 33, 36, 91,
  Thomas, deced. [Will proved -51],
  Thomas, Exr. of Thomas, deced. -51,
BRIDGMAN.
  Thomas 90, 100, 101,
BRITTAINE.
  Frances -47, 87, 104,
  Francis, deced. -87, 104,
BRODIE.
  Alexander 46, 92, 96,
  David -98,
BROWNE.
  Henry 60,
  Thomas [Rioter -75, 76, 86], 94,
  William -104,
BRYANT.
  John -80, 88, 92, 106,
  Katharine [imported -48],
BRYERLY / BRYERY
  Frances, Exrx. of Robert deced. -60,
  Robert -12, 16, 21,
  Robert, deced. [Will proved -60],

BUCKLEY.
  Samuel -37,
BURBURROUGHS
  Thomas 72, 73,
BURBURY.
  Thomas -3,
BURGESS.
  Richard [Levy free -1],
BUTLER.
  John 46,
BYRAM.
  Abraham -26,
  Peter -7, 10, 21, [m. Anne Exrx. of Samuel Goche, deced -37], 38-40, 47, 49, 55, 59, 61, 63, 69, 71, 72, 75, 86, 90, 102,

CAMMELL.
  William [Cert. for Linen -1, 4], 100,
CANTWELL.
  Henry 66,
CARTEE
  Dennis -37, 50, 66, 80, 90, 102,
CARTER.
  Dennis -8, 29, 43,
  Thomas [Master of Ketch "Susanna of Boston" -25], ,
CHAMBERLAIN
  Robert [Surveyor -5], 21,
CHAMBERS
  Mary Servant to Richard Hull -5,
CHAMPION
  John -7, 13, 15, 41, 45, 46, 68, 74, 84, 102,
CHANDLER.
  Thomas -82,
CHARLES.
  Henry [imported -21],
CHERRY POINTE
  -1, 14, 31, 60,
CHEWNING.
  Thomas -27, 34, 41, 46,
CHICACONE
  -1, 60,
CHILTON.
  Edward 23,
CHIN.
  Michael -105,
CHURCHILL.
  Samuel -1,
CLARK.
  John -82, 83, 88, 89, 93,
  William -47, 103, 104,
CLARKERETT.
  Stephen [imported -105],
CLAUGHTON
  James -3, 5-7, 9, 14, 19, 20, 28, 32, 45, 82, 89, 96,
  John 16, 42, 105,
COCKERELL.
  John 3, 20, 57,
CODD.
  St. Leger, Collo. -35, 37,
COLES.
  Cornelius 89, 90,

INDEX, NORTHUMBERLAND ORDERS 1683-1686

COLES [contd.]
  John [apptd. Constable -1], 53, 57, 67, 84, 105,
COLLINS
  Thomas 87,
CONDON.
  Ann, Exrx. of Edmund, deced. -50,
  Edmund deced [Will proved -50],
CONOWAY./ CONWAY
  Edward -6, 9,
  Edwin 18, 25, 27, 38, 42, 68,
CONSTANCE./ CONSTANT
  Peter -18, [apptd. Constable -60], 88,
COOPER.
  George, Capt. -17, 23, 45, 63,
COPEMAN.
  Thomas -90, 94, 97, 104,
COPPAGE.
  William 21, 73,
CORBELL.
  John -5, 39, 59, 86, 89, 95, 100, 103,
CORBETT.
  John -75,
COSSENS./ COZENS
  John -41, 43, 44,
COTMAN.
  Benjamin -42, 47,
  Elizabeth, Wife of Benjamin, Dau. of William and Mary Thomas, deced. -42,
COTOON.
  Anthony Servant to Clement Latimore -48,
COUNTIES
  Lancaster -100,
  Rappahannock -86,
COUNTY LEVY
  16, 42, 43, 94, 95,
COUTANSHEW./ CONTANCEAN
  John -5, 12, 78, 86, 94, 105,
  John Junr. -51,
  John Senr. -51,
  Peter -105,
COX.
  James, Servant to John Bowrne -48,
  Mathew -32, 95,
  Richard -36, 37, 49, 76, 79, 86, 93, 106,
  Richard, Admr. of George Knight, deced. -82,
CRALLE.
  John 59, 65, 90, 94, 101,
CRANE.
  Margarett, Servant to Thomas Williams -60,
CRAVEN
  John -63, 86,
CROST.
  John, Servant to Peter Maxeell -48,
CROUCH.
  Symon -65, 101,
CURTIS
  John -15, 17, 53, 55, 67, 70, 78, 80, 90, 98, 102,

DACRES.
  Charles 60,
DALE.
  Edward 41, 45,
DAMERON.
  Bartholomew 22,
  George 65, 66, 69, 71-73,
DAVIS.
  Hester [imported -105],
  John, [Certificate of land -105],
  John Junr. [imported -105],
  John Senr. [imported -105],
  Mathew [imported -105],
  Thomas [Levy free -31],
DAWKINS.
  George -17, 18,
DAWSON.
  Henry -5, 21, 64, 106,
  John 21,
  William 52, 64, 71-73, 95, 98,
DEBRIE
  James -62,
DELABRIE
  John -75,
DERMOTT
  Owen -42, 52, 53, 71, 89,
DIAMOND.
  Nicholas -94,
DONALDSON.
  John -62,
DONAUGH
  Patrick [Rioter -75, 79, 86], 93,
DONAWAY.
  John -17, 39,
DOOLY.
  Daniel [imported -48],
DOWNING.
  John 17, [Cert. for Land -21], [Cert. for cloth -30], 33, 53, 86, 89, 95,
  John, Churchwarden 35,
  Mary, Exrx. of William Junr. deced. -1, 11, [m. John Hughlett Junr. -23], 97,
  Margarett, Exrx. of William deced. -9, [m. Edward Tipton -26],
  William -49, 86,
  William, deced [Will proved - 9], 26, 97,
  William Junr. -1, 11, 23,
DRAKE.
  Philip -8, 56,
DRAPER.
  William -62,
DUKE.
  Jane, Orphan bound out -30,
  John -92,
  John, Orphan of Sylas bound out -17,
  Mary, Orphan bound out -30,
  Sylas -14,
  Sylas, deced. -17,
DUNNE.
  Walter -4,
DYER.
  Thomas 36, 42, 97, 98, 99, 101, 103, 104, 106,

EATON.
  Richard -104,

ECOCK.
  Thomas [imported -48],
EDGAR.
  John 50,
EDNEE
  James -70, 78, 85, 92, 96,
ELLIOTT.
  George [Levy free -31],
  Thomas 43, 47, 48, 58, 62, 67, 89, 96,
ENGLISH
  Alexander -80, 102,
  John 15,
EUSTACE
  John [apptd. Constable -1], 53,
EVANS.
  John -12, 47, 53, 68, 70, 73, 78, 85, 86, 89, 90, 100, 102,
  Thomas -8, 10, 63,
EVES.
  William -69, 71-73, 86, 89, 90,
"EXETOR LODGE"
  House of John Rice -43,
EYES / EYSE
  Dennis 11-14, 34, 35, 100,

FALLONS,
  Charles 3,
FARIGON.
  John [imported -21],
FARMER
  Anne, Widow of William deced. -85, 99, 105,
  William 54, 63,
  William deced. -77, 78, 85,
FARNEFOLD.
  John -12, 54. 55, 58,
FARRINGTON.
  John -34,
  Richard 12, 13, 33, 34, 46,
FERNE
  Thomas 100,
FIELDING.
  Ambrose, deced -7,
  Edward Admr. of Ambrose, deced. -7,
  Richard -8,
FISHER.
  William -73,
FITZHUGH.
  Collo. -83,
  William 89,
FLEET.
  Elizabeth -5,
  Henry -83, 88, 89, 96, 102,
FLOOKER / FLUKER
  David -7, 10,
FLOWERS.
  John -64, 66, 71-73, 75, 83, 86, 89, 90, 97, 100, 102, 103,
  John, Admr. of William deced. -60, 61,
  Thomas -89,
  William -38, 57, 58,
  William, deced. -60, 83,

FLOYD.
  David 53,
  John -47, 80, 90, 102,
FLYNT.
  Peter -24, 64, 66, 89, 89,
  Peter Son of Richard, deced. -25,
  Peter, Admr. of John Knott, deced. -1, 7,
  Richard -19, 22-26, 35, 37, 43-45, 49, 61, 63, 81, 88, 90, 98, 103,
  Richard, deced. -25,
  Thomas 32, 45, 49, 95, 98, 105,
  Thomas, Son of Richard, deced. -25,
FORD.
  John [m. Aunt of Mary Morton -9], 55,
FOSTER.
  John, Servant to Henry Metcalfe -84,
FOWLER.
  James -49,
FOX.
  William -57,
FREEMAN
  John -65,
FRIEND.
  Thomas -105,

GAMMONDS.
  Philip [imported -48],
GARLINGTON.
  Christopher -27, 39, 41, 53, 58, 61, 64, 65, 94, 105,
GAWLER.
  Henry -51, 52,
GAYLARD.
  Anne, Mrs. -30, 34, 101, 105,
  Anne, Admrx. of James, deced. -87,
  James, deced. -87,
GENESIS.
  Ezekiel -4, 22, 29,
  Ezekiel, deced. [Will proved -32], 37, 40, 41, 53, 58,
  Rebecca, Wife of Ezekiel, an Orphan of John Shaw, deced. -4,
GENN / GINN
  James -37, 43. 94, 101,
GEORGE.
  Elizabeth 34,
  Elizabeth, Admrx. of Thomas, deced.-36, 42, 79, 86,
  Thomas -23, 85,
  Thomas, deced -36, 42-44, 79, 86,
GERRARD.
  Elizabeth Admrx. of Samuel, deced. -14, 19, 22, 26, 29, 41, 43, 49, 71,
  Greves 16,
  Samuel -5,
  Samuel deced -14, 19, 22, 29, 41, 49, 71,
GIBBONS.
  Edmund 12,
GLASCOCK.
  Thomas -66, 75, 90, 97, 100,
  Thomas, Admr. of Roger Walters, deced. -67, 71,

INDEX, NORTHUMBERAND ORDERS 1683-1686

GOCH[E]
  Anna [m. Peter Byram -39],
  Samuel 8, 38,
  Samuel, deced. (Will proved -32], 33, 39, 40, 44, 49,
GOLDMAN.
  Alice, Admrx. of Thomas, deced. -69,
  Thomas, deced. -69,
GOLDSMYTH
  Thomas -7,
GRACTON.
  Thomas 93, 94,
GRADEY.
  Walter -62,
GRAHAM.
  John -4, 5, 61, 62, 79, 96,
GREEN.
  Timothy, Orphan of Timothy, deced. -84, 92,
  Timothy, deced. -84,
GREENSTED.
  John -94,
  William -97, 106,
GREENSTON.
  Anne, Dau. of John bound out -51,
  John -51,
GRIFFIN.
  Samuel, Collo. -27, 28, 60, 79, 81, 82, 86, 87,
GRIMSTEAD.
  John, Son of William bound out -51,
  Thomas Son of William, bound out -51
  William 51,
GRINSTEAD
  William -23,

HADWELL.
  James [Levy free -60],
HAMBLETON.
  Boye -17,
  George -18, 24, [apptd. Constable -60], 96, 98,
HAMMONDS. / HAMMON
  Thomas -5, 29, 35, 37, 53,
HANKING
  Mark -89, 96,
HANNAH.
  Mr. -77,
HARCUM
  Hannah, Wife of William 103,
  William 4-6, 9, 13, 15, 18, 20, 21, 31, 33, 56, 68-70, 75, 83, 89, 90, 96, 100, 101, 103,
HARRIS.
  Charles [Attorney's Lic. -36], 40, 43, 50, 53-55, 57, 58, 61, 64, 71, 80, 88, 90, 94, 96, 97, 101,
  Hugh -97,
  Jeremiah [imported -21],
  John -5, 24, 37, 40, 44, 58, 60, 61, 80, 84, 87, 89, 103,
HARROLD.
  Gilbert [apptd Constable -68], 71, 92, 95, 98,
HARTLAND.
  William -4, 6, 13, 18, 55, 56, 71, 73, 83, 91,
HARTLEY.
  Henry 16, 30, 34, 43, 44,

HARTNELL.
  Samuel 31, 68, 74, 84,
HARVEY.
  Henry -8,
  William 47,
HATFIELD.
  Gervas -18, 20, 99,
HATTON.
  William Justice of St.Mary's Parish in Maryland -74,
HAY.
  George [Surveyor -5],
HAYNIE,
  Anthony -86,
  John, Capt. [Justice -1], 2, 4, 5, 12, 14, 18, 22, 25, 33, 36, 38-40, 45, 55, 58, 59, 63, 64, 74, 78, 81, 86, 91, 95, 103,
  John, Capt. Admr. of John Shaw, deced. -4,
  Richard -23, 26, 57, 79, 96, 98, 99, 101,
HESTER.
  Isaac 40,
HICKMAN.
  Thomas -26, 27, 49, 56,
HIGGINS.
  Thomas, Servant to John Hull -51,
HIGH.
  Thomas -57,
  Thomas, Admr. of Edward Maxwell, deced. -76,
HILL.
  Anna, Exrx. of William, deced. -60,
  Ezekiel -40,
  William -16, 42,
  William deced. [Will proved -60],
HOBSON.
  Elizabeth, Servant to Lt. Collo. Samuel Smyth -17,
  Thomas -4, 10, 15, 18, 20, 24, 34, 61, 92, 95, 104,
  Thomas [apptd. Sheriffe -13],
  Thomas Junr. [sworn Clerk of County -16], 99,
  Thomas Senr. -23, 41, 46, 54, 63, 64, 66, 68, 73, 96, 102,
  Thomas, Senr. [an Exr. of Richard Flynt deced. -25,
  Thomas Senr. [sworne Sheriffe -31], 32, 70,
HOCKLEY.
  John -102,
HOOKE.
  William, deced. -74,
HOPPER.
  Thomas [apptd. Constable -31],
HORNBY.
  James -27,
HOWARD.
  Doeothy [imported -21],
  William 15, 20, 29, 32, 33,
HOWLAND.
  Charles, Servant to Robert Sech -59,
HOWSON.
  Leonard Capt. [Justice -1], 2, 5, 15, 40, 42, 47, 54, 59, 64, 98,

HUDNALL.
   Alice, Exrx. of Ezekiel Genesis, deced. 32, 37, 40.
      41, 47, 53, 58,
   Alice Admrx. of John deced. -17, 37, 39, 45, 47,
   John, deced. -17, 37, 39, 45.
   Partin 40, 41,
HUDSON.
   Henry Servt. to John Coutanshew, Junr. -51,
HUGHLETT.
   John -4, 11, 16, 23, 32,
   John Junr [m. Mary, Relict of William Downing,
      Junr., deced. -23], 24, 35, 53, 97, 98,
   John, Senr. 20, 33, 95, 98,
   Mary, Wife of John Junr., Relict of William
      Downing, Junr., deced.-23, 97,
   Thomas 14, 24, 98,
HUGHS
   George -18, 23,
   John, Brother of Thomas, -55,
   Thomas -55,
HULL.
   John 22, 51, 52, 54,
   Richard -4, 5, 16-18, 23, 25-27, 30, 52, 60, 86, 92,
   Richard, Exr. of Walter Moor, deced -7,
   Richard, Exr. of Henry Willoughby, deced. -91,
HULL's CREEKE
   -60,
HUTCHINS
   Mathew -92,
HUTTON.
   George -5, [apptd. Constable-12], 14, 20, 60, 92,

INDIAN
   Servant to Richard Hull -60],
   Slave, age adudged 3,
INGRAM.
   Thomas 40, 80, 87, 102,

JACKMAN.
   Charles -98, 99, [m. Widow of Thomas Towers,
      deced. -101], 103, 106.
   Dorothy -97, 104,
   Dorothy, Wife of Charles -106.
JACKSON.
   Tabtby -93,
JAMES.
   Mary, Servt to Cuthbert Span -36, 45,
JAMES CITTIE
   -106.
JANES.
   Thomas, Servt. to Daniel Neale -25,
JEFFERSON.
   Samuel -12,
JEFFERYES
   John Esqr. & Co -86, 97,
JENKINS.
   Walter -66, 70,
JENNY.
   John 34,

JOHNSON.
   Jacob -48,
   James -5, 11, 14, 15, 20, 24, 32, 33, 45, 53, 59, 61,
      64, 66, 69, 71-73, 76, 95, 97, 98,
   James, Gdn to Timothy Green -84, 92,
   Jeffery 21, 63, 71, 72,
JONES.
   Edward of Bristoll 26,
   Edward, Exr. of Roger Bagnell, deced. -8,
   Francis, Servant to Daniel Neale -31,
   George 71,
   James 8, 11, 15, 21, 29, 90, 97, 102,
   John 6, 26, 69,
   John, deced. -44,
   Richard, deced. [Will proved -64], 81,
   Richard, Orphan -92,
   Samuel -29, 53, 86,
   Thomas -2, 6, 9, 21, 56, 80, 82, 83, 90, 100, 101,
      103, 104, [King's Attorney -105],
   Thomas, Capt. 11, 15, 16, 29, 30, 44, 63, 68, 75,
      82, 83, 87-90, 93, 98, 100,
   William 40, 44, 53, 61, 70, 76, 78,
JOYCE
   Abraham 21, 52, 61, 62, 66, -106.
JULIAN.
   John -12, 16, 34, 49,
   John, deced. [Will proved -50], 85, 88, 98,
JUSTICES [first appearance at a Court]
   BRERETON, Thomas   51,
   HAYNIE, John Capt   1,
   HOWSON, Leonard Capt   1,
   KENNER, Richard Mr.   1,
   KNIGHT, Peter Capt.   1,
   LEE, Charles   84,
   MATHEW, Thomas, Capt   1,
   MOTTROM, John Major   1,
   NEALE, Christopher Mr.   1,
   OWEN, Nicholas Mr.   1,
   PRESLEY, Peter Mr.   1,
   PRESLEY, Peter Junr. Mr.   86,
   ROGERS, Richard   59,
   ROGERS, William   3,
   SHAPLEIGH, Philip Mr.   1,
   SMYTH, Samuel Lt. Collo.   1,

KANNE.
   Judith [imported -48],
KEELY.
   John -94,
KEEN.
   Elizabeth, Mrs. -75, 100,
KENNER.
   Richard -1, 12, 76,
   Richard Gent. [Justice -1], 64, 66.
KER
   Charles -57,
KESTERSON.
   Margaret -90,
KETTLE.
   Susanna, Servant to John Coutanceau -105,

INDEX, NORTHUMBERLAND ORDERS 1683-1686

KEYNE./ KEEN
   Elizabeth -95,
   Elizabeth, Exrx. of William, deced. -59,
   John -105,
   William -5, 10, 21, 25, [Cert. for Cloth -30], 105,
   William deced. -59,
KING.
   William[Uncle to Jane Morton, Dau. of John Morton, deced. -12], 91,
KIRK.
   Christopher -5, 6, 9,
KNIGHT.
   George -2-4, 6, 8, 11, 15-17, 72, 73, 80, 88,
   George, deced. -82, 83,
   Leonard -73,
   Peter -2, 51, 57, 73, 101, 103,
   Peter, Capt. [Justice -1], 8, 11, 14, 40, [Burgess -42], 44, 55, 61, 62, [Burgess -94],
KNOTT.
   John, deced. 1, 7,

LAMBERT.
   William 21,[Rioter -75. 7, 86], 90, 96, 102,
LAMPREY./ LAMPERY
   Richard -4, [apptd Constable -31].
   Richard. Admr. of Bartholomew Yeamans, deced. -33, 53, 95,
   Richard, deced. -86,
LANCASTER./ LANKESTER
   Nicholas 58, 68,
LANE.
   Martha 13,
LATHERAM
   John -98, 100,
LATTIMORE
   Clement -6, 9, 12, 13, 39, 47, 48, 55, 56, 61, 65, 66, 69, 71-73, 75, 83, 86, 89, 90,
   Richard 7, 64. 66, 69, 71, 72, 91, 92, 94,
LAWRENCE.
   John -6, 10, [levy free -16], 23, 60, 83, 88, 96, 100, 102, 106.
   Thomas -98,
LAWSON.
   Robert -99,
LEHEGE.
   Daniel [imported -105],
LEE.
   Charles, Gent. [Justice -64], 66, 98,
   John -35,
   William -15, 17, 94,
   William [apptd High Sheriffe -59], 78. 80, 81, 83, 86, 89, 93, 102, 103,
LEWIS.
   John -6, 13, 15, 50, [apptd. Constable -60],
   Thomas -7,
LITTLEPAGE.
   Richard -44,
LIVERSAGE
   William [Levy free -79,
LOE.
   Thomas -27,

LONG.
   Josias -61, 64, 66. 69, 83, 103, 106.
LONGHAM.
   Katherine [imported -105],
LOYD.
   Richard -19,
LUKE.
   Ann, Wife of Edmund -77,
   Edmund 45, 49. 55, 57, 59, 69. 70, 77, 85, 95,
   John -27, 48,
LYNDSAY./ LYNSAY
   David -50,
   Robert 65, 98,
LYSER.
   John -95, 98, 100,
   John, [m. Exrx. of Edward Allgood, deced. -79,

MAHON.
   Samuel 6, 9, 39,
MANDLEY.
   Edmund, Servant to Richard Hull -84,
MARMADUKE.
   Miles -99,
MARSHALL.
   James -102,
MARYLAND.
   St. Mary's Parish -74,
MASEY.
   Henry -51,
MATHEW
   Rebecca, Mrs. -37,
   Thomas, Capt.)Justice -1], 2, 5, 12, 19, 22, [Cert. for cloth -27], 28, 58, 65, 82, 83, 88, 89, 97, 101, 104,
MATTAPONY
   1, 12, 31, 60, 68,
MAXFIELD.
   Edward -67,
   Peter -79,
MAXWELL.
   Edward, deced. -76,
   Mary, Wife of Peter 30, 31,
   Peter -23-25, 30, 31, 48, 64, 66, 92,
MAYSE./ MAIZE
   Henry -53, 98, 100,
MELTON.
   Michael -26, 101,
MERCHT.
   Elizabeth -4,
METCALFE / MEDCALFE
   Henry -51, 84,
   Sarah -3,
MICHAELL.
   Richard -6,
MILLER.
   Thomas 11, 37, [Rioter -75, 76, 86],
MOLINAX.
   John -75,
MONGOMERY.
   James 50,

MOOR.
- Anna, Dau. of Walter, deced., Wife of Henry Rider -7, 79,
- James -19, 32, 37, 38, 49, 60,
- Sarah, Dau. of Walter, deced. -7, 79,
- John, Son of Walter, deced. -79,
- Walter, deced. -7, 12, 13, 30, 79,

MORELAY.
- Ellinor, Servant to John Corbell -59,

MORRIS.
- Anthony, deced. 12-14, 18,
- Dorothy, Relict of Anthony, Wife of Cuthbert Span -12], 13, 18,
- Jane, heir of Anthony, deced. 12-14, 18,
- Thomas 16,
- Thomas deced. [Will proved -75], 79, 91,

MORTIMORE.
- James, Servant to John Coutanshew, Senr. -51,

MORTON
- Andrew, deced. -9,
- Mary, Dau. of Andrew deced -9,

MOTTROM.
- John, Major [Justice -1], 7, 8,
- John, Major [deced -54], 55, 62, 78, 86, 99

MOUNTJOY.
- Thomas -48,

MUNSLOW / MUNSLOE
- Grace, Wife of Valentine 13,
- Valentine 13, 19, 22,

MUTTOONE.
- John 72,
- Sarah, Wife of John 72,

NEALE.
- Christopher, Gent. [Justice -1], 12, 24, 25, 29, 30, [Cert. for cloth -31], 40, 44, 61, 63-66, 77, 80, [Burgess -94], 103,
- Daniel -4, 25, 61, 96,

NEGROES.
- Age adjudged -1, 35, 84, 85,
- Attached -78,
- Levy free -28, 61, 83,

NELMES.
- John [Levy free -60], 81,
- Richard -69, 81, 103,
- Richard Junr. -17,
- Thomas, deced. [Will proved -32], 36.

NELMES als. MATTOCKS
- Thomas -41,

NESBETT.
- Edward -26, 27, 91,

NEWHAM.
- William 47, 53, 61,

NEWMAN's NECK
- 1, 60,

NEWTON.
- Christopher -69, 73, 93, 104,

NICHOLS.
- John 2, 11, 42, 58, 84,

NICKLESS.
- John -94, 105,

NIPPER
- James 22,

NORRIS.
- Abraham -4,
- Mary [imported -21],

NUTT.
- John -12,
- Richard, Exr. of Richard, deced. -60,
- Richard, deced [Will proved -50],
- William -12,
- William, Capt. deced. -12,

NUTWELL.
- Arthur [a mad man -14], 56, 57, 62,

OAGE.
- Israell 30,

OKEANE
- Lawrence [imported -105],

OLDAM
- John -5, [Cert. for Linen -6], 64, 67,

OLDIS.
- Robert -29, 48, [escaped from Prison -59],

ONEALE.
- Roger 41, 43,

ORLAND.
- David deced. -85,
- Richard. Son of David deced. 85,

OWEN.
- Nicholas Gent. [Justice -1], 40, 59, 64, 76, 79, 81-83, 86, 93, 94,
- Nicholas, Exr. of John Julian, deced. -50, 85, 88, 99,

PALMER.
- John -23, 35, 37, 56, 57,
- Joseph [apptd Constable -60],

PARKER.
- Azarcam -27, 28, 49, 53, 60,
- Azarcam, deced. [Will proved -76], 84, 98, 100, 102,
- Elizabeth 35, 90,
- Elizabeth, Relict & Exrx. of Azarcam, deced. 76, 84, 98, 100, 102,
- William -10, 51, 78, 86, 89, 90, 92, 95, 98,

PARRIS.
- Nicholas -47,

PARSONS
- Emanuell -91, 92,

PASKALL
- Hannah, Exrx. of John deced. -1,
- John, deced., [Will proved -1],

PATE.
- Thoroughgood -51,

PAUL.
- Charles -29, 56, 58, 68,

PEMBERTON.
- -89,
- Richard -6, 10, 11, 15, 19, 20, 23, 25, 29, 32, 33, 41, 43, 52, 53, 60, 64, 71, 82, 89, 94-97, 100, 105,

PERCIFULL
- William -68, 78, 80, 94,

PERYNE.
  Alice -8,
  Alice, Wife & Admrx. of Thomas, deced. -20,
  Thomas deced. -20,
PICKMORE.
  Lymon, Chirurgeon -99,
PICKRIN.
  Edward 46,
PINCKARD.
  John 46,
PITCHER.
  Emmanuell 15, 26,
PITTS.
  Josias 38,
  Josias, Admr. of William Thomas, deced. 20, 42,
  Rebecca, Wife of Josias, Dau. of William Thomas
    deced -20,
PLATT.
  Peter -34,
POLLOCK / POLLICK
  Patrick [apptd Constable -31], 56, 61, 64. 66. 68,
    69, 71-73, 106.
POPE.
  [?] -102,
POTOMACK CREEKE
  21,
POTTER.
  John -25,
PRESLEY.
  Peter, Gent. [Justice -1], 2, 4, 40, [Burgess -42],
    66.
  Peter Junr. -1, 24, 35, 70, 75, 92, 95, 99,
  Peter Junr., Gent. [Justice -36], 64, 66, 80,
  Peter, Junr. Son of William, deced. -63, 66.
  Peter, Senr. -12, 31,
  Peter Senr. an Exr. of Richard Flynt, deced. -25,
  William -24,
  William, deced. -63, 66.
PRICE.
  Elizabeth, Servant to Thomas Flynt -105,
  William -73,
PRITCHARD / PRICHARD
  Robert -82, 102,
  William -5,
PRITT.
  Robert, deced. [Will proved -51], 70, 77, 95,

QUICK.
  Thomas a poor man, deced. -51,
QUIGG.
  Richard, deced. [Will proved -60],

RABLEIGH / RABLY
  Thomas -23,
REASON.
  John -47, 74, 75,
RENNOLLS
  William 14,
REYNOLDS.
  Elinor 32,
  Henry -69, 71,

RHODES
  [? Nestor] bound out -65,
RICE.
  -89,
  Dominick 22,
  Dominick [imported -48],
  John -27, 28, 32, 39, 43, 45, 48, 51, 61.
  Richard 14, 19, 20, 24, 33. 61, 65, 85,
  Richard, Exr. of Robert Pritt, deced. -51, 70, 77,
    95,
RIDER.
  Anne, Wife of Henry, Dau. of Walter Moor, deced
    -7, 79,
  Henry -7, 16, 17, [apptd. Constable -60], 79,
ROACH.
  John 53, 61,
ROBERTS.
  David, Servant to William & John Keen -105,
  Robert 12,
ROBINSON.
  John -47, 94,
  Thomas -9, 10,
ROGERS.
  Joane -20, 81, 86,
  Joane, [Relict of John, deced. -47],
  John, deced. 47,
  Richard -5, 12, 59, 91, 92,
  Richard, Brother of William 16,
  Richard, Gent. [Justice -59], 66.
  William, Gent. [Justice -3], 6, 14, 16, 24, 41, 47,
    55, 56, 62, 63, 80, 83, 88, 91, 93,
ROOT.
  Richard 43,
ROSSE.
  Henry -5, 12, 23,
ROUT.
  Thomas [apptd. Constable -1],
RUSSELL.
  Thomas -48,

SADLER.
  Miriam, Admrx. of Thomas, deced. -4.
  Thomas, deced. -4.,
SALLOWES
  Stephen -69, [m. Mother of Richard Orland -85],
SALTER.
  John [Rioter -75, 76, 86],
SAMPSON.
  William -64,
SANDERS.
  Ebenezer -7, 14, 53, 60, 83,
  Ebenezer, Son & an Admr. of Mrs. Mary Thomas,
    deced. -20, 29, 32, 37, 38, 42, 46, 48,
  Edward, Son & an Admr. of Mrs. Mary Thomas
    deced.-20, 42, 48,
SANFORD.
  Elizabeth, Wife of Samuel, Exrx. of Edward
    Elliott, deced. -74,
  Samuell [m. Elizabeth Exrx. of Edward Elliott]
    -74,
SEABORNE.
  Nicholas -2,

SEABRIGHT.
  John -56,
SECH.
  Robert -5, 12, 59, 64, 65, 69, 71-73, 92, 99, 100,
SHAPLEIGH.
  Philip Gent. [Justice -1], 2, 6, 10, 19, 22-26, 44, 55, 56, 62, 65, 77, 96, [Cert. for Land -105],
SHARP.
  John -90,
SHAW.
  John, deced. -4,
  Rebecca, Dau. of John, Wife of Ezekiel Genesis -4,
SHEARES.
  Abraham, 65, 71-73, 94,
SHELTON.
  Robert -67,
SHERWOOD.
  William -80, 87,
SHIPS & VESSELS
  Barque called "The Vine" -27,
  "Susannah of Boston" -25,
SHIRLEY.
  Frances -96,
  Jane, Servant to Peter Presley Junr. -95,
SHOARES.
  William -5, 14, 21, 86, 91,
SIMPSON.
  Hannah 35,
  James -8,
SIMS.
  Walter -6, 9, 10, 95, 96, 100,
SMYTH.
  Charles [Rioter -75, 76, 86],
  John, Exr. of Richard Quigg, deced. -60,
  Margaret, Servant to Robert Sech -99,
  Richard -18, 38, 46, 50, 53, 58, 68, 69, 71, 79, 81, 103,
  Samuel, Lt. Collo. [Justice -1], 13, 15, 17, 27, 28, 30, 41, 47, 54, 57, 58, 61, 64, 65,
  Thomas -103,
  William -9, 13,
SNELL.
  Thomas 46,
SOUTHERLAND.
  John 24, 100,
SOUTHING.
  William -1,
SPAN[N]
  Cuthbert 12-14, 36, 45, 53, [apptd. Constable -60], 67, 102,
  Dorothy, Wife of Cuthbert, Relict of Anthony Morris, deced. -12, 13,
  John [Brother of Cuthbert -53],
SPARKES.
  John -51,
SPENCER.
  Nicholas, Esqr. -10, 24, 26, 44, 54-57, 62, 63, 77, 85,
SPICER.
  Arthur -49, 51,

INDEX, NORTHUMBERLAND ORDERS 1683-1685

SPRAG
  Anne [imported -48],
STANLEY.
  John 43,
STATHEM.
  Hugh -67, 106.
STEWARD.
  Elizabeth 65,
STRECHLEY
  John -74,
STRINGER.
  Edmund -43, 52, 82,
SWANN
  Alexander -37, 39,
SWANSON.
  John 6, 9,
  John, deced. 39, 44,
  Mary, Relict & Exrx. of John, deced. 39,
SWEATMER
  Mathew -64,
SWETNAM
  William -47, 87, 98,
SYMMONS.
  John 20,
  Lawrence 14,

TAVERNER.
  John -43, 48,
TAYLOR.
  Henry [imported -48],
  John Junr. [Cert. for cloth -30], 94,
  Richard -106.
  William -51, 67, 85, 87, 89, 90, 94,
TEMPLAR.
  William -52,
THOMAS.
  Christopher -97,
  Edward 23,
  Elizabeth, Dau of William & Mary, deced. Wife of Benjamin Cotman -42,
  Mary, Admrx. of William deced. -14, 15, 17,
  Mary, Mrs. deced. 20, 21, 29, 32, 37, 38, 42, 46, 48,
  Mary, Dau. of William & Mary, deced., Wife of Edward White -42,
  Mr. -7,
  Rebecca., Dau. of William Thomas, deced. Wife of Josias Pitts -20,
  Rebecca, Servant to Mrs. Jane Wildey [freed from the Levy -3,
  William, deced -14, 15, 20, 21, 42,
  Zachariah [apptd. Constable -1], 24, 57,
THOMPSON./ TOMSON
  Richard -27, 28, 34, 76, 77,
THORNE.
  Richard 22,
THORNTON.
  Jeremiah -51,
THORP.
  Thomas, Exr. of Thomas Nelmas, deced. 32, 36,
THRUSTON.
  Malachy -87,

INDEX, NORTHUMBERLAND ORDERS 1683-1686

TIDWELL.
  Richard -105,
TIGNALL.
  William, Churchwarden -35,
TIGNOR.
  William 60, 74, 75, 80, 86, 90, 91,
TIPTON.
  Edward [m. Margarett Downing, Exrx. of William Downing deced -26], 48, 53, 92, 106.
  Margaret, Wife of Edward -26],
  Samuel -3, 7, 8,
TOP[P]
  Thomas 21, 40, 44, 70,
TOPPING.
  John, [apptd. Sub Sheriffe -13, 16, 31],
TORRINGTON.
  Richard -12,
TOWERS.
  Dorothy, Wife & Exrx. of Thomas, deced. -64, 67
  Thomas -6, 9, 10,
  Thomas, deced. [Will proved -64], 67, 101,
TREIP.
  Thomas 41,
TRESSRY.
  James 64, 96,
TULLOS.
  Cloud [apptd. Constable-1], 4, 64, 105.
  Cloud, Son of Cloud, [Levy free -4],
TURBERVILLE.
  John -51, [apptd. Sub Sheriff -59], 76,
TUTT
  Mary 78, 84, 85,
TUXBURY.
  James -75,

UPTON.
  Elizabeth 22,

VANLANDEGHAM
  Michael [apptd. Constable -60], 97,
VEALE
  Humphrey [imported -105],

WADDING.
  Thomas -102,
WADDINGTON.
  Ralph, Junr. -95, 98,
WADDY
  James -78, 83-85,
  James Exr. of his Father, John, deced. -105,
  John -21, 25, 34, 40,
  John, deced. [Will proved -105],
  Thomas -27, 28, 37, 50, 64, 66, 68, 84,
WADE.
  John -3, 11,
WALKER.
  George -6,
  Joseph -95,
WALTERS.
  Ellinor Widdow -3, [deced, Will proved -43], 47,
  John -1, 82, 90, 100,

WALTERS [contd]
  John, Exr. of Richard Jones, deced. -64],
  John, Gdn. Richard Jones -92,
  Peter 64,
  Roger -38, 39,
  Roger, deced. -67, 71,
WARD
  John -9, 10, 67,
WARNER.
  John 38,
WARRINGTON.
  Ralph Junr. 22,
WARWICK.
  William 50,
WATERMAN.
  Thomas -18, 44, 49,
WATT
  Isaac -74,
WATTS.
  Edward 19, 26, 41, 43, 49, 56, 87,
  Elizabeth 47,
WAUGHOP / WAHOP
  Thomas -2, 10,
WEATHERSTONE
  Alexander 91, 92, 96, 103,
WEBB.
  John -5, 16, 28, 42-44, 67, 87, 94, 100,
  Thomas -11, 20, 33, 53, 61, 67, 98, 100,
WEEKES.
  Henry -60,
  Thomas 22, 26, 27,
WELLS.
  Stephen 50, 82, 102,
WEST
  John Collo. -39,
WHEELER.
  Thomas, Servant to Thomas Brower -91,
WHITE.
  Edward -20, 32, 40, 42, 48, 103,
  Lawrence [Rioter -75, 76, 86],
  Mary, Wife of Edward, Dau. of William & Mary Thomas deced. -42,
  Thomas -57,
WHITFORD.
  David 40, 44,
WICOCOMICO
  Great -1,
WILDEY.
  Jane Mrs. [Cert. for wool cloth -1], 2, 5, 18, 24, 86, 104,
  Jane, Exrx. of Wiliam deced. -3,
  William, deced. -3,
WILKS / WILKES
  Robert, Servant to John Bowin -91,
  Thomas -43-47,
WILLIAMS.
  Edward 15, 16, 29, 32, 33, 35, 36, 42, 64-66, 87, 95,
  Edward, Senr. deced. Father of Edward -32,
  Elizabeth -5, 6,
  Howell -84,
  Richard -91,

INDEX, NORTHUMBERLAND ORDERS 1683-1686

WILLIAMS [contd]
 Roger -93,
 Temperance, Wife of Edward Senr. -32, 33,
 Thomas 9, 50, 55, 60, 95,
WILLOUGHBY.
 Henry 12, 13,
 Henry, deced. [Will proved -91],
WINTER.
 Thomas -8, 10, 12, 27, 34, 37, 61, 80, 84, 87, 90, 92-94, 101, 105,
WISE.
 Sarah -48, 59,
WOOLDRIDGE.
 Edward -8,
WORMLEY.
 Christopher Esqr. 101,
WORNAM.
 John 11-13, 33, 36, 47, 53, 83,
WORSHAM
 John -67,
WRIGHT.
 Mottrom 47, 58, 62, 67, 68, 70, 78,
 Thomas -27, 37,

YARRET / YARRATT
 Adam -24,
 Jane, Wife of William -51,
 Rachell -105,
 William 16, 51, 67,
YATES.
 Robert -27,
YEAMANS.
 Bartholomew -29,
 Bartholomew, deced -33, 53, 86, 95,
YEOCOMOCO POINTE
 14,
YOUNG.
 James -84, [Levy free -104],

Heritage Books by Ruth and Sam Sparacio:

Abstracts of Account Books of Edward Dixon, Merchant of Port Royal, Virginia, Volume I: 1743–1747
Abstracts of Account Books of Edward Dixon, Merchant of Port Royal, Virginia, Volume II
Albemarle County, Virginia Deed and Will Book Abstracts, 1748–1752
Albemarle County, Virginia Deed Book Abstracts, 1758–1761
Albemarle County, Virginia Deed Book Abstracts, 1761–1764
Albemarle County, Virginia Deed Book Abstracts, 1764–1768
Albemarle County, Virginia Deed Book Abstracts, 1768–1770
Albemarle County, Virginia Deed Book Abstracts, 1776–1778
Albemarle County, Virginia Deed Book Abstracts, 1778–1780
Albemarle County, Virginia Deed Book Abstracts, 1780–1783
Albemarle County, Virginia Deed Book Abstracts, 1787–1790
Albemarle County, Virginia Deed Book Abstracts, 1790–1791
Albemarle County, Virginia Deed Book Abstracts, 1791–1793
Augusta County, Virginia Land Tax Books, 1782–1788
Augusta County, Virginia Land Tax Books, 1788–1790
Amherst County, Virginia Land Tax Books, 1789–1791
Caroline County, Virginia Order Book Abstracts, 1765
Caroline County, Virginia Order Book Abstracts, 1767–1768
Caroline County, Virginia Order Book Abstracts, 1768–1770
Caroline County, Virginia Order Book Abstracts, 1770–1771
Caroline County, Virginia Order Book, 1765–1767
Caroline County, Virginia Order Book, 1771–1772
Caroline County, Virginia Order Book, 1772–1773
Caroline County, Virginia Order Book, 1773
Caroline County, Virginia Order Book, 1773–1774
Caroline County, Virginia Order Book, 1774–1778
Caroline County, Virginia Order Book, 1778–1781
Caroline County, Virginia Order Book, 1781–1783
Caroline County, Virginia Order Book, 1786–1787
Caroline County, Virginia Order Book, 1787, Part 1
Caroline County, Virginia Order Book, 1788
Culpeper County, Virginia Deed Book Abstracts, 1795–1796
Culpeper County, Virginia Land Tax Book, 1782–1786
Culpeper County, Virginia Land Tax Book, 1787–1789
Culpeper County, Virginia Minute Book, 1763–1764
Digest of Family Relationships, 1650–1692, from Virginia County Court Records
Digest of Family Relationships, 1720–1750, from Virginia County Court Records
Digest of Family Relationships, 1750–1763, from Virginia County Court Records
Digest of Family Relationships, 1764–1775, from Virginia County Court Records
Essex County, Virginia Deed and Will Abstracts, 1695–1697
Essex County, Virginia Deed and Will Abstracts, 1697–1699
Essex County, Virginia Deed and Will Abstracts, 1699–1701
Essex County, Virginia Deed and Will Abstracts, 1701–1703
Essex County, Virginia Deed and Will Abstracts, 1745–1749
Essex County, Virginia Deed and Will Book, 1692–1693
Essex County, Virginia Deed and Will Book, 1693–1694
Essex County, Virginia Deed and Will Book, 1694–1695
Essex County, Virginia Deed and Will Book, 1753–1754 and 1750
Essex County, Virginia Deed Book, 1724–1728
Essex County, Virginia Deed Book, 1728–1733
Essex County, Virginia Deed Book, 1733–1738
Essex County, Virginia Deed Book, 1738–1742
Essex County, Virginia Deed Book, 1742–1745

Essex County, Virginia Deed Book, 1749–1751
Essex County, Virginia Deed Book, 1751–1753
Essex County, Virginia Land Trials Abstracts, 1711–1716 and 1715–1741
Essex County, Virginia Order Book Abstracts, 1699–1702
Essex County, Virginia Order Book Abstracts, 1716–1723, Part 1
Essex County, Virginia Order Book Abstracts, 1716–1723, Part 2
Essex County, Virginia Order Book Abstracts, 1716–1723, Part 3
Essex County, Virginia Order Book Abstracts, 1716–1723, Part 4
Essex County, Virginia Order Book Abstracts, 1723–1725, Part 1
Essex County, Virginia Order Book Abstracts, 1723–1725, Part 2
Essex County, Virginia Order Book Abstracts, 1725–1729, Part 1
Essex County, Virginia Order Book Abstracts, 1727–1729
Essex County, Virginia Order Book, 1695–1699
Fairfax County, Virginia Deed Abstracts, 1799–1800 and 1803–1804
Fairfax County, Virginia Deed Abstracts, 1804–1805
Fairfax County, Virginia Deed Book Abstracts, 1799
Fairfax County, Virginia Deed Book, 1798–1799
Fairfax County, Virginia Land Causes, 1788–1824
Fauquier County, Virginia Minute Book, 1759–1761
Fauquier County, Virginia Minute Book, 1761–1762
Fauquier County, Virginia Minute Book, 1766–1767
Fauquier County, Virginia Minute Book, 1767–1769
Fauquier County, Virginia Minute Book, 1769–1771
Hanover County, Virginia Land Tax Book, 1782–1788
Hanover County, Virginia Land Tax Book, 1789–1793
Hanover County, Virginia Land Tax Book, 1793–1796
King George County, Virginia Order Book Abstracts, 1721–1723
King George County, Virginia Deed Book Abstracts, 1721–1735
King George County, Virginia Deed Book Abstracts, 1735–1752
King George County, Virginia Deed Book Abstracts, 1753–1773
King George County, Virginia Deed Book Abstracts, 1773–1783
King George County, Virginia Will Book Abstracts, 1752–1780
King William County, Virginia Record Book, 1702–1705
King William County, Virginia Record Book, 1705–1721
King William County, Virginia Record Book, 1722 and 1785–1786
Lancaster County, Virginia Deed and Will Book, 1652–1657
Lancaster County, Virginia Deed and Will Book, 1654–1661
Lancaster County, Virginia Deed and Will Book, 1661–1702 (1661–1666 and 1699–1702)
Lancaster County, Virginia Deed Book Abstracts, 1701–1706
Lancaster County, Virginia Deed Book, 1710–1714
Lancaster County, Virginia Order Book Abstracts, 1656–1661
Lancaster County, Virginia Order Book Abstracts, 1662–1666
Lancaster County, Virginia Order Book Abstracts, 1666–1669
Lancaster County, Virginia Order Book Abstracts, 1670–1674
Lancaster County, Virginia Order Book Abstracts, 1674–1678
Lancaster County, Virginia Order Book Abstracts, 1678–1681
Lancaster County, Virginia Order Book Abstracts, 1682–1687
Lancaster County, Virginia Order Book Abstracts, 1729–1732
Lancaster County, Virginia Order Book Abstracts, 1736–1739
Lancaster County, Virginia Order Book Abstracts, 1739–1742
Lancaster County, Virginia Order Book, 1687–1691
Lancaster County, Virginia Order Book, 1691–1695
Lancaster County, Virginia Order Book, 1695–1699
Lancaster County, Virginia Order Book, 1699–1701

Lancaster County, Virginia Order Book, 1701–1703
Lancaster County, Virginia Order Book, 1703–1706
Lancaster County, Virginia Order Book, 1732–1736
Lancaster County, Virginia Will Book, 1675–1689
Loudoun County, Virginia Order Book, 1763–1764
Loudoun County, Virginia Order Book, 1764
Louisa County, Virginia Deed Book, 1744–1746
Louisa County, Virginia Order Book, 1742–1744
Madison County, Virginia Deed Book Abstracts, 1793–1804
Madison County, Virginia Deed Book, 1793–1813, and Marriage Bonds, 1793–1800
Middlesex County, Virginia Deed Book, 1679–1688
Middlesex County, Virginia Deed Book, 1688–1694
Middlesex County, Virginia Deed Book, 1694–1703
Middlesex County, Virginia Deed Book, 1703–1709
Middlesex County, Virginia Deed Book, 1709–1720
Middlesex County, Virginia Order Book, 1686–1690
Middlesex County, Virginia Record Book, 1721–1813
Northumberland County, Virginia Deed and Will Book, 1650–1655
Northumberland County, Virginia Deed and Will Book, 1655–1658
Northumberland County, Virginia Deed and Will Book, 1662–1666
Northumberland County, Virginia Deed and Will Book, 1666–1670
Northumberland County, Virginia Deed and Will Book, 1670–1672 and 1706–1711
Northumberland County, Virginia Deed and Will Book, 1711–1712
Northumberland County, Virginia Order Book, 1652–1657
Northumberland County, Virginia Order Book, 1657–1661
Northumberland County, Virginia Order Book, 1665–1669
Northumberland County, Virginia Order Book, 1669–1673
Northumberland County, Virginia Order Book, 1680–1683
Northumberland County, Virginia Order Book, 1683–1686
Northumberland County, Virginia Order Book, 1699–1700
Northumberland County, Virginia Order Book, 1700–1702
Northumberland County, Virginia Order Book, 1702–1704
Orange County, Virginia Deeds, 1743–1759
Orange County, Virginia Order Book Abstracts 1747–1748
Orange County, Virginia Order Book Abstracts 1752–1753
Prince William County, Virginia Deed Book, 1749–1752
Prince William County, Virginia Order Book Abstracts, 1752–1753
Prince William County, Virginia Order Book Abstracts, 1753–1757
(Old) Rappahannock County, Virginia Deed and Will Book Abstracts, 1656–1662
(Old) Rappahannock County, Virginia Deed and Will Book Abstracts, 1662–1665
(Old) Rappahannock County, Virginia Deed and Will Book Abstracts, 1663–1668
(Old) Rappahannock County, Virginia Deed and Will Book Abstracts, 1665–1677
(Old) Rappahannock County, Virginia Deed and Will Book Abstracts, 1668–1670
(Old) Rappahannock County, Virginia Deed and Will Book Abstracts, 1670–1672
(Old) Rappahannock County, Virginia Deed and Will Book Abstracts, 1672–1673/4
(Old) Rappahannock County, Virginia Deed and Will Book Abstracts, 1673/4–1676
(Old) Rappahannock County, Virginia Deed and Will Book Abstracts, 1677–1678/9
(Old) Rappahannock County, Virginia Deed and Will Book Abstracts, 1678/9–1682
(Old) Rappahannock County, Virginia Deed and Will Book Abstracts, 1682–1686
(Old) Rappahannock County, Virginia Deed and Will Book Abstracts, 1686–1688
(Old) Rappahannock County, Virginia Deed and Will Book Abstracts, 1688–1692
(Old) Rappahannock County, Virginia Order Book Abstracts, 1683–1685
(Old) Rappahannock County, Virginia Order Book, 1689–1692
(Old) Rappahannock County, Virginia Will Book, 1682–1687

Richmond County, Virginia Deed Book Abstracts, 1692–1695
Richmond County, Virginia Deed Book Abstracts, 1695–1701
Richmond County, Virginia Deed Book Abstracts, 1701–1704
Richmond County, Virginia Deed Book Abstracts, 1705–1708
Richmond County, Virginia Deed Book Abstracts, 1708–1711
Richmond County, Virginia Deed Book Abstracts, 1711–1714
Richmond County, Virginia Deed Book Abstracts, 1715–1718
Richmond County, Virginia Deed Book Abstracts, 1718–1719
Richmond County, Virginia Deed Book Abstracts, 1719–1721
Richmond County, Virginia Deed Book Abstracts, 1721–1725
Richmond County, Virginia Order Book Abstracts, 1694–1697
Richmond County, Virginia Order Book Abstracts, 1697–1699
Richmond County, Virginia Order Book abstracts, 1699–1701
Richmond County, Virginia Order Book Abstracts, 1714–1715
Richmond County, Virginia Order Book Abstracts, 1719–1721
Richmond County, Virginia Order Book, 1692–1694
Richmond County, Virginia Order Book, 1702–1704
Richmond County, Virginia Order Book, 1717–1718
Richmond County, Virginia Order Book, 1718–1719
Spotsylvania County, Virginia Deed Book, 1722–1725
Spotsylvania County, Virginia Deed Book, 1725–1728
Spotsylvania County, Virginia Deed Book: 1730–1731
Spotsylvania County, Virginia Order Book Abstracts, 1742–1744
Spotsylvania County, Virginia Order Book Abstracts, 1744–1746
Stafford County, Virginia Deed and Will Book, 1686–1689
Stafford County, Virginia Deed and Will Book, 1689–1693
Stafford County, Virginia Deed and Will Book, 1699–1709
Stafford County, Virginia Deed and Will Book, 1780–1786, and Scheme Book Orders, 1790–1793
Stafford County, Virginia Deed Book, 1722–1728 and 1755–1765
Stafford County, Virginia Order Book, 1664–1668 and 1689–1690
Stafford County, Virginia Order Book, 1691–1692
Stafford County, Virginia Order Book, 1692–1693
Stafford County, Virginia Will Book, 1729–1748
Stafford County, Virginia Will Book, 1748–1767
Westmoreland County, Virginia Deed and Will Abstracts, 1723–1726
Westmoreland County, Virginia Deed and Will Abstracts, 1726–1729
Westmoreland County, Virginia Deed and Will Abstracts, 1729–1732
Westmoreland County, Virginia Deed and Will Abstracts, 1732–1734
Westmoreland County, Virginia Deed and Will Abstracts, 1734–1736
Westmoreland County, Virginia Deed and Will Abstracts, 1736–1740
Westmoreland County, Virginia Deed and Will Abstracts, 1740–1742
Westmoreland County, Virginia Deed and Will Abstracts, 1742–1745
Westmoreland County, Virginia Deed and Will Abstracts, 1745–1747
Westmoreland County, Virginia Deed and Will Abstracts, 1747–1748
Westmoreland County, Virginia Deed and Will Abstracts, 1749–1751
Westmoreland County, Virginia Deed and Will Abstracts, 1751–1754
Westmoreland County, Virginia Deed and Will Abstracts, 1754–1756
Westmoreland County, Virginia Order Book, 1705–1707
Westmoreland County, Virginia Order Book, 1707–1709
Westmoreland County, Virginia Order Book, 1709–1712